JEWISH EDUCATION

Key Words in Jewish Studies

Series Editors

Deborah Dash Moore, University of Michigan
Jonathan Boyarin, Cornell University

JEWISH EDUCATION

ARI Y. KELMAN

RUTGERS UNIVERSITY PRESS
New Brunswick, Camden, and Newark, New Jersey
London and Oxford

Rutgers University Press is a department of Rutgers, The State University of New Jersey, one of the leading public research universities in the nation. By publishing worldwide, it furthers the University's mission of dedication to excellence in teaching, scholarship, research, and clinical care.

Library of Congress Cataloging-in-Publication Data

Names: Kelman, Ari Y., author.
Title: Jewish education / Ari Y Kelman.
Description: New Brunswick : Rutgers University Press, 2024. | Includes
    bibliographical references and index.
Identifiers: LCCN 2023041112 | ISBN 9781978835627 (paperback) |
    ISBN 9781978835634 (hardback) | ISBN 9781978835641 (epub) |
    ISBN 9781978835658 (pdf)
Subjects: LCSH: Judaism—Study and teaching. | Jews—Education. | Jewish
    religious education. | Neusner, Jacob, 1932–2016.
Classification: LCC BM70 .K45 2024 | DDC 296.6/8—dc23/eng/20231002
LC record available at https://lccn.loc.gov/2023041112

A British Cataloging-in-Publication record for this book is available from the British Library.

References to internet websites (URLs) were accurate at the time of writing. Neither the author nor Rutgers University Press is responsible for URLs that may have expired or changed since the manuscript was prepared.

∞ The paper used in this publication meets the requirements of the American National Standard for Information Sciences—Permanence of Paper for Printed Library Materials, ANSI Z39.48-1992.

rutgersuniversitypress.org

To my parents, Vicky and Stuart. Lifelong Jewish educators who sent me to all the institutions (day school, overnight camp, Israel, synagogue), but who still showed me how the best stuff is learned elsewhere.

Contents

Foreword

The Rutgers book series Key Words in Jewish Studies seeks to introduce students and scholars alike to vigorous developments in the field by exploring its terms. These words and phrases reference important concepts, issues, practices, events, and circumstances. But the terms also refer to standards, even to preconditions; they patrol the boundaries of the field of Jewish Studies. This series aims to transform outsiders into insiders and let insiders gain new perspectives on usages, some of which shift even as we apply them.

Key words mutate through repetition, suppression, amplification, and competitive sharing. Jewish Studies finds itself attending to such processes in the context of an academic milieu where terms are frequently repurposed. Diaspora offers an example of an ancient word, one with a specific Jewish resonance, which has traveled into new regions and usage. Such terms migrate from the religious milieu of Jewish learning to the secular environment of universities, from Jewish community discussion to arenas of academic discourse, from political debates to intellectual arguments and back again. As these key words travel, they acquire additional meanings even as they occasionally shed long-established connotations. On occasion, key words can become so politicized that they serve as accusations. The sociopolitical concept of assimilation, for example, when turned into a term—"assimilationist"—describing an advocate of the process among Jews, became an epithet hurled by political opponents struggling for the mantle of authority in Jewish communities.

When approached dispassionately, key words provide analytical leverage to expand debate in Jewish Studies. Some key words will be familiar from long use, and yet they may have gained new valences, attracting or repelling other terms in contemporary discussion. But there are prominent terms in Jewish culture whose key lies in a particular understanding of prior usage. Terms of the past may bolster claims to continuity in the present, while newly minted language sometimes disguises deep connections reaching back into history. Attention must be paid as well to the transmigration of key words among Jewish languages—especially Hebrew, Yiddish, and Ladino—and among languages used by Jews, knitting connections even while highlighting distinctions.

An exploration of the current state of Jewish Studies through its key words highlights some interconnections often only glimpsed and holds out the prospect of a reorganization of Jewish knowledge. Key words act as magnets and attract a nexus of ideas and arguments as well as related terms into their orbits.

This series plunges into several of these intersecting constellations, providing a path from past to present.

The volumes in the series share a common organization. They open with a first part, Terms of the Debate, which defines the key word as it developed over the course of Jewish history. Allied concepts and traditional terms appear here as well. The second part, State of the Question, analyzes contemporary debates in scholarship and popular venues, especially for those key words that have crossed over into popular culture. The final part, In a New Key, explicitly addresses contemporary culture and future possibilities for understanding the key word.

To decipher key words is to learn the varied languages of Jewish Studies at points of intersection between academic disciplines and wider spheres of culture. The series, then, does not seek to consolidate and narrow a particular critical lexicon. Its purpose is to question, not to canonize, and to invite readers to sample the debate and ferment of an exciting field of study.

Deborah Dash Moore
Jonathan Boyarin
Series Coeditors

JEWISH EDUCATION

Introduction

Jewish education is exceedingly difficult to define. A recent study of Jewish educators found little internal logic that either held the field together or united members of the profession, save their common understanding that they all identified as Jewish educators and engaged in something called Jewish education.[1] Schools certainly qualify as Jewish education, as do summer camps, especially if we broaden the definitional door to include locations of "informal" or "experiential" education.[2] Synagogues generally fit under the definition, but operationally they divide their "educational" offerings and their ritual ones. People who participate in weekly Torah study probably see themselves as engaging in Jewish education, as do people preparing for their b-mitzvah. But what about the b-mitzvah itself? Is that ritual educational? What about other rituals like, say, the Passover Seder? What about scholarship about Jews or Judaism? Many of the people who write books about Jews intend to inform their readers about their subject, but do scholars see their work as Jewish education? What about the field of scholarship known as Jewish Studies? It emerged from American higher education, but many of its members would chafe at the idea that they do Jewish education. What about documentary filmmakers? Musicians? Poets? Chefs? Graphic novelists? Viral video makers? Jewish meme makers? Journalists? What about other practices: Political organizing? Journalism? Commentary? Theater?[3]

In making this contribution to a book series called Key Words in Jewish Studies, I am wary of the warning issued by literary theorist Raymond Williams, who noted in his own volume of key words that "culture," a term that he used frequently, was among the most difficult words to define in the English language.[4] We might make a similar claim about education in the context of Jews, Judaism, and Jewish culture. But Williams went a step further, offering an insight about key words, themselves. Difficult definitions, he argued, are what make dictionaries or explications of keywords interesting, valuable, or useful. "The dictionaries most of us use, the defining dictionaries, will in these cases, and in proportion to their merit as dictionaries, list a range of meanings, all of them current, and *it will be the range that matters.*"[5] He continued, "The variations and confusions of meaning are not just faults in a system, or errors of feedback, or deficiencies of education. They are in many cases, in my terms, historical and contemporary substance."[6] Divergences and deviations in the evolution of a word, he cautioned, should not distract from its use but rather reveal subtleties and implications that the term has accrued and shed over time, showing traces of its evolution, its uses, and its meanings.

The term "education" applies to so many features of modern Jewish life—from the work of the smallest synagogues to the efforts of the largest transnational organizations, and from concerns as diverse as philanthropy and publishing—that it would not be too far a stretch to conclude that Jewish communities dedicate more resources to education than they do to any other single cause, including politics, human services, and spirituality. There have been some writers and thinkers who believe that study qualifies, alongside or instead of prayer, as an essentially devotional act.[7] Education, it might be said, is what Jewish communities do. But this still does not help us answer this question: What do we mean by "Jewish education"? Over the following chapters, this book proposes to answer that question not by drawing lines that separate things that are educational from things that are not. Instead, it answers this question by following Williams and expanding the range of the term to include instances of the production and transmission of Jewish knowledge.

Why Production? Why Transmission? Why Knowledge?

This book focuses on education at the intersection of two related processes regarding knowledge: production and transmission. We can begin with an obvious educational matter like curriculum or a textbook. They are almost self-evidently material intended to facilitate the *transmission* of knowledge from their authors, through teachers, to students. But they also *produce* knowledge by representing editorial, authorial, and scholarly decisions about what to include, what to exclude, what to ignore, and what to amplify. What is excluded can be as important as what is included, and studies of textbooks or curricula, though not the same as studies of classrooms, can provide valuable insights into propositions about what knowledge is acceptable, significant, or even appropriate within a given historical or cultural or political context.[8] It is not difficult to apply a similar logic to other educational media that are, effectively, guided by a similar concern for production and transmission.

Production and transmission also provide a broader analytical berth for the discussion that follows because they are not hamstrung by the modern associations with the term "education," which entered the English language only around the sixteenth century (more on this in chapter 1). To refer to premodern efforts to teach children or train clergy, as in book titles like *Jewish Education and Society in the High Middle Ages* and *Jewish Education and History*, is to frame past practices in terms of present concepts in ways that the subjects of those books may not have recognized.[9] I do not wish to diminish the insights of those books, nor do I seek to marginalize the work of other scholars who have written about scribal schools, medieval private tutors, aural recitational culture, instructional texts, grammar books, or any other efforts to codify or systematize knowledge. But I do wish to resist efforts that use the modern term "education" to imply connections between schools then and schools now or that suggest that ancient approaches to knowledge work should be understood as "education" in its modern or contemporary form.

The impulses that led to the invention of Jewish education are clearly present throughout Jewish history, well before "Jewish education" came to be. Even the key word itself—rendered in English as a compound phrase consisting of the modifier "Jewish" affixed to the more general term "education"—needed an English-speaking community to formulate it in the first place. The emergence of a Hebrew analog—*chinuch Ivri* or *chinuch Yehudi*—emerged as a core element of Zionism around the turn of the twentieth century, appearing only sporadically before then.[10] The late arrival of the terms relative to the long arc of Jewish history indicates that the concept is a relatively recent development within the history of Jews and their communities, despite much longer concerns with the presentation, transmission, and production of knowledge as a driving force for the perpetuation, maintenance, and definition of those same communities.

The concern for the production and transmission of knowledge invites questions about what common purpose, if any, all of the efforts that compose this phenomenon served. How did different people or different communities understand their investments in knowledge work? What did they imagine would transpire as a result? The responses (explored in greater detail in chapters 2 and 3) varied by place and time, and their diversity demonstrates that it is exceedingly difficult to identify a unifying purpose shared by these varied and various efforts. As a result, this book is less concerned with questions about the content of Jewish educational efforts and more interested in its social processes, structures, and dynamics.

Different claims about what types or forms of knowledge people think is important or valuable have preoccupied writers in Jewish Studies and Jewish education for some time. In the introduction to their widely cited anthology, *Visions of Jewish Education*, Seymour Fox, Israel Scheffler, and Daniel Marom recalled the prompts given to the volume's contributors: "What is an educated Jew? What does an educated Jew need to know? What would you consider to be the product of a successful Jewish education?"[11] By answering these three questions, the contributors hoped to identify some kind of overarching theory or vision for the enterprise. But their questions predicted their answers rather rigidly, constituted as they were around the assumption that the purpose of Jewish education was to manufacture something called an "educated Jew." More troubling was the circularity of their logic: their version of "an educated Jew" was defined by what they thought such a person would need to know, and knowing it would make someone an "educated Jew." But who is really an "educated Jew," and who is to judge?

This book does not answer those questions and it rejects the figure of the "educated Jew" entirely in order to focus on the ways in which Jewish communities have produced and transmitted knowledge. Knowledge has long functioned like a commodity in that it could be shared, traded, and disbursed. As such, it has power, which meant that it was important and useful to control who had access to what forms of knowledge.[12] Women, for example, were afforded different access to certain sources of Jewish knowledge than were men, and these differences generated separate spheres of action, influence, and behavior. Children were supposed to know certain things and adults others. Jews were given access to some kinds of knowledge from which non-Jews were excluded. Young men deemed most capable (or, occasionally, just well-connected) were given access to still other, more difficult, more coveted sources. Jews in some parts of the world focused on certain sources of knowledge, while elsewhere Jews privileged others. Other knowledge, such as the Talmud's acknowledgment of the many manifestations of gender, have been suppressed, ignored, or marginalized.[13] Others, such as the system of Torah cantillation that often features in b-mitzvah training, have been elevated to quasi-mandatory status, even if they only occasionally become part of a person's repertoire for living a Jewish life.

The specifics about what mattered when and to whom have differed over time and across space as people disagreed about who was supposed to know what, what certain people thought other people should know, how best to ensure that the right people (whomever they were) knew the right things (whatever those were), and how to most efficiently ensure that all of this happened. People disagreed about what kinds of knowledge was important, what was trivial, and what constituted knowledge in the first place. Disagreements led to schools, schisms, towering intellectual achievements, and no small measure of anxiety about the future of knowledge and its ability to do all of the work that people had invested in it.

Jewish Studies and Jewish Education

Jewish Studies and Jewish education are two relatively recent developments in a long history of knowledge in Jewish life, and they will occupy the focus of chapter 1. Each represents a response to the Enlightenment, though they see their commitments to Jewish knowledge production differently. Reductively, practitioners of Jewish Studies tend to see themselves as responsible for knowledge about Jewish life, culture, history, and so on. Practitioners of Jewish education tend to see themselves as responsible for knowledge that people can and should apply to their lives. As a result of these different knowledge commitments, members of each sometimes regard the other with a measure of suspicion.

Principally, the field of Jewish Studies upholds the values of academic freedom and what would later be called "value-free" study directed more or less by the principles of the scientific method and university-based scholarship.[14] Scholars and their universities actively sought to differentiate their efforts from those of their more religiously oriented predecessors, drawing lines between "science" and "religion" and, more subtly, between "religious studies" and "theology."[15] The scholarly movement that preceded the contemporary formation of Jewish Studies was the Wissenschaft des Judentums or the academic or scientific study of Judaism. The purpose of the Wissenschaft was to apply the tools of critical, empirical modern scholarship to Judaism and to situate it in the academy rather than the synagogue.

Jewish education can also be understood as a product of the Enlightenment, insofar as the ideas and values that undergird many conceptions of education can be traced back to some key Enlightenment thinkers: John Locke, Jean-Jacques Rousseau, and Johann Gottfried von Herder principally among them (more on this in chapter 1). The approach to education advanced in the Enlightenment emphasized individual and societal uplift through study and the development of one's critical faculties via what Herder called *Bildung*. Theoretically, education was open to everyone and becoming educated meant that one could enter the deracinated, unmarked world of civil, cultural, and social affairs. Education, it was believed, could help teach people to assimilate and become modern citizens of the emerging world order of nation states. In practice, this proved not to be universally available, as the promises of education were effectively off-limits to colonized people, women, and, sometimes, Jews.[16] Nevertheless, in the late nineteenth century, American Jewish leaders began using the phrase "Jewish education" to refer to their efforts. Central to this new concept was the belief that approaches to teaching Jewish subjects needed modernization and that by modernizing the production and transmission of Jewish knowledge, Jewish education could both capitalize on the promise of Enlightenment education and inspire people to retain their commitments to the specificities of Jewish community, custom, culture, and practice. Jewish education thus emerged both as a response to the prospect of assimilation as imagined by the Enlightenment and as a bulwark against it.

The result has been something of a cold peace between Jewish Studies and Jewish education. Many Jewish educators regard Jewish Studies as not sufficiently engaged with Jewish life, and too removed, abstract, or otherwise dispassionate. Scholarship can be interesting, but to what end? Yet, when I tell people that I study Jewish education in a Graduate School of Education, they sometimes ask if I train Hebrew school teachers. Many of my colleagues in the field of Jewish Studies do not think of themselves as engaging in Jewish education because of the term's association with children, religious instruction, synagogues, Hebrew school, b-mitzvah training, the belief that it is an instrument of Jewish communal anxieties, the presumption that it is largely a failure, and that it is education largely in name but not in practice, and the list goes on and on. There is a gendered dimension to this criticism as well, which assumes that Jewish education is largely child-centered and low status and thus constitutes a kind of "women's work," with all of the suggestively derisive and misogynistic overtones that phrase recalls. In Russian Canadian writer David Bezmozgis's short story, "An Animal to the Memory," one of the characters mock-congratulates another on his victory in a schoolyard fight, saying, "Congratulations, you're the toughest kid in Hebrew School."[17] It was not meant as a compliment.

When I told a senior scholar in Jewish Studies that I was applying for the position I currently hold, he remarked, "There are no *gedolim* [great scholars] in Jewish education." The comment struck me less as an observation than as a warning about the field: the study of Jewish education is not serious enough to warrant the attention of a "great" scholar, and neither are its opportunities rich enough to produce one. Jewish education, he implied, is too applied, too parochial, too ethnocentric, too focused on convincing young people of their Jewishness, and too dedicated to survival or continuity. In his mind, this contrasted with Jewish Studies and its commitments to meticulous explorations of the intellectual intricacies of rabbinics, Jewish history, literature, or culture. Jewish Studies, he suggested, is a forum for learning *about* Jews and their societies, not about teaching people *to be* Jews or, in fact, to be anything at all.[18] In my colleague's formulation, Jewish education's flaw is that it is devotional and confessional, whereas Jewish Studies is intellectual, dispassionate, critical. Jewish Studies operates according to the conventions of academic freedom and open inquiry, while Jewish education is an agent for alleviating concerns about Jewish communal survival. In this formulation, Jewish Studies becomes and promises to be everything that Jewish education is not, and it becomes the corrective for everything that Jewish education has become. In response, Jewish education becomes the response to what the arid, abstract scholarship emerging from Jewish Studies cannot provide.

To understand the tension between Jewish Studies and Jewish education, we might use the language of philosopher Gilbert Ryle, who differentiated between two kinds of knowledge: "knowledge-how" and "knowledge-that."[19] The former refers to knowledge regarding operations or practices: how to fly a kite or how to chant from the Torah scroll according to the system of cantillation. The second refers to observable claims about the world: *this* is a kite and *that* is a Torah scroll. Learning scientists and philosophers of knowledge gave them slightly fancier names: "procedural knowledge" and "propositional knowledge."[20] Jewish education is often thought to foreground knowledge-how regarding the ways in which one ought to live a Jewish life. Jewish Studies can be understood to privilege knowledge-that, given its commitments to scholarly objectivity.

But Ryle proposes a slightly more complicated relationship between these two forms of knowledge. He argues that although "knowledge-that" is often privileged as the "ideal model of all operations of intelligence," it is grounded fundamentally in knowledge-how.[21] Action, not pure cognition, is the demonstration of true intelligence, or knowing. Ryle explained: "In short the propositional acknowledgement of rules, reasons or principles is not the parent of the intelligent application of them; it is a step-child of that application."[22] One can, he continued, know a great deal of facts, but the measure of intelligence he sought lay in how those facts are applied in the world. While Jewish Studies and Jewish education have retrenched around two knowledge propositions, Ryle reminds us that they are not as distinct as they might seem.

Yet, the mutual antipathy between Jewish Studies and Jewish education illustrates what is at stake in their respective efforts: their camps have to care enough about their perceived differences to bother disagreeing. Though they differ sharply about the best way to make good on their intentions, Jewish Studies and Jewish education share a commitment to the production and transmission of knowledge. By foregrounding this commitment, this book offers an account of Jewish Studies and Jewish education that pulls on their similarities to explore how pervasive and persistent knowledge work has been in Jewish communities and cultures throughout a long historical frame and across broad geographical terrain. It includes accounts of efforts in places as diverse as Salonika, Kairouan, Jerusalem, Buenos Aires, New York, Odessa, Warsaw, and Paris. It examines the visions that created Bais Yaakov (a school for Orthodox girls), the Jewish Sunday school, the Alliance Israelite Universelle, various yeshivas, summer camps, and other institutions. It draws on sources from the Talmud to the philosophy of the Enlightenment and postmodern epistemological theory because each of these influences has helped shape the ways in which Jews and their communities have tried to produce and transmit knowledge.

This book is born of the tension between Jewish Studies and Jewish education and the sense that they share more than either cares to admit. Resisting the image of the "educated Jew" as well as the binary logics of scholarship and practice, procedural and propositional knowledge, or communal concern and intellectual purity, and drawing on historical precedents that preceded the invention of Jewish education, this book seeks to shift the locus of inquiry from "an examination of the *contents* of knowledge to the investigation of *forms and practices* of knowing."[23] This effort will play out in the following pages by recalibrating our working understanding of Jewish education around a concern for *how* people know and not just *what* they know. By critically engaging Jewish education and Jewish Studies' respective knowledge commitments (chapter 1), by highlighting instances in the production and transmission of knowledge (chapters 2 and 3), and by turning to an appreciation of learning (chapter 4), this book argues for an appreciation of knowledge work as constitutive of Jewish life.

PART I

TERMS OF THE DEBATE

1   Estranged Siblings

The debate, as I'm framing it here, turns on the distinction between propositional knowledge and procedural knowledge in Jewish education and Jewish Studies. Jewish education, it could be said, trades primarily in procedural knowledge insofar at its practitioners seek to instill in their students a sense of *how* to be Jewish. Jewish Studies has largely served as a framework for the transmission of propositional knowledge, as its practitioners teach people *about* Jews, Judaism and Jewish culture, religion, knowledge, and so on. The debate contains elements that are both terminological and conceptual: Does the production and transmission of knowledge in Jewish Studies resemble that of Jewish education? How does each go about its work with regard to knowledge, how do they imagine their audience, and what they might do with the knowledge they gather? Chapters 2 and 3 respond to these questions by illustrating that the difference between them is less clear than it seems. Still, the debate between Jewish Studies and Jewish education turns on this difference, so it is worth exploring here.

The conceptual divide derives from the assumption that scholars of Jewish Studies are not practitioners of Jewish education and vice versa. This belief holds even though most scholars of Jewish Studies are employed by universities, teach students, write syllabi, lecture to audiences of adults on occasion, write books, appear on podcasts, pen articles in the Jewish and general press, and think at least occasionally about how best to explain their ideas to other people such that they can be understood. In short: they engage in a content area—Jewishness—and they teach people about it. Meanwhile, Jewish educators are thought not to produce knowledge but only transmit it, with an aim to guide the minds and hearts of their students toward a greater commitment to Jewish life, culture, practice, or identity. The difference between them hinges on how each regards their knowledge work in relation to the other, and this difference has shaped a series of binaries: If Jewish education is the domain of volunteer teachers, the professoriate is professional. If Jewish education is child-centered, Jewish Studies concerns young adults and adults seeking intellectual stimulation. If Jewish education is driven by Jewish communal agendas, Jewish Studies is guided by academic freedom. If Jewish education is about an identity proposition, Jewish Studies is about intellectual rigor. If Jewish education teaches Judaism, Jewish Studies teaches about Judaism. The result has been the emergence of two neighboring fields whose conflict, like that of estranged siblings, is fueled by their shared background.

The divide employs and reproduces stereotypes. Jewish education's stereotype of Jewish Studies tracks with stereotypes of scholars and higher education more generally: it is overly concerned with petty differences, with footnotes and citations. It is too theoretical, too removed from the lives or interests of actual people, and too abstract to matter much. The work produced by Jewish Studies might be interesting, but ultimately the world of the ivory tower bears little resemblance to the world in which most people live, and its scholarly contributions might line the shelves of libraries, but who has the patience for another four-hundred-page tome that excavates some long-forgotten figure or some arcane concept? In short, Jewish Studies appears to engage too deeply in propositional knowledge that can explain a phenomenon in great detail but offers little in the way of practical utility or inspiration.

Jewish Studies' conceptions of Jewish education typically turn on a belief that it is and has been the delivery mechanism for a set of coercive ideologies intended to boost religious practice, ethnic coherence, and Jewish identity, but not really, at the end of the day, to "educate" people or to inspire them or to entrust them with whatever riches one believes that Judaism might have. It is too interested in outcomes and not committed enough to critical engagement, thought, or even substantive knowledge. These concerns lead to a situation in which Jewish education is thought to be largely child-centered and thus neither serious nor worthy of status.[1] It might engage kids at summer camp or get them through their b-mitzvahs,[2] but Jewish education will readily trade good feeling for solid teaching.[3] According to this logic, Jewish education is not really education at all but just an elaborate set of institutions and programs designed to carry out a survivalist agenda at the behest of Jewish communal organizations and their funders.[4]

The stereotypes run deep, even among those who seek to destabilize one or both terms. Andrew Bush, in his volume on Jewish Studies for this series in Key Words in Jewish Studies, offered a trenchant critique of the field, but he still employed Jewish education as a foil. Critical of Jewish Studies' roots in the European Enlightenment, Bush writes,

> As a field in the setting of nonsectarian institutions of higher learning, Jewish Studies is charged with the reproduction of "Europe" . . . : to inculcate the value of the individuated self as the locus of free will, expressed through critical thinking, for instance, and the related valorization of certain kinds of individuals whose positions within structures of power allow them to exercise agency and voice. The institutions of Jewish learning reproduce Jewish values—fulfillment of the covenantal obligations revealed at Sinai, above all—and authorize some members of the covenantal community to interpret the obligations and oversee their fulfillment.[5]

Bush's juxtaposition of "studying" and "learning," though meant to destabilize the privileges associated with certain practitioners of Jewish Studies and the institutions that support them, nevertheless offers a caricature of "institutions of Jewish learning." Though later he notes that "the educational institutions of Jewish learning and Jewish Studies can sometimes serve one another's goals of social reproduction," the opposition he proposes serves a rhetorical function meant to clarify Jewish Studies against its implied inverse: Jewish education.

Stereotyped versions of each and both grow from an often-unarticulated but nevertheless strongly held investment in what education is and what it ought to be. Jewish education has been constituted around a paradox, namely that the values and ideals of "education," as a product of the universal ideals of the Enlightenment, can be marshalled to cultivate commitments to the particularistic concerns of Jewish communal life. I refer to this as the paradox of Jewish education. Jewish Studies has taken shape around a similar concern, most forcefully articulated by Jacob Neusner, a scholar of Judaism and prolific author, who believed deeply in the value of scholarship of Judaism. Neusner held this belief so strongly that he rejected the idea of "Jewish Studies" because of his concerns that it would just end up looking like Jewish education, but in college. Instead, he advocated for the scholarly study of Judaism, which he believed could buffer scholars and scholarship from parochial concerns of either Jewish communities or the researchers themselves. I call this the Neusnerian Fallacy.

Albeit implicitly, both the paradox of Jewish education and the Neusnerian Fallacy grow out of normative understandings of the preferred relationship between people and knowledge and a sense of what kinds of knowledge ought to preoccupy teachers and their students: Jewish education's preference for procedural knowledge that will enable students to live engaged Jewish lives and Neusner's preference for propositional knowledge that can stoke scholarly innovation. Both, however evidence a suspicion about the values implicit in the other. Yet, as will be demonstrated in chapters 2 and 3 and advanced in chapter 4, the distinction and the caricatures that underwrite it obscure more than they clarify. Together, they recall the old joke about Jews complaining about the food at a Catskills resort: it is not something they do, and they do not think particularly highly of it anyhow.[6]

The only scholarly volume that foregrounds connections between Jewish Studies and Jewish education, Harvey Shapiro's *Educational Theory and Jewish Studies in Conversation*, still invests in keeping its two titular terms distinct from each other.[7] Shapiro explains that he seeks "neither a synthesis nor an amalgam. No reduction or dilution is implied. And I am not suggesting a combining of two fields to address each's insufficiency."[8] Although he argues that each field can benefit from an engagement with the other, he nevertheless recruits "interdisciplinarity" as the modality of engagement and in the process further reifies Jewish Studies and Jewish education as distinct "disciplines." Even this lone effort to put these two fields (they are not disciplines) in conversation nevertheless affirms their distinction.

The sense of mutual exclusion carries into the structure of the respective fields as well. The field of Jewish Studies has effectively ignored scholarship and research in Jewish education, which contributed to the creation of the Conference on Alternatives in Jewish Education in the 1970s and the Network for Research in Jewish Education, which held its first conference in 1989. During the 2010s, the Association for Jewish Studies created a division in its annual conference called "pedagogy," but it does not feature research on pedagogy; instead, it typically hosts panels of professors talking about how they teach.[9] The field of Jewish education, in turn, has almost totally ignored Jewish Studies. The two-volume *International Handbook of Jewish Education* includes only a single essay on the academic study of Judaism, a reworking of an article on the history of the Association for Jewish Studies by Judith Baskin.[10] Stuart Kelman's 1992 handbook, *What We Know about Jewish Education*, omits Jewish Studies and ignores the academic study of Judaism more generally.[11] Throughout its nearly hundred-year history, the *Journal of Jewish Education* has scarcely addressed these topics.[12] Birthright Israel, one of the largest single Jewish educational programs, partnered with Hillel International and drew participants from people ages eighteen to twenty-six but never engaged significantly with Jewish Studies scholars, nor did it include any substantive consideration of Jewish Studies programs, centers, or courses in its evaluations of the program's impact on participants.[13] The same is true, largely, of Hillel International's research efforts, despite their engagement with college students and their association with universities.

To get past the caricatures and explore the relationship between Jewish education and Jewish Studies, we need to explore each term individually, to understand how each has been constituted around a conception of what knowledge is and how to produce or transmit it. This will require looking at the historical and cultural conditions that led to the emergence and conceptual underpinnings of each. Though teaching and learning have long been features of Jewish life, it was not until the late nineteenth century that the term "Jewish education" emerged, and Jewish Studies did not coalesce as a field until the late 1960s. Situating each phenomenon historically will help explain why they emerged in the ways that they did and how they constituted themselves and each other around concerns for and about knowledge.

The Invention of Education

There is no shortage of terms in Hebrew for some of the activities that are associated with education: learning, study, teaching, instruction, direction, knowledge, and so on (more on all of these in chapters 2 and 3). But the emergence of the term "Jewish education" or even "education" more generally has been relatively recent, so using it to describe instances of study, learning, or schooling in Jewish societies is a presentist misapplication of the concept. As we will see below, the term "Jewish education" is a particularized version of a more general phenomenon. So before we can investigate "Jewish education," we have to first understand the ideological, political, and cultural overtones of the term "education" and its emergence in and through the European Enlightenment.

The English term "education" did not come into circulation until the middle of the sixteenth century.[14] The earliest examples provided by the *Oxford English Dictionary* point to its usage in describing a child who had been taught or otherwise acquired appropriate manners and behavior. Over time, the concept expanded to suggest a more systematic approach to instruction that included some formalized instruction. But its emergence was closely tied to the end of the Middle Ages and the early promises of the Enlightenment, namely that science, knowledge, politics, and art could fuel the revival of Europe.

It was also closely tied to the Protestant Reformation, which was kicked off, in part, by the disgruntled priest Martin Luther, who in 1517 posted his famous Ninety-five Theses to the local parish door. Chief among Luther's claims was that individuals did not need church hierarchies or elaborate rites to commune with the divine. Luther, in a direct challenge to the power of the Catholic Church, argued that individuals could cultivate their own beliefs without the intercession of the clergy and could read the Bible directly and without Church-approved interpretations or commentaries. Accelerated by the invention of the printing press in the middle of the fifteenth century, Luther's ideas about the power of individuals to read and come to their own conclusions about the meaning of the Bible and their relationship to God helped to transform common understandings of both religion and education in Europe.

As Luther's ideas spread, so too did new ideas about the power of science, universalism, and individualism and the prospect that nation states could become the basis for a new world order based on natural rights and not religious orders or empires. Political emancipation promised "the inclusion of the excluded and the elevation of the oppressed" within the emergent social and political order.[15] But emancipation was easier promised than delivered, and with it came a host of questions about how exactly to treat people who did not, for one reason or another, resemble the people who came up with the concept in the first place. Race, region, gender, language, and religion all figured as challenges to the universalized promise of political emancipation, as did efforts to forge new nations out of disparate people who lived within both its borders and its colonial imagination. How do people become citizens of a nation? How do they learn to understand their roles and responsibilities? How to mitigate differences between people and orient them toward a common set of values, concerns, and goals? How can empires expand and colonize other lands and create reliable, devoted subjects from the people who lived there? How to forge a collective out of disparate, diverse people with individual wills? The answer, in part, was education.[16]

Among the first to formulate a theory of education was English philosopher John Locke (1632–1704), who advanced the notion that children were blank slates and that corruption ensued through improper teaching.[17] The obvious answer was not just that people ought to improve instruction, but that the cultivation of people's values and virtues could make them self-governing agents, capable of controlling their own desires and rationally and reasonably engaging in public and civil discourse. Freedom, in the form of the innate freedom of the human intellect, laid the foundation for education. Locke's ideas proved broadly influential across Europe and left a particularly deep impression on French philosopher Jean-Jacques Rousseau (1712–1778), who outlined his own educational vision in his 1762 book *Emile*.[18] *Emile* tells the story of the eponymous youth and maps out an educational trajectory that largely falls in line with Rousseau's understanding that society corrupts the natural goodness of humanity. In the book, Rousseau argues against rigid instruction and for an approach to education that can leverage children's natural curiosities and proclivities without tainting them with concepts drawn from the corruptions of society. Like Locke, he railed against strict religious instruction and its emphasis on memorization and advocated for education that cultivated what he thought were children's natural interests. Rousseau wagered that the less corrupted children would be by society's ills, the more likely they would be to find fellowship and commonalities with others. This could be taught, he argued, but only by tapping into the natural state of humanity.

Rousseau's theory of education as a kind of moral training grounded in humanity's innate curiosity, intellect, and orientation found resonance among philosophers of the Enlightenment who wedded intelligence to the human spirit, highlighting it as the engine for the Enlightenment itself. German philosopher Immanuel Kant (1724–1804) said it most plainly at the beginning of his essay, "What is Enlightenment?" "Enlightenment is man's emergence from his self-imposed nonage. Nonage is the inability to use one's own understanding without another's guidance. This nonage is self-imposed if its cause lies not in lack of understanding but in indecision and lack of courage to use one's own mind without another's guidance. Dare to know! (Sapere aude) 'Have the courage to use your own understanding,' is therefore the motto of the Enlightenment."[19] Central to Kant's claim was his belief in the innate capacity for understanding and reason. One must be taught: "Man can only become man by education. He is merely what education makes of him."[20] Yet true enlightenment could be achieved only by virtue of one's own intellectual bravado. In this way, Kant followed Locke and Rousseau in framing education not as a matter of instruction but as an approach to the careful cultivation of innate characteristics.[21]

Johann Gottfried von Herder (1744–1803), another German philosopher, operationalized this concept as Bildung, or cultural and moral formation.[22] Herder believed deeply in the power and utility of education and understood that it was a defining quality of European culture. The scientific or systematic pursuit of knowledge that characterized the Enlightenment in German universities was known as Wissenschaft, and it came to be intimately connected to the ideology of Bildung. Allan Bloom, one of Rousseau's translators, called *Emile* the first Bildungsroman, a genre of fiction that advanced the concept.[23] In nineteenth-century Germany, what one knew and how one came to know it came to be components of the new, modern approach to knowledge and new political orders. "The barbarian rules by force," Herder asserted, "the cultivated conqueror teaches."[24] The distinction is forceful and plain. Education can be as powerful as force for conquering the world. The difference is one of sensibility.

With respect to Jews, historian David Sorkin explained how this played out. Referring to Herder, Sorkin observed that the German states of the early nineteenth century believed that their job "was to educate Jews to become worthy of citizenship by transforming their occupations and endowing them with true moral character through education (*Bildung*)."[25] Jewish leaders, he noted, eagerly went along with the plan, hoping that the state would make good on its promise of political emancipation. But historian Michael Meyer noted that the term chafed against Jewish conceptualizations of scholarship and study. "Education, in the sense of Bildung, was not conceived as inherent within Judaism but involved a cultivation of intellect, taste, and manners that were seen to emanate from outside of it. A Jew qua Jew might be 'learned' but not educated. An 'educated Jew' in Central or Eastern Europe was one who had broadened his perspective beyond the confines of Judaism through the acquisition of non-Jewish culture and values."[26] To be educated, then, was to embrace ideas, values, and orientations from beyond the Jewish community. Because the terms of Bildung were set by the German elite, they reflected those concerns, not those of Jewish communities. When Jews did adopt the term, it signaled a shift away from previous conceptions of learnedness, or at least it echoed a willingness to distinguish between them. Insofar as the term meant "education," it referred not to the study of Jewish texts but to the adoption of mores and values of the non-Jewish German majority. To become educated under these conditions may have been accompanied by political, cultural, social, and economic benefits, but at the time it was not considered a modality for sustaining a commitment to Jewish life and its values and mores, or even its conception of knowledge.

Education, of course, could also become a tool for socialization or other political ends. In nineteenth-century Russia, for example, Tsar Nicholas I made education more accessible to Jews by allowing them to enroll in state schools and establish Jewish-run institutions. His intention was clear: to use education to transform Jewish peasants into subjects of the Russian regime.[27] He believed that by exposing them to state schools he could force them to modernize. His plan, however, did not unfold as he intended, as "the Jews attending these schools, rather than becoming assimilated Russians, became Jewish intellectuals."[28] Later in the century, Tsar Alexander III banned Jews from schools and shuttered other schools, fearing that too much access to education would foment Jewish political agitation and activity.

In the United States, these ideas translated into approaches to education that aspired to balance commitments to individual liberty and social cohesion. Historian of American education Carl Kaestle wrote that the founders of the United States "shared a sense of opportunity, of responsibility to mankind, a sense that a real revolution had been made, that they build a new society based on enlightened ideas about the perfectibility of men and institutions."[29] Again, education would play a key role in the fulfillment of this ideal, though in practice it would prove a continual challenge. The first half century of the United States' existence saw many experiments with schooling and education, most of which were managed by individual states, and with varying degrees of success.

In the early nineteenth century, Massachusetts educator Horace Mann outlined one of the first and most influential visions of American education, advocating for the creation of a system of "common schools," which became the precursor to America's public schools. Mann's common schools would be freely available to all citizens and provide a shared, unifying experience that would train an increasingly diverse and dispersed American population to be informed citizens of the emerging nation.[30] Concerned about social divisiveness, Mann tried to forbid the teaching of controversial issues and advocated for regular Bible readings "without comment," so as to reduce the threat that religious sectarianism might pose to his unifying belief in education.[31] Jews, who represented a tiny fraction of the American population at that time, did not concern him.

But Jews did figure in the broader history of European education, which has been formative to the conceptualization of Jewish education and Jewish Studies. Specifically, they were often included in state-initiated educational endeavors, but only so that they could be educated out of their Jewishness. Some Jewish communities welcomed the opportunity, others grudgingly went along with it, and others resisted. Still, education paved the path to modernization, to political emancipation, to participation in the sciences and the cultural arts. Jews could become educated according to the terms laid out by emerging nation states, but it often meant shedding their Jewishness. As historian Peter Gay put it, the philosophers of the Enlightenment believed that the "absorptive capacity of Judaism did not give it a philosophical world view." Consequently, "the path to the scientific mentality lay elsewhere."[32]

Crystalized in the concept of Bildung, education sought to instill in its subjects a sense of moral purpose and common cause. Following Herder's comment about civilized conquerors, one could claim that nearly all forms of state education constitute a form of cultural imperialism, as Michael Apple, Stanley

Aronowitz, Henry Giroux, and other critics of education have argued.[33] But there is always room for resistance and refashioning even within this most universalizing of concepts. And for Jews, the possibility that they could adopt the terms and ideals of education for the purpose of advancing their own communal aims proved irresistible, if fraught.

The Invention of Jewish Education

When Rebecca Gratz opened her Hebrew Sunday school in Philadelphia in 1838 and Adolphe Crémieux led the Alliance Israelite Universelle (AIU) to build its first school in Tetouan, Morocco, in 1862, neither used the term "Jewish education" to describe their efforts.[34] They spoke of teachers and teaching, students and learning, schools, values, books, and subjects. They certainly spoke of the value of schooling to Jewish youth and their communities, but they did not speak of "Jewish education" as such. Writing in the German newspaper *Shulamith* in 1821, Eduard Israel Kley outlined a vision for Jewish schools that highlighted the difference between what he observed and what he wished, though he too did not use the language of Jewish education. Instead, he wrote that Jewish schools "should not be merely instructional institutions but rather educational institutions. . . . Youth in the elementary schools should therefore not only be instructed but much more so educated." Driven by the ideals of the Enlightenment, Kley explained his hope that Jewish schools would produce modern citizens: "To this end and before all else the young generation ought to become educated and refined. Out of this refined humanity will come forth a refined Israelite and a refined citizen."[35] Kley, Gratz, and the founders of the AIU all embraced the value of education and its benefit to Jewish communal interests, though they did not yet think in terms of "Jewish education" as such.

Historian of Israeli education Rachel Elboim-Dror wrote of the various valences of the term "education" during what she called the "Zionist revolution" of the early twentieth century. "Hebrew education," (*chinuch ivri*) she wrote, "presented radical goals for the transformation of society and people, hence the emphasis on Hebrew education, in contrast to traditional Jewish education and general education, which was the fruit of the culture of other nations."[36] By "Hebrew education," she meant both an approach to teaching that revolved around Hebrew instruction but also something broader, which suggested an approach to education that was powerfully rooted in Jewish values and the cultural revival of the Jewish nation. By distinguishing between general, traditional Jewish, and Hebrew education, Elboim-Dror indicated how centrally education figured in the Zionist vision, and how significant it was to establish a particularly "Hebrew" instance of it.

When the English term emerged in the late nineteenth century, American Jews had already embraced both the ideals and some of the practices of American public schooling. Beginning in 1881, Jewish immigrants from Eastern

Europe began arriving in the United States in larger and larger numbers, settling in cities and turning to the systems of free and compulsory public education as the primary pathway toward Americanization.[37] The structures and
values of American public schooling, fraught though they might have been,
made an impression on Jewish leaders charged with educating immigrant
youth, as did the pressures to both enable their acculturation to their newly
adopted homes and bolster their commitment to Jewish life. Some of the earliest references to "Jewish education" in English can be found in the work of the
Jewish Chautauqua Society, a late nineteenth-century initiative that envisioned
itself as a training institute for Jewish teachers.[38] Drawing explicitly on the language and orientations of American public schooling, the Jewish Chautauqua
Society tried to bring approaches to the teaching and learning of Jewish subjects into alignment with expectations and conventions of modern American
education by providing curricular materials and professional development
for teachers working in the nascent field. The Jewish Chautauqua Society
"organized the first national Jewish teachers institute, a correspondence school
for religious-school teachers, and was a pioneer in the areas of adult education,
textbook publication, audio-visual production, and curricular development."[39]
The purpose was to create and support an approach to the teaching of Jewish
materials that drew on their resemblance to the educational system with
which most immigrant Jews were already familiar. By grafting its conception of
American education onto its commitment to train teachers of Jewish children,
the Jewish Chautauqua Society bestowed on their project both an immediate leg-
ibility and a sense of credibility among a community eager to take advantage of
"the wonders of America."[40]

A few decades later, Samson Benderly, the architect of the Jewish supplementary school approach in the United States, transformed the ideas of the
Jewish Chautauqua Society into a vision for Jewish education that even more
explicitly styled itself on American public education. For Benderly, this included
materials and pedagogic techniques as well as the adoption of new technologies
like single-student desks, chalkboards, and report cards alongside an administrative structure that emulated the centralized organization of public schools
into districts led by superintendents.[41] His purpose was clearly to draw on the
conventions of general education in order to invest his vision of Jewish education with the gravity and seriousness of public schooling. Benderly regularly
emphasized the compatibility between Jewish education and public education,
arguing that the more closely the former resembled the latter, the better it
would be able to complement but not directly compete with the withering
effects of a purely secular education.[42]

As late as 1914 the term "Jewish education" had still not yet coalesced, as
indicated in a footnote affixed to the title of a report filed by Israel Friedlander,
a professor of Bible at the Jewish Theological Seminary who also served with

Benderly on the Board of Trustees of the Bureau of Education of the Jewish Community in New York. The report, called "The Problem of Jewish Education in America," was published as part of a larger volume issued by the United States Bureau of Education, where it appeared alongside a number of other articles on specialized topics like Catholic and Lutheran education, but also vocational, agricultural, and rural education. The editor of the volume found it necessary to add a note to Friedlander's title to clarify the contribution's focus. "This paper relates to Jewish education, not the education of the Jews. The schools fostered by the Bureau of Jewish Education are designed to impart a knowledge of Judaism and its religious institutions. The children who attend them are also pupils of the public schools."[43] The editor's need to make such a distinction, and the distinction that it made, indicate that the term "Jewish education" was not yet widespread enough to be meaningful on its own.

Though new, the term had begun to find wider use in the Jewish community. Alexander Dushkin, a scholar of Jewish education in the United States and another student of Benderly's, found it necessary to explain his choice of language in his 1918 survey titled *Jewish Education in New York City*. "The phrase 'Jewish education' is used throughout this book instead of the more technically correct 'Jewish training' or 'Jewish instruction,' because of the sanction of popular usage."[44] In opting for the more popular term instead of the more precise one, he implied that "Jewish education" was not the best choice for his study, but that he would give in to popular opinion.

Following Dushkin, other scholars also adopted "Jewish education" to generically refer to premodern practices of teaching, schooling, instruction, and study. Often, the phrase is used without critical comment to make a broad claim about the significance of Jewish education across space and time, drawing implicit continuities between ancient and contemporary practices and values. For example, Joseph Bentwich's history of education in the State of Israel begins by declaiming, "Education, among the Jewish people, has a long tradition."[45] More recently, the preface to the *International Handbook of Jewish Education* asserts, "Jewish education has topped the agenda of Jews whenever and wherever they lived."[46] Hebraist and historian Zevi Scharfstein captured the universalizing dimension of this approach in his introduction to a three-volume history of the phenomenon: "The goal of Jewish education in the diaspora has been the continuation of the existence of our nation and the continuation of the foundation of the tradition, developed atop the culture of the day."[47] Sweeping claims like these retroject the modern concept of education onto premodern social forms. More subtly, these claims impute historical continuities in values and practices, blurring understanding of and insight into how the invention of education shaped its formulation in Jewish communities and contexts. In so doing, scholars appear to employ ostensibly historical studies to find answers to contemporary challenges or to justify their own interests in Jewish education.

What results is a blurring of historical practices in the name of present concerns. Philosopher of Jewish education Barry Chazan erroneously claimed that "for pre-modern Jews, education was ipso facto Jewish education."[48] Similarly, in their analysis of Christian hegemony in American education, Kevin J. Burke and Avner Segall make a similar claim by counting the number of times versions of the verbs "teach" (261) and "learn" (244) appear in the Hebrew Bible before concluding that "God's interactions . . . are all inherently educational."[49] Historian Moshe Aberbach used a similar logic to explain the response of Jewish communities to the destruction of the Temple in Jerusalem in 70 CE: "Education became the new Temple; and the study of what was lost replaced what was lost."[50] Historian Emanuel Gamoran used the term throughout his 1924 volume *Changing Conceptions in Jewish Education*, including in its title. Gamoran's book covers a lot of ground and surfaced a great deal of data about how Jews organized, paid for, and carried out schooling of adults and children under a variety of social, cultural, and political conditions. Yet his application of the term "Jewish education" to premodern Jews reveals his own concerns, born of his own social and political context. Describing his work as a study "on the educational adjustment of the immigrant Jew," he adds that "the writer aims to give a historical, descriptive account of Jewish education. . . . Besides the historical value that this study may have, a knowledge of Jewish education in Russia and Poland has significant practical implications for the adjustment of the Jew to America."[51]

In one sense, these scholars are not wrong. The children in Chazan's study did not attend formal schools outside of their own communities, Burke and Segall correctly count the number of times certain words appeared in the biblical text, and Aberbach's account of scholarship in the wake of the destruction of the Temple is more or less the accepted version of those events. But using the term "education" to refer to the conditions and instances to which they were referring allows them to perform some scholarly sleight of hand by applying a contemporary concept to past practices. The term was not widely used by the people to whom it is being ascribed, and they may not even have recognized it as applying to their efforts to teach, study, or school. Given the history of the concept of education and its emergence from the Enlightenment conception of Bildung, the application of the term "education" to premodern efforts to teach, school, study, or learn blurs our understanding of how Jewish communities regarded those processes and put them into action. With all due respect to Dushkin's acknowledgement of the popular convention, these scholarly efforts distort the past in light of the present by imagining that people *back then* thought of themselves and their activities in the same ways and for the same reasons that people do *now*.

By applying the term "Jewish education" to phenomena that predated the emergence of the term by its avowed practitioners, scholars of schools and study have flattened the diversity of approaches and concerns regarding the production and transmission of knowledge in the premodern period. Additionally, they have reified "Jewish education" by imagining it as a transhistorical feature of Jewish life and culture, rather than approaching it as a response to specific historical and political conditions. It also offers the promise of an unbroken chain of connection between an ancient culture and the contemporary one, a chain that weaves through the vicissitudes of migration, exile, diaspora, political disenfranchisement, and the challenges and opportunities of emancipation and modernity. "Jewish education" can then be mobilized in support of the logic of communal survival or "continuity."

Jewish Education for What?

The concept of Jewish education would have been utterly foreign for much of Jewish history. The norms and conventions of Jewish life that emphasized the study or teaching of sacred texts put little daylight between study and action, between what one learned and what one did, between knowledge-that and knowledge-how. At least, the intention was that the more one learned—if one did so the right way—the more apt one was to engage in Jewish life either at home or in the community. Even with concerns about Bildung and education, the impulse in Jewish teaching and learning was closer to that of math education or history education, in which one is not only taught *about* a subject but taught to embody the thought and practices of the subject.[52] Thus, the tension between Jewish Studies and Jewish education can be understood to be the exception rather than the norm, with respect to the transmission and production of Jewish knowledge.

In premodern times, scholars and teachers sought to provide their students with the basic knowledge necessary to participate in Jewish communal life. For boys, this typically meant a familiarity with liturgical Hebrew and ritual performance. For girls, this often meant focusing on the customs and laws regarding family conduct, foodways, and menstrual purity. For those boys who proved capable, advanced study became an option. But there was no sense that study and practice were distinct from each other, nor was there an understanding (as there was in modernity) that the study of Jewish texts could be distinct from the Jewish people who studied them. Study was not universal, though commentator after commentator lamented the fact that Jewish people were not as knowledgeable as they wished they were. The corresponding idea that Jewish people should engage in the study of Jewish sources was largely self-evident, on the assumption that the sources contained the information necessary for Jews to fulfill their divinely appointed mission.

The historian of medieval Jewish education Moses Güdemann wrote that commentators of the time "were so occupied with the actual work of educating that they had little time left to write about education."[53] This is not entirely accurate. It would be more accurate to say that they found study and teaching so ubiquitous that they did not require additional comment or theorization. For men at least, learning, interpreting, and studying were communal activities that were part and parcel of Jewish social life. The weekly recitation of a portion of the Five Books of Moses, read from a Torah scroll, the compilation of the prayer-book, and other apparently ritualistic elements presented elements of knowledge for learning. Synagogue sermons and ethical wills, too, included instructions about what people thought to be worth paying attention to. This is not to suggest that people spent their days cloistered in studies and poring over texts, but rather that the prevailing perspectives on learning, at least as they have been handed down to us, understood it as part of Jewish life because it promised to orient people toward serving God, which was part of what they understood to be the unique mission of Jews in the world.

Those commentators and writers who gave some indication about why they were writing seemed largely to do so because they feared that people either were not knowledgeable enough, according to whatever measure they were using, or were learning the wrong things or studying the right things but doing so incorrectly. Each successive text that claims to illuminate and elucidate Jewish law, lore, and custom makes an implicit argument for better, more accurate, more authentic approaches to learning. The extraordinary chain of commentaries from the Rambam's *Mishne Torah* to Rabbi Jacob ben Asher's *Arbah Turim* to Joseph Karo's *Beit Yosef*, which then became the basis for his *Shulchan Aruch*, is perhaps the best example of this intergenerational dialogue about what kinds of knowledge matter and how to make it accessible. The point was to keep people Jewishly on track, and people would propel themselves down that track through study.

With the arrival of modernity, political emancipation, and the Enlightenment, Jewish communities in Europe and beyond faced new challenges, new opportunities, and new ideas about what one had to know in order to participate in or properly resist this emerging world. The chance to participate widely in political and cultural movements or to become citizens of new nation states challenged assumptions that the imperative to study derived from the unique divine mission of the Jews. Instead, Jewish responses to the conditions of modernity tended to approach Jewishness as something that no longer seemed to be an a priori condition for Jews and Jewish communities. This required the creation of an additional layer of theorization or rationalization, absent from the writings of Güdemann's teachers, that outlined both *how* and *what* people ought to know. More importantly, the conditions of modernity demanded that people writing about teaching and thinking about their applicability to Jewish life begin to express *why* they thought people ought to know what they were hoping to teach.

One set of responses embraced the opportunities of modernity and tried to formulate visions for how best Jews could leverage study to make inroads into the new political, social, and economic orders. Another set of responses embraced Jewish nationalism and its promises of cultural renewal through art, literature, and politics. Still another group saw modernity as a threat to Jewish life and mapped out new relationships between life and study that tried to keep it from encroaching on what they understood to be Judaism and Jewish culture. Figureheads and leading thinkers of these groups often disagreed sharply, but their frameworks also overlapped, leading to formulations like religious Zionism, diaspora nationalism, or efforts to reform religious practice.

Though people differed in approach, content, strategy, and ideology, each of these three responses to modernity—one assimilationist, one nationalist, and one archly religious—agreed that the production and transmission of knowledge was central to their larger strategies, and they worked to communicate—to *teach*—their ideas to whoever would listen. Their leaders wrote tracts and gave lectures. They fundraised for and built schools (both physical and ideological). They debated with themselves and others, all in the pursuit of refining and publicizing their ideas so that others might internalize and adopt them. Beneath these varied approaches, however, also lay a shared set of concerns for the survival of Jewish communities in this new modern world. Each of these responses made a different bet on what approach would succeed, but they all tethered the future of the Jewish people to the production and transmission of knowledge about and for Jewish life. Education was to be the fuel for the survival of the Jewish people.

This sentiment pervades writing on Jewish education to the extent that it is often advanced but rarely explained. It can be found in writings from practically every ideological camp and representing virtually every perspective. The Tarbut (culture) schools in Russia and Poland offered secular, Zionist-oriented education that employed modern approaches to education like the immersive *Ivrit-be-ivrit* (Hebrew in Hebrew) approach to teaching Hebrew, to prepare students for immigration to Palestine as part of the revitalization of Jewish culture.[54] Historian Glenn Dynner noted that religious leaders in interwar Poland expressed their fears around cultural attrition and religious diminution: "But their anxiety was tempered by an abiding faith in the restorative power of devotional ('Torah') study, and their optimism began to seem justified as traditionalist schools were revamped across Poland and institutes of advanced Jewish learning (Hebrew: yeshiva) enrollments swelled beyond capacity."[55] Also in Poland, Sarah Schenirer applied this logic to the religious education of young women through her creation of the Bais Yaakov school, about which she explained, "My main intention is to arouse [my students'] desire to be Jewish."[56]

In the United States and Canada, the belief in the power of education to repel fears about the loss or weakening of Jewish identification was even more powerfully expressed. The secular Yiddishist Sholom Aleichem schools (founded in 1913), the Farband, and the Workman's Circle were all motivated by a shared intention "to educate a generation that will be bound to Jewish culture, and that will, in time, be able not only to be the consumer but also the creator of new Jewish culture."[57] Around the same time, Samson Benderly and his acolytes imbued their vision for Jewish education with an explicitly survivalist, retention-focused orientation from the very beginning.[58] In a 1955 reflection, Benderly's student, Samuel Dinin, penned an "analysis and critique of Jewish Education in America" in which he surveyed the scene and fretted about the effort it would require to ensure the transmission of Jewishness to an Americanized generation. "Unless there is a diffusion of the know-how of Jewish life among the masses so that it has a certain pattern, a distinctiveness, a quality all its own," he warned, "we will not be a cohesive Jewish community able to maintain its own unity, let alone its unity with Israeli Jewry and other Jewries."[59]

At the end of the 1960s, as Jewish Studies was beginning to take shape, Walter Ackerman reiterated this approach amid an otherwise searing indictment of the blandness of the larger effort: "The broad purpose of the Jewish school is to contribute to the continued existence of the Jews as an identifiable group."[60] Shortly thereafter, sociologist Steven M. Cohen opened his study of Jewish day school graduates by recapitulating this logic: "The distinctive purpose of parochial education is to develop and maintain favorable attitudes toward the values and practices of a particular religious group."[61] This attitude persisted in bolstering the conceptualization of Jewish education as the most likely strategy for retaining or perpetuating Jewish communal survival. As Jonathan Krasner noted, "By the 1980s, Jewish education was acknowledged as a communal desideratum even as educators, communal professionals, and lay people alike expressed dissatisfaction with the status quo and the lack of a coordinated strategy for systemic renovation and renewal."[62] But the language of survival sounded a little bleak, so in the late 1980s, American Jewish communal leaders advanced a program of "Jewish continuity" to replace the language of "survival," though it meant, in effect, the same thing.[63]

All of this momentum and investment led historian Jack Wertheimer, writing at the end of the twentieth century, to observe, "And perhaps never before has a Jewish community pinned so much of its hopes for 'continuity'—for the transmission of a strong Jewish identity to the next generation—on programs of formal and informal education."[64] By the turn of the twenty-first century, the rationale of Jewish education had been affirmed as a central pillar of Jewish communal life and as the most likely driver of Jewish commitment for the future.

The Paradox of Jewish Education

The hope that Wertheimer identified, and the persistent claims that Jewish education held the key to the perpetuation of the Jewish people, however, cannot quite cover over the paradox inherent in the term "Jewish education."

Clearly, it refers to a specific kind of education—like math education, science education, or religious education. The term connotes an implicit but necessary distinction between education that is Jewish and another, unmarked concept of education that bears no such modifier. The existence of marked and unmarked forms of education implies a relationship between them in which the general serves as the model for the particular. Otherwise, the two terms would be redundant. What benefit would be garnered by applying the term "education" to a Jewish concern, and what benefit would be gained by affixing the particularistic modifier "Jewish" to the more universal notion of "education"? The process of adapting the universalistic claims of education to the particularistic needs of the Jewish community in the neologism "Jewish education" has resulted in something of a paradox: How can the values of universalistic education, with its roots so strongly in the assimilationist logic of Bildung, serve the particularistic needs of a community seeking to retain its characteristics as a unique group? Is "education" even the right word?

The paradox can be traced back to the emergence of the term in both Hebrew (typically translated as *chinuch*) and English. Jewish Enlightenment reformer Naphtali Herz Wessely (1725–1805) used the term in his writings, including in the subtitle of his 1782 book, *Words of Peace and Truth*, which was among the first to outline a systematic approach to the schooling of Jewish youth. Wessely's educational vision hinged on his division of knowledge into two clusters: *Torat ha'adam*, or secular teaching, and *Torah Hashem*, God's teaching.[65] The aim of instruction, he argued, was to teach the content of both and, in the process, demonstrate how the former laid the foundation for the latter. But how to balance secular and sacred knowledge, and how to calculate the relationship between the two? Wessely feared that too much attention to secular knowledge might lead Jews astray, and too much of God's teaching would fail to avail Jews of the promise of modernity.

This tension courses through many of the Jewish educational efforts that followed. Historian Aron Rodrigue explained that one of the aims of the AIU, an educational program and network of schools meant to serve Jewish communities throughout the French colonies, was to "have Westernization go hand in hand with a real attachment to Judaism by the students."[66] Ahad Ha'am asked how to undertake "national education" (Hebrew: *hachinuch haleumi*) without lapsing into "chauvinism" ("like we see in France," he added).[67] Philosopher Paul Mendes-Flohr detected this tension more broadly among cultural Zionists during the early twentieth century who were wedded at once to the liberal, secular vision of culture, while passionately committed to the national reconstruction of their own people.[68]

Among American Jews, we can find the tension deep in the writings and approaches of Samson Benderly by looking at the influence of philosopher John Dewey on his educational thinking. Chief among Dewey's educational contributions was his understanding that education provided the foundation for productive, deliberative citizens of democratic societies and that schools should help train youngsters to be citizens.[69] Benderly had read Dewey and internalized his theories of education, and many of Benderly's students wrote their dissertations about philosophical matters that drew on Dewey's core ideas.[70] Benderly tried to model his vision of Jewish education on Dewey's in order to provide an educational approach that he believed would teach American Jews to be both committed Jews and thoughtful actors in a democratic society. As he explained, Jewish education was to create American Jews: "The future Jews of America, we felt, are not going to be Reform or Orthodox, Zionists or anti-Zionists, but Just American Jews. . . . The problem before us was to form a body of young Jews who should be, on the one hand, true Americans, a part of this republic, with an intense interest in upbuilding American ideals; and yet, on the other hand, be also Jews, in love with the best of their own ideals, and not anxious merely to merge with the rest and disappear among them."[71] Deepening the echoes of Dewey, Benderly concluded that Jewish education "is not merely a religious, but a civic problem." Benderly's formulation bears the distinct imprints of Dewey's thinking, but it also reverberates with the concerns of Wessely, the AIU, and Ahad Ha'am, each of whom envisioned Jewish education that could balance commitments to enlightened learning and to the specific construction or reconstruction of Jewish communal life.[72]

Jewish education scholar Isa Aron proposed that a better framework for thinking about these efforts was that of "enculturation," which she defined as "the process by which an individual is initiated into all aspects of a culture, including its language, values, beliefs, and behaviors."[73] This would be a more accurate conceptual framing for the efforts of Jewish institutions that currently fall under the umbrella of "Jewish education," and it more closely reflected the approaches of Ahad Ha'am and other Zionists who believed that they had to train a generation of Jews to commit themselves to the project of national revitalization. Yet even though the values of enculturation align well with the intention of much that is referred to as "Jewish education," the appeal of education persists, in part, because of its resonance with modernity, with free inquiry, democratic citizenship, and the promise of Bildung. Enculturation, by contrast, suffers from associations with parochialism and can border on indoctrination. Enculturation gives up on enlightenment in favor of cultivating particularistic commitments. Writing toward the end of the twentieth century, philosopher of Jewish education Michael Rosenak offered a philosophical reframing of this tension: "How does one really educate a young person, really help a young person to become loyal, disciplined by the regimen of revealed norms and, at the same time, curious, open and endowed with an expansive spirituality?"[74] How, Rosenak's question asks, does one provide the tools of enlightenment to young people and still ensure their commitment to the particular formations and beliefs of the Jewish community?

This question lies at the heart of the paradox of Jewish education. For critics of Jewish education who assert that the endeavor is driven too directly by desired outcomes, the paradox reveals Jewish education's indoctrinating intentions and thus undermines any claim the effort makes on "education" proper. The paradox provides easy fuel for people ready to dismiss Jewish education as an avenue for adults to conscript children into becoming "good Jews," however that might be understood. This critique is a bit too cynical (and too dismissive of learners, as we will explore in chapter 4). Instead, we might hear in Rosenak's question a measure of optimism that underwrites the paradox. Rosenak, like many who preceded him, believed that it was possible to draw on both the inspiration of the Enlightenment and the allure of Jewish tradition in the service of something called "Jewish education."

Read in this light, the paradox might not undermine Jewish education but define it. It certainly does not make it any less worthwhile or less intellectually rich, though it has opened up Jewish education to withering criticism for being both insufficiently educational and insufficiently Jewish. It has provided fodder for critics who see the undertaking as little more than indoctrination, and it has driven scholarly efforts to reinforce the invention of Jewish education as a transhistorical value. Yet it also provides the dynamism necessary for any sustained effort to produce and transmit knowledge under circumstances in which there is no obvious authority, and where social and cultural boundaries are defined more by their porosity than by the limitations they are supposed to represent. It allows for the adaptation of new technologies, new modalities, and new combinations of commitments to emerge in unpredictable ways. The paradox holds a logic that appeals to religionists as well as secularists, nationalists as well as diasporists, traditionalists and modernists, and everyone in between and beyond. It frames an approach to schooling and study that can draw on contemporary pressures while allowing those ideas, wisdom, and knowledge to become part of the explanatory framework for the remarkable resilience of communities that identify as Jews. By focusing on the production and transmission of knowledge in and among modern communities, the paradox of Jewish education is both its Achilles' heel and one of its most potent strengths.

The Neusnerian Fallacy

Religious Studies scholar Jacob Neusner, introduced above, had no patience for the paradox of Jewish education. To concern oneself or one's studies with ethnic or communal concerns, he argued, undermined the whole project of the academic study of Judaism and gutted the initial promise of Enlightenment approaches to education and scholarship. The purpose of studying Judaism, he forcefully argued, was not to produce people who behaved a certain way or felt certain commitments to Jewish practice or community. Rather, it was to subject Judaism to critical inquiry and, through that process, to illuminate the wisdom and power of the tradition. Neusner is important to this discussion because his understanding of the field has set the terms for its own self-conception since its beginning. Neusner invested a lot of time and no small amount of writing in outlining his own dissatisfaction with Jewish Studies as an academic field, which led, ultimately, to his rejection of it. Nevertheless, it is his outsider's conceptualization of the field, not the definition of those who went ahead and helped to build it from the inside, that has held sway over at least two subsequent generations of scholars. This is perhaps the greatest irony of his many legacies: in rejecting Jewish Studies as a scholarly proposition, he accidentally became the field's primary theorist.

Neusner drew a sharp distinction between his academic study of Judaism and Jewish Studies as a field. The former, he asserted, leveraged the best of Enlightenment and scientific thinking, and it was in that capacity that it could prove its worth ("prove to whom?" is a question we'll address below). By contrast, he regarded the effort to create a distinct field called "Jewish Studies" as little more than a slightly grown-up version of Jewish education: too obsessed with ethnic outcomes and too influenced by Jewish communal concerns to represent the values of either Judaism or education.

To be clear, he did not write extensively about K–12 Jewish education, but he cared passionately about research and teaching in higher education.[75] Similarly, he was not opposed to the work of Hillel or campus chaplains but simply saw their work as completely independent of his. He approached his role as a professor with gravity and with a commitment to the deepest of Enlightenment educational ideals. "A professor of Judaic studies," he explained,

> does not advocate Judaism but ultimate seriousness about the problematic of Judaism, about the interpretation of Judaism as an aspect of the humanities, a very different thing. We are not agents of the Jewish community or rabbis. . . . We are not missionaries, but professors. The professor leads, says, 'follow me,' without looking backward to see whether anyone is there. The missionary pushes, imposes self upon other, autonomous selves. That is the opposite of teaching and bears no relevance to university scholarship. Our task indeed is to teach, which means, not to indoctrinate; to educate, never to train.[76]

Neusner's definition of scholarship and teaching in the academic study of Judaism has become central to the self-definition of Jewish Studies, which evolved in sharp distinction to Jewish education. It offers a useful framework for distinguishing the world of scholars from the worlds of the community. Neusner doubled down on knowledge-that, and left knowledge-how to the rabbis and communal professionals.

The distinction Neusner drew between professors and missionaries stretches back to the various births of the field of Religious Studies and the desire to distance scholarship *on* religion from normative or doctrinal instruction *in* religious traditions.[77] The creation of the modern research university channeled the center of intellectual gravity to a growing body of scientific experts who rejected clerical and religious authority and much of what accompanied it. With regard to scholarship on religion, it also fueled the advent of Higher Criticism in German universities in the nineteenth century and new scholarship into the historical Jesus. German research universities housed scholars who used the newest scholarly techniques to advance powerful arguments about religion, which distinguished them from their more theologically minded counterparts. Excluded from university positions because of their Jewishness, scholars like Leopold Zunz (1794–1886) and Hermann Geiger (1810–1874) borrowed the popularity of Wissenschaft and employed it in the formulation of the Wissenschaft des Judentums, the name adopted by practitioners of the academic study of Judaism in nineteenth-century Germany. It constituted a response to Christian hegemony over the study of religions, especially ancient Judaism.[78] The point, at least for Geiger and Zunz, was not only to offer a counternarrative to the Christocentric one that was then dominant but also to offer a more modern framework for the revivification and rejuvenation of Jewish communal life that was not exclusively religious in nature.[79]

Neusner's emergence as a young scholar in the 1960s drew on these century-old dynamics, and he eagerly took up some of their arguments, especially within the rapidly growing postwar field of Religious Studies.[80] For Neusner, Judaism could be best understood as a religion, to be studied alongside other religions and only with the best and most rigorous scholarly methods. Its place alongside other religions would subject it to comparative rigor that would reveal whatever it was about Judaism that Neusner found so irresistible and valuable to the humanities as a whole. Neusner rejected the idea that scholars of Judaism should segregate themselves from other scholars of like phenomena, claiming that doing so would diminish its value, which extended well beyond the Jewish community. When Neusner spoke of the Jewish community, he referred to the organized networks of Jewish charitable organizations known as "federations," among other national Jewish membership organizations that claimed to represent American Jews and their interests: B'nai B'rith, Hadassah, the American Jewish Congress, the American Jewish Committee, as well as the bodies representing the three major religious movements in American Judaism.[81] He worried regularly that communal interests might weaken scholarship on Judaism by infusing the kind of pure scholarly inquiry that he advocated with concerns about ethnic survival or ritual performance. Neusner believed that he taught ideas, not people.

By and large, the organizations that Neusner thought of as encroachments into the work of scholarship had been founded to represent or serve the needs of American Jewry. By the late 1960s they developed significant concerns about the situation of American college students, who, they worried, arrived on campus with a strong enough basis in Jewish knowledge but ill-equipped to reject or deflect whatever pressures or threats they might encounter.[82] The source of the problem was the perceived laxity of Jewish education. In an article typical of this perspective, Rabbi Irving Greenberg, an Orthodox rabbi and professor at Yeshiva University, called campuses a "disaster area for Judaism, Jewish loyalty and Jewish identity," concluding, "The failure of Jewish identity on campus must also be seen as a further revelation of the insufficiency and irrelevance of much of Jewish education in America."[83] One answer, following the paradox of Jewish education, was to increase investment in campus resources, including the burgeoning field of Jewish Studies.[84]

Greenberg's concerns led some scholars of Judaism to advocate for the creation of a scholarly field known as Jewish Studies, which, they believed, could respond to these concerns through scholarship.[85] Speaking at a conference he organized to explore this possibility, historian Leon Jick asserted that "we must act in concert to strengthen the contemporary expressions of Judaic culture and to secure the continuity of that culture."[86] Sociologist Marshall Sklare agreed, framing scholarship and communal concerns as inseparable. "There may be some who fear that concern and involvement with the identity problem, and by extension with the welfare of the Jewish community, will pervert the nature of modern Jewish scholarship. Let them be strong and of good courage, for the opposite is the case. Without such concern, modern Jewish scholarship will be neither modern nor Jewish."[87] Others, like historian Gerson Cohen, noted that the presence of Jewish Studies on campus is "by their presence an affirmation of the corporate identity of the Jews. But," he warned, "to make our positions tools of propaganda and preachment for any cause, ultimate or contingent, is so reprehensible and unthinkable that if that should ever be the price of their inclusion it would be better for them not to be part of the campus complex."[88] Decades later, this position has not softened. Writing about the teaching of "Jewish Civilization," historian Robert Chazan sharply claimed that any concern that Jewish Studies had with "Jewish survival or Jewish identity lie outside the pale."[89]

Neusner might have agreed with Chazan's rejection of identity and with Greenberg's assessment about the sorry state of Jewish education and the low levels of knowledge held by Jewish students, but he rejected Jick and Sklare's belief that Jewish Studies should occupy itself with contemporary concerns or with larger considerations of Jewish communal life or survival. Scholarship was not confessional. "It is not the responsibility of the historian of Judaism, or of Hebrew, to interest himself in the state of the soul of his students, whether Jewish or gentile," he wrote.[90] As his colleagues discussed the possibility of creating a formal organization for scholars of Judaism, Neusner feared the possible influence that Jewish communal organizations might exert over their scholarship through funding or other means. "The 'Jewish community' is not our business and even if it were, nothing worthwhile is likely to come from it, though it, or with it."[91] In his biography of Neusner, Aaron Hughes summarized his approach and its emphasis on intellectual rather than identitarian concerns. "Neusner sought to teach Judaism as an example of an intellectual system to students interested in the study of religion without regard to personal religious commitment. Judaism, for him, was not an ethnic or cultural affiliation, but a thinking person's religion. . . . Judaism was not about Israel nor about the Holocaust; rather, it was about the life of Torah and of thinking."[92]

These concerns shaped Neusner's approach to teaching. He explained,

> We do not pray in classrooms. We do not advocate that students adopt belief in God, let alone specific theological positions. Our lectern is not confused with a pulpit. We do not preach. We teach. We do not teach religion, moreover, but we teach about religion, a distinction absolutely fundamental to our work. . . . The academic world is made of words, not supernatural experience. We do not sing, we do not pray, we do not meditate, we do not repeat sacred formulas, we do not fast, burn incense, dance or otherwise move or control our bodies and attain visions. All we do is talk and think.[93]

In defining himself and his profession in these terms, Neusner defended himself from associations with others whom he derided as being too narrowly ethnocentric. He drew a sharp line between the practices of Jewish ethnicity and the study of Jewish religion. "Conflict arises when matters are confused, so ethnic opinion is taken to represent religious tradition, and religious tradition is made to stand for the Jews, their histories and cultures, without differentiation."[94] Ultimately, Neusner's position on Jewish Studies, among other personal factors, resulted in his decision to distance himself from the enterprise of Jewish Studies. He predicted that it would become, essentially, an arm of the Jewish community, a hub for ethnic boosterism, a confessional enterprise that violated his deeply held sense of the value and power of scholarship on and teaching about Judaism in higher education. For Neusner, there was no middle ground.

Although Neusner rejected the creation of Jewish Studies as an independent field and situated himself as a scholar of Judaism within the field of Religious Studies, his conceptualization of Jewish Studies stuck and helped shape the field and its anxieties about its potential susceptibility to Jewish communal concerns.[95] Running through so much of his writing in this vein was his rejection of "the theory of advocates of survival through Jewish learning."[96] He rejected it on two counts. First, he believed that it violated the spirits of scholarship and the professoriate. Second, and perhaps worse, he believed that it sneakily and disingenuously advanced a communal agenda that was clad in the trappings of education but was really, secretly, indoctrination.

Neusner's vision of Jewish Studies recapitulates the paradox of Jewish education. But rather than seeing the paradox as a defining characteristic, Neusner
tried to pry it apart, detaching education from its Jewish modifier and transforming Judaism into an object of pure study. Study and action, for Neusner, were
unrelated. At least, this was the case in his classroom and his larger scholarly
mandate. His own personal life was beside the point—and that *was* the point. To
teach about Judaism to people who wanted to *be* Jews was not something that his
vision of education could countenance. Education could provide the tools for
critical discourse and teach people to use them. To forget the university's roots in
Wissenschaft, Neusner warned, was to lose the thread and become a "missionary," or an agent of the Jewish community. He clarified the difference he saw
between different modalities of study. "Talmud Torah, the Hebrew words which
signify the study of holy books, does not take place in a university classroom
because Talmud Torah happens only in the community of Israel. It follows that
what we do in the classroom is something quite different, even though the
form—the act of study of books deemed by Judaism to be sacred and the processes of learning in them—is on the surface the same. . . . The classroom is
incongruous to the religious quest. The holy community is the appropriate
locus."[97] To make the university classroom a vehicle for Talmud Torah would
be to undermine both by expecting of them the wrong kinds of inquiries and
outcomes. Instead, he offered two modalities of learning, each independent of
the other, with no overlap except with regard to the books that each regarded
as interesting enough to examine.

But Neusner's scholarly center cannot hold because his commitment to
Judaism is too strong. His writings about Jewish Studies are littered with
implicit arguments about Judaism's significance to the world and, notably, about
the role that he felt it should assume in Jewish communal life more generally.
Better teaching and better scholarship, he argued, would land scholarship where
he thought it belonged: leading the Jewish community rather than taking orders
from it. "Commitment to the Jewish community as we now know it," he argued,
"*should* be replaced by commitment to the values of the academic community,
so that in time, the Jewish community will be reshaped by the values of learning, gain renewed access to its own intellect."[98] With full-blown echoes of Zunz
and Geiger, Neusner tried to recalibrate the Jewish community around the
academy and resist impulses to do the inverse.

Therein lies the crux of the Neusnerian Fallacy, namely that he saw himself
and his efforts as utterly independent of concerns about Jewish life as it was lived
and organized outside of the academy. Yet, he cared deeply and passionately
about Jewish life and community and knowledge. Despite his fervent protestations, he was obsessed with the Jewish people. Noting the changes in attitude
toward Jewish students in Ivy League schools, Neusner stated, "The fact
remains that what must be said at Yale is that we [Jews] are what we are; we are

proud of ourselves; and we do not apologize for being different than the rest."[99] Elsewhere he concluded an essay about the contribution of Judaism to "western Civilization" by returning not to ideas but to people. "That is why I offer you," he told his audience, "as the principal and most interesting Judaic component of Western civilization, the Jewish people itself."[100] Neusner reached these concerns in his own inimitable scholarly and rhetorical styles, but they bear evidence of concerns that transcend (or maybe subscend) his stringent warnings against Jewish Studies as concerned with Jewish people.

The Neusnerian Fallacy holds only if one maintains a scrupulous distinction between Talmud Torah and the university classroom, between people and their knowledge, between learning and studying, between knowledge-how and knowledge-that. These distinctions, too, prove problematic for Neusner, who concerned himself with investigations not just of the textual traces of Jewish thought as a product but of the inner workings of what he called "the mind of Judaism."[101] He explains,

> When I speak of "the making of the mind of Judaism," I refer, specifically, to the setting forth of those processes of thought that taught people to see things in one way and not in some other and to say things in this way, not in that way. . . . Minds may change on this and that. But mind does not, mind meaning modes of patterned thought on ephemera. . . . How people think dictates the frontiers of possibility. The mind of Judaism, that is to say, process, is what will define Judaism in age succeeding age, so long as a Judaic system endures.[102]

To teach *about* Judaism, therefore, is to teach people how to inhabit or at least simulate "the mind of Judaism." But by teaching people to inhabit "the mind of Judaism," he is teaching people to "see things in one way and not in some other and to say things in this way, not in that way," at least temporarily. It is not a confessional kind of pedagogy, but it does suggest that one of his goals is to teach his students to think in a particularly Jewish way. He was trying to change their minds, if only through sheer force of his scholarship, insight, and rhetoric.[103]

His rhetorical fireworks about the importance of the objective, academic study of Judaism mask just how steeped he was in the particular Jewish knowledge of his own area of expertise. His passion for objective scholarship appears to be at odds with what feminist critic of science Donna Haraway calls "situated knowledge."[104] Haraway advocates for a "practice of objectivity that privileges contestation, deconstruction, passionate construction, webbed connections, and hope for transformation of systems of knowledge and ways of seeing."[105] Haraway's vision would almost certainly have resonated with Neusner. Haraway, however, pushes forward, rejecting the "god trick" of both objectivity and relativism, and advocating instead for ways of knowing that are more foundationally grounded in subjectivity and experience. Central to her claim is an observation about the limitations of objectivity and the place of identity within it. "The knowing self is partial in all its guises, never finished, whole, simply there and original; it is always constructed and stitched together imperfectly, and therefore able to join with another, to see together without claiming to be another. Here is the promise of objectivity: a scientific knower seeks the subject position, not of identity, but of objectivity, that is, partial connection."[106] Haraway challenges Neusner's strong commitment to objectivity, suggesting that no matter how hard one studies or applies the tools of an ostensible objectivity, whatever knowledge emerges will always be partial anyway.

One cannot enter Neusner's "mind of Judaism" objectively. Reading Neusner through Haraway reveals evidence that the very stark distinction that he made between communal concerns and scholarship was not nearly as clear as he hoped because the kind of pure scholarship to which he aspired is plainly impossible if one's aim is to teach people to enter the "mind of Judaism." What kind of scholarly positionality is required for such imaginings? One cannot draw a sharp line distinguishing oneself from the communities with which one is in conversation. Even Neusner's beloved field of Religious Studies has been the site for ferocious debates about whether or not a scholar can properly "know" what a religious person does about their religion. While some find the "insider/outsider" debate reductive, Neusner's intention was to teach people to become Judaic "insiders," revealing his belief that such a transformation was possible through careful study.[107]

Aaron Hughes, Neusner's biographer, makes a curious comment to this end. Making note of the copious editorials, book reviews, letters to the editor, and other nonacademic writings that Neusner penned in various Jewish media outlets, Hughes writes, "He was always able to draw a line between academic work in Judaism and being a Jewish public intellectual." But the explanation Hughes gives for Neusner's ability to do so is tautological. "The two must never blur into one another because, if they did, Jewish studies would be an ethnic enclave and, thus, only of parochial importance."[108] Neusner's role as a public intellectual, which he relished, was underwritten by his scholarship, and his scholarship was shaped by his role as a public intellectual. He wrote about Jewish issues and tried to shape public discourse about them because he cared about them, and he could not simply cordon off his scholarship from his popular writing. He appears to have applied the same level of scholarly rigor to all his writing and all of his subjects regardless of the outlet. Indeed, that was his larger point, which was not to suffer fools or shortcuts or simple answers when it came to Jewish life, whether the life of the mind or the body or the mouth or the heart. The sheer volume of his writing and range of topics indicate that he could not help but express himself. His popular essays frequently refer to "we Jews," locating him within, not outside of, American Judaism. His popular writing also evidences a profound commitment to helping improve the state of Jewish intellectual affairs. Why else would he write as much as he did, as ferociously as he did, in as many venues as he did?

To make good on his own promise of what the academic study of Judaism could be, Neusner would have had to abandon the Enlightenment's promise of objectivity and embrace the fact that he was trying to change how people think. Otherwise, teaching and writing might impress his peers but would not be worth much at the end of the day, even to Neusner. If the aim was to effect changes in his students, then he was something of a missionary, albeit a missionary for the Enlightenment, the university, or scholarship, rather than for Judaism or the Jewish people specifically. And one does not have to be a shill for Jewish jingoism or communal organizations to try to teach someone to understand how to see the world in a particular way or to hope as he did that one's teaching makes a difference in the lives of their students. His fallacy gathers momentum from the claim that this was not his concern, or that it was possible to distance his scholarship from his commitments to Jewish life. Protestations aside, he cared passionately about Jewish people and Judaism, and his whole body of work represents an argument about why others should too. In a sense, he could not help himself. He wrote so much and so often, and tried to encourage his students to enter "the mind of Judaism" because he was trying to get people to change their minds, to think critically and rigorously in ways that might even alter their behaviors in the world. He was not trying to missionize his students or bolster their "Jewish identities." But he certainly believed that study mattered, and that scholarship mattered to and for Jews and how they lived.

Jewish Studies as an Educational Enterprise

When I began this chapter by writing that Jewish Studies is Jewish education, I did not mean that Jewish Studies has become what Neusner feared it might: a shill for Jewish communal interests. Though he did not support the creation of a field of Jewish Studies, Neusner nevertheless helped establish the conceptual and theoretical terms that have framed the field, and his terms have become the terms of debate. The terms divide procedural knowledge from propositional knowledge and subjective understanding from objective understanding. The two former terms have been assigned to Jewish education and the latter two to Jewish Studies, resulting in the caricaturing of each by the other. But, as I have shown, the two share more than they care to admit insofar as both have been constituted around a tension central to their respective enterprises.

Jewish education has taken shape around a paradox that promises the benefits of Enlightenment-informed education to the particularistic Jewish situation. The self-conception of Jewish Studies has taken shape around the Neusnerian Fallacy, which held that it was possible and desirable to remain at a critical remove from communal concerns that bear on one's scholarly investigations. As this chapter has explained, neither framework fully holds. But their convergence around the production and transmission of knowledge reveals the ways in which the motivating concerns of Jewish education owe a debt to those of Jewish Studies and vice versa. In effect, they are committed to quite similar ends, motivated by similar aims that are grounded in the converging narratives about how people know what they know.

To be clear: this does not mean that Jewish Studies is or ought to be confessional or prescriptive. Similarly, it does not mean that every fourth-grade Sunday school class ought to undertake original historical or philological research. But if the purpose of Jewish Studies is to understand Jewish concepts as conveyed through text or cultural practices on their own terms, then the aim may be not to make Jews in a reductive survivalist mode but to encourage people to think in modalities that allow them to change their minds about all kinds of things. And if the purpose of Jewish education is to access the benefits of modern education, then it too can engage more readily in intellectual pursuits and loosen its grip on concerns about survival. Perhaps both Jewish Studies and Jewish education would do better if they allowed for the greater possibility of change by approaching their efforts with greater acceptance of their limitations and their similarities to each other.

Chapter 4 will explore this proposition in greater detail by shifting the terms of debate from a concern for what Jewish education and Jewish Studies are trying to convey to their students, to focus on how students learn. Chapters 2 and 3 will trace some of these connections through a set of case studies that explore the convergences between propositional and procedural knowledge in Jewish history. The next two chapters will offer snapshots of historical examples of ideas, approaches, settings, people, and practices that have mobilized knowledge in Jewish life and complicated the distinction between propositional and procedural knowledge in Jewish societies and cultures. They will also highlight just how central knowledge has been as a feature of Jewish culture, practice, community, syncretism, debate, and mobility. Chapter 4's proposal for a new key is an effort to recenter learning in both Jewish education and Jewish Studies by focusing on how people produce and transmit knowledge, recalling the book's larger argument that Jewish Studies is a Jewish educational enterprise, paradox and all.

PART II
STATE OF THE QUESTION

2   Logics of Production

VALUES, QUALITIES, FRAMEWORKS

Chapter 1 set out the terms of debate, staked out in the tension between Jewish education and Jewish Studies. Chapter 4 will argue for the possibility of hearing this tension in a new key that is pitched around learning. Chapters 2 and 3 provide a bridge between them by presenting a series of case studies and vignettes chosen to illustrate how central concerns about the production and transmission of knowledge have been within and across Jewish history. One of the challenges of these two chapters is that it is almost impossible to pull apart Jewish knowledge from Jewish history itself. What one knows or is supposed to know about Jewish life or practice has derived from questions about the kind of Jewish life one was supposed to live. The modes that have been used to transmit knowledge deemed important pervade Jewish life: Rabbinical responsa, codes of law, children's bibles, heritage travel, museums, cookbooks, bedtime stories, liturgy, sermons, viral videos, reading primers, and the list goes on. Virtually every dimension of Jewish life could be considered elemental to the production and transmission of knowledge.

Jewish education and Jewish Studies both represent efforts to organize this phenomenon, and to divide efforts that could be considered properly "educational" from others that might be better regarded as cultural or social.[1] They are modern constructs that both propose modes for the production of knowledge as well as frameworks for imagining how people taught and learned in the past. The next two chapters are an effort to look beyond Jewish education and Jewish Studies to try and account for the pervasiveness of Jewish knowledge work in Jewish life. In the process, the chapters attempt to resituate Jewish education and Jewish Studies as a matched pair of formal structures that help to explain broader and more diffuse currents of knowledge work, but are not the only instances of it. The chapters are organized thematically. Chapter 2 explores the logics of knowledge production, and chapter 3 focuses on the modes of knowledge transmission. Chapter 2 is divided into three clusters that explore values, frameworks, and qualities. The "Values" section features discussions of some of the prominent value propositions for Jewish knowledge. The "Frameworks" section addresses some of the approaches that have guided the transmission and production of knowledge, and the "Qualities" section highlights theories for approaching engagements with knowledge. Chapter 3 is divided into two sections: "Catalysts," which contains discussions of events or concerns that sparked ongoing knowledge work, and "Technologies," which focuses on specific cultural forms for organizing that work.

Though the division of the next two chapters suggests a neat distinction between production and transmission, the division is artificial (recall Raymond Williams's warning about the value of definitions). Is writing a book an act of production or transmission? How would one characterize the act of teaching a lesson from a well-regarded curriculum? What about a podcast? An improvised speech? Are teachers producing or transmitting knowledge in their classrooms? What about students? The twin terms can best be understood as distinct dimensions of a mutually constitutive set of practices for engaging with knowledge, and a lot has hung on the dynamic relationship between them. Jewish Studies and Jewish education are but two relatively recent instances of a much longer and broader historical story, some of which will unfold over the next two chapters. But most of the time Jews and their communities have been trying to produce and transmit knowledge in ways that both precede and exceed the boundaries of either Jewish Studies or Jewish education.

The case studies that compose chapters 2 and 3 were chosen to follow a fairly conventional educational conceit: the alphabetical primer.[2] This is a book about Jewish education, and so much of Jewish education begins with the letters of the alphabet. Basic literacy, mystical interpretations, and poetic flights of fancy all try to make sense of the shapes and symbols that make literacy possible, inscribing upon them all semblances of practical and mystical knowledge.[3] The scribal arts, the history of book printing and publishing, even sending a text message are all elements of the ways in which people have produced and transmitted Jewish knowledge from person to person and from generation to generation by using the letters of the alphabet, arranged into words.

These chapters, however, do not unfold in alphabetical order. Rather, they are told through thematically related but disorderly fragments because that is the only way to acknowledge the diversity of approaches to knowledge in and among Jewish communities. Their layout is also a nod to the fragmentary nature of knowledge itself and to the sporadic and largely uncoordinated ways in which approaches to teaching and learning have taken shape. There was nobody directing it from "on high," no school district or superintendent coordinating individual communities, no state-mandated curriculum, no singular ideology, no final exam, no measure of what would constitute knowing "enough." Though some efforts—the establishment of Bais Yaakov schools, the invention of Jewish Sunday schools, the work of the Alliance Israelite Universelle, the creation of the field of Jewish Studies, the redaction of the Talmud, the compilation of the Jewish Encyclopedia—have had tremendous influence, there has never been a single center of Jewish learning, so it cannot hold. Instead, this chapter provides an array of portraits that together make a compelling but necessarily incomplete picture. Together, though, they capture the pervasiveness of concerns for the production and transmission of knowledge throughout Jewish history.

Values

Vav—Veshinantam

With an assist from Crosby, Stills, Nash, and Young, one of the most popular sources for understanding Jewish education comes from the paragraph known as the *ve'ahavta* ("and you shall love"). The paragraph follows the Shema (the proverbial "watchword of the Jewish faith") in Deuteronomy, and the two are usually recited together as part of the prescribed daily prayer service and often as part of bedtime rituals. It includes the charge *veshinantam levanecha*, which is usually translated as "and you shall teach your children."[4] Some have taken this verse as a literal commandment to teach their own children, while others have approached it metaphorically to mean that the parent-child relationship should serve as the model for all teacher-student interactions. Indeed, for much of the history of Jewish people and communities, the family was the primary locus for teaching and learning of all kinds. For boys this usually amounted to ensuring basic familiarity with the elements of Jewish ritual life, while for girls this meant learning to run and maintain a Jewish household.[5]

But the verb that is conjugated as *veshinantam* is unclear. In biblical and rabbinic literature, it does not directly mean "to teach." Instead, it can be taken to mean "to sharpen," as it shares its root with the word for "tooth." Taken in this way, veshinantam could mean "to speak sharply or clearly" or "to memorize," as in "to keep it in your mouth." More poetically, it could mean something like "to impress upon," as in "to bite" or "to incise." Some scholars believe that the root of the Hebrew word is not *shin-nun-nun* (which is the root for "tooth") but *shin-nun-hey*, which would be closer to the verb "to repeat," derived from the Hebrew for the number two (Hebrew: *shnayim*), as well as the word for "year" (Hebrew: *shanah*), both of which suggest a rhythm of regular repetition. In the latter case, the charge would be not to "teach your children" but to repeat the lessons regularly, or, as Robert Alter has translated it, "to rehearse" them.[6]

But if most parents were not scholars, how and what were they supposed to teach their children? Yehoshua ben Gamla, a rabbi who lived in the first century CE, offered a solution: in cases where parents were "not capable of teaching their own children," towns would band together to hire teachers for them. The Gemara reports that "Ben Gamla came and instituted an ordinance that teachers of children [Hebrew: *lamdei tinokot*] should be established in each and every province and in each and every town, and they would bring the children in to learn at the age of six and at the age of seven."[7] The text continues to describe how one should discipline students (with the strap of a sandal, so it doesn't hurt) and what to do with students who cannot read (let them learn with students who can, so as to encourage them), and it prescribes a student-teacher ratio of twenty-five to one (for classes greater than twenty-five, the teacher is permitted to hire an assistant, paid for by the town). The text was almost certainly speaking only of male children.

The Gemara does not specify the institutional settings in which appointed teachers ought to teach, and neither does it call them "schools." Ben Gamla's ordinance, however, helped professionalize the teaching of children and absolve parents of the responsibility for teaching their own children. He made teachers accessible to everyone, regardless of whom their parents were, but he also brought the practices of instruction under rabbinically appointed teachers and took it out of people's homes. His proposal at once democratized knowledge and centralized it.

Almost undoubtedly, Ben Gamla's newly authorized teachers did not teach whatever it was that parents might have rehearsed with their children. Instead, they likely turned to whatever they had learned from their own rabbinic teachers. When the Mishna (a compendium of rabbinic writings from the first century CE, which, together with the Gemara, composes the core of the Talmud) known as Pirke Avot ("Ethics of the Fathers") proposes a course of formal study, it does so in ways that emphasize rabbinic rather than parental or domestic knowledge. "At five years of age the study of Scripture; At ten the study of Mishna; At thirteen subject to the commandments; At fifteen the study of Talmud." According to this plan, students reach certain forms of maturity or responsibility in the years that follow too (marriage, children, a profession), culminating in the achievement of "wisdom" at age forty.[8] If this is the preferred course of study, then it replaces the countless parental lessons about how to eat or treat one's siblings or how to navigate sticky social situations and how to prepare a meal, with knowledge authored and authorized by the ancient rabbis.

This approach favored rabbinical knowledge over what might be termed "familial" or "folk" knowledge. As scholar of rabbinics Jeffrey Rubenstein has written, "Classical rabbinic literature was produced within rabbinic educational institutions, by the sages who taught and studied there, for the purpose of educating those who attended them."[9] The result was an inclination in the written record toward the production and transmission of knowledge authorized by those most invested in it and the institutions that they served and that, in turn, served them. Rubenstein was referring to the contributions of two prominent Babylonian schools, located in Sura and Pumbedita, both in present-day Iraq, which played a foundational role in the formulation of the texts that became the Talmud and the establishment of what came to be known as "Rabbinic Judaism."[10]

The concept of "Rabbinic Judaism" took shape in the wake of the destruction of the Second Temple in 70 CE and through the formation of the Gemara and the Mishna as the central compendia of authoritative knowledge. As S. D.

Goitein, scholar of the Cairo Geniza, observed, compiling comprehensive accounts of local knowledge was common practice during the first centuries of the first millennium. "The pervading spirit of Near Eastern and European civilization at that time was in favor of authoritative compendiums that were regarded as containing in final form the entire content of a certain field of knowledge. This tendency prevailed in secular sciences, such as medicine, not less than in religious studies."[11] Creating such bodies of knowledge invites a slew of questions: Whose knowledge is considered part of the "entire content" and whose is not? What knowledge is considered "essential" and what is considered marginal? And, of course, the most important question of all: who has the authority to decide, and what does their authority rest upon?

The term "Rabbinic Judaism" highlights the role that rabbis like Yehoshua ben Gamla and others played in formulating it. It refers to the form of Judaism crafted and codified by ancient rabbis, following the destruction of the Temple in Jerusalem. Religious Studies scholar Moulie Vidas explains that the emergence of a codified body of law and lore in ancient Israel is best understood not as a reflection of rabbinic authority but as part of an apparatus through which that authority was produced by the rabbinic elite.[12] Their creation of a comprehensive body of knowledge cannot be distinguished from the authority generated in the process. The social dynamics of knowledge in the Mishna and the Gemara, which include lengthy debates and stories about interactions between rabbis, reflect the power inherent in the process of producing it as an authoritative account of knowledge deemed significant (or at least it was significant enough to have been included). As one might predict from a book compiled by, for, from, and in some senses *about* rabbinic scholarship, the Mishna and the Gemara have a great deal to say about the status and significance of knowledge.

Following Alter, we find the term *veshinantam* also at work also in the name Mishna, which can refer either to the whole corpus of writings (as in "the Mishna") or to a single passage within the larger text (usually referred to as "a Mishna"), but the term derives from the repetitive ways in which people have approached the practices and habits of study and recalls the biblical injunction to parents to teach their children through repetition and rehearsal. Whatever it is that parents or appointed teachers were supposed to teach, the term *veshinantam* suggests that it ought to be done repetitively, cyclically, and that wherever important lessons are learned, they are never learned just once.

Chet—Chinuch

Chinuch serves as the modern Hebrew word for education, as in designations like "special education" or institutionally, as in the Israeli Ministry of Education. In biblical and rabbinic contexts, it meant "to train" or "to initiate." The oft-quoted verse from Proverbs, "Train a child in their way, so that they will not depart from it even in old age," uses a form of the verb *chinuch*, indicating a specific kind of preparation rather than a general, open-ended course of inquiry or exploration.[13] Though popular in modern educational contexts, the proverb is something of an outlier in its use of the term *chinuch*.

Ben Gamla does not use it, and it appears to be absent from the documents in the Cairo Geniza, though they contain numerous references to teaching, learning, and study.[14] Neither does it appear in the *Sefer Hasidim*, a medieval German pietistic text that devotes significant attention to the ways of teachers and the importance of study.[15] Its first significant appearance is the title of the *Sefer Hachinuch* (the Book of Education), written and compiled in Spain during the late thirteenth century. Although the book's author remains anonymous, his intention in writing the book was clear: "to arouse the heart of the youth—my son and his friends—each and every week about the tally of the commandments after they study that [reading]. And [this is also in order] to accustom them to [the commandments] and to attach their thoughts to the thought of purity; and to the calculation of the essential, before they put in their hearts, calculations of joking and 'what is it to you,' and of 'what is the point.' And [so] 'even when they age, it will not depart from them.'"[16] The *Sefer Hachinuch* presented itself as a kind of prophylactic, intended to cultivate certain sensibilities (purity, seriousness) in the minds of male youngsters as part of their training for adulthood. It was meant to train its readers, to discipline them, but not necessarily to "educate" them in the modern sense of that term.

Chinuch emerged as a concept slowly and unevenly during the Enlightenment. The tumultuous transition to modernity led to an explosion of interest in schools and schooling and to an array of responses to emerging conditions brought on by the range of political, cultural, geographic, economic, and religious changes. Because it landed at the intersection of local, Jewish community control and the authority of larger state actors and emerging political formations, schooling emerged as a central locus of concern for nearly everyone at every level of the social order. Insofar as they concerned the cultivation of youth for adult participation in society, schools became sites of struggle over competing visions for what those youth ought to know and, consequently, the world for which they were being prepared. Among the first to adopt the term were Isaac Daniel Itzig, David Friedlander, and others in the Berlin Jewish Enlightenment in the formation of the Chevra Chinuch Ne'arim, or the Society for the Education of Youth, a group that helped establish and support the Berlin Jewish Free School, which was established in 1778. Also in Berlin at this same time, Jewish Enlightenment reformer Naphtali Herz Wessely (1725–1805) used it in his writings, including in the subtitle of this 1782 book, *Words of Peace and Truth*, which reads, "The science of man and the science of education for Jewish youth."[17] His book was among the first to outline a systematic approach to the schooling of Jewish youth, but still the word chinuch appeared only a handful of times.

The term picked up more widespread use with the advent of Hebraism and Zionism in the late nineteenth century, but even then, somewhat unevenly. For example, Ahad Ha'am, the Zionist thinker who wrote extensively about the necessity for a Jewish cultural revival, used chinuch inconsistently in his writings.[18] When he did use the term, as in his essay "Hachinuch haleumi" (National Education), he clearly understood that it would serve the purpose of national revitalization through instruction and training of a new generation of Jews who could become the engine for the new nation.[19]

Educational questions played an important role in Jewish settlements in Palestine under the British Mandate, as approaches to schooling in Jewish settlements drew on modern educational ideologies, and school administrators, teachers, and thinkers began to see themselves not just as individual agents but as participants in a shared enterprise called "chinuch."[20] Some concerns focused on how to utilize education to cultivate a sense of national unity, while others were concerned with trying to wrest control of Jewish schools from the British. On this latter point, historian Suzanne Schneider has shown that Jews were divided between Zionist and religious school systems, and the British Department of Education in Palestine agreed to recognize Zionist schools as "public entities," but nevertheless assigned their oversight to Zionist leaders.[21] This agreement effectively ensured that talk of chinuch in the Yishuv would be informed by the political orientations of those who controlled the schools. On the former, historians of education Nirit Raichel and Tali Tadmor-Shimony have written extensively about the schooling in the Yishuv, arguing that the "modern educational approach [of Yishuv schools] went hand in hand with the idea of Jewish solidarity espoused by the nineteenth-century Jewish emancipation. The leaders of this movement considered the principles of modern society as a framework that would enable the Jews to embrace several different identities, one of them Jewish and the other, as part of the country in which they lived."[22] But the emergence of the term *chinuch* at this time indicated the emergence of an increasingly coherent field of concerns that cut across institutional and conceptual aspects of Zionism.

The establishment of the Hebraist-Zionist Teachers' Union in 1903 evidences one aspect of this emerging educational consciousness, as does the union's 1927 launch of *Hed Hachinuch* (Echo of Education) as its general organ.[23] The invitation to the founding gathering of the teachers' union outlined the mission of its members in national terms. Together, they could "teach and raise a strong and vigorous generation, healthy in body and spirit, that will know and love their nation, their land, and its language."[24] The ideas of teaching and schooling clustered under the larger concept of education as chinuch, as a feature of a modern nation taking responsibility for educating its youngest citizens. When the State of Israel drafted its first education law in 1953, it did not require the study of Judaism's religious ideas or concepts in secular schools.

Instead, paragraph 44 of the state's basic law outlined its educational vision in the following way: "The object of State education is to base elementary education in the State on the values of Jewish culture and the achievements of science, on love of the homeland and loyalty to the State and the Jewish people, on practice in agricultural work and handicraft, on pioneer (chalutzic) training, and on striving for a society built on freedom, equality, tolerance, mutual assistance and love of mankind."[25] Different leaders understood this passage differently. David Ben-Gurion, Israeli prime minister, advocated for "Hebrew culture," and the soon-to-be-appointed minister of education, Zalman Aranne, advanced his vision through the establishment of the Center for Fostering Jewish Consciousness in the Ministry of Education.[26] Aranne hoped his concept of "Jewish consciousness" would foster a sense of global connections with and affinity for Jews who did not live in the State of Israel without sacrificing the state-centered approach of Israeli education.

On the ground, the Center for Fostering Jewish Consciousness ran into trouble operationalizing its vision, as historian Walter Ackerman explained: "Teachers on all levels complained that they were required to teach material that they neither understood nor believed. More broadly, the Ministry was accused of using the seemingly neutral and generally acceptable idea of Jewish Consciousness to introduce religion into schools defined by law as secular and chosen by parents for that reason."[27] This tension shaped Israeli secular schooling for decades and contributed to "a decline in the degree of overlap and correlation between [students'] Jewish and Israeli identities," as reported in a study of Israeli students from 1989.[28]

It is notable, then, that the term that emerged is *chinuch* and not something like *educatzia*, which would follow the pattern of adoption for other academic terms like *sotziologia*, *philosophia*, *historia*, and *politica*, as neologized Hebrew versions of popular English or German ones. Drawing on its roots in rabbinic literature, the term, in theory, evoked a broad concern for preparation for the conditions of modern life, but channeled through the distinct requirements or desires of an ethno-religiously defined nation state. Chinuch in the Israeli context speaks to a version of national training for membership in a polity, even as it also bears the overtones of Enlightenment ideals. Insofar as it reverberates with both of these ideological overtones, Israeli chinuch is, in some ways, among the best illustrations of the paradox of Jewish education.

Gimel—Good for the Jews

It works as a punchline, a refrain in published editorials, and the title of at least three books and one record album. Jewish education is supposedly "good for the Jews" because it has long been invested with the power to sustain Jewish communal life. Though there is general agreement about the value of knowledge in general, there has been (and continues to be) debate about what kinds of knowledge matter and what people ought to know. Some of the most significant debates emerged as modernity and the Enlightenment ascended across Europe (approx. 1700–1900). Communities, scholars, leaders, and writers argued passionately about whether or not the ideas and methods of the Enlightenment could or should be integrated into Jewish study. Different schools of thought divided into different movements committed to particular forms of knowledge production based in large measure on their respective ideological positions regarding what was good for the Jews. These differences emerged in terms of how people might respond to certain conditions, but they also exhibit a shared underlying logic: that the production and transmission of knowledge *was* good for the Jews. It might even be the Jews' best hope.

Leaders of the Jewish Enlightenment, known as the Haskalah, argued that a revival of Jewish life could be fueled by the application of Wissenschaft ideals, which meant the creation of Jewish schools. Throughout Europe, schools for both boys and girls were founded to transmit these ideas and orientations to children. Berlin opened the Hinuch Ne'arim (Education for Youth) school in 1778, and Prague and Trieste saw the establishment of similar Jewish schools in 1782. Many Jewish communities in France had Jewish religious schools at the time of the Revolution in 1789, but the first secular Jewish schools were not organized until 1817.[29] Odessa opened its first Jewish school in 1826 and included in its curriculum the study of multiple languages along with math, bookkeeping, and other subjects whose mastery would better position young Jews in Odessa for successful careers.[30] Later, Zionist educators advocated for education that they believed promised the most likely pathway toward a rejuvenation of Jewish community, culture, and commitment. Though these approaches differed substantially in their orientations, they nevertheless agreed both on their social diagnoses and on the prescription of schools as the cure.

But schools were not always intended to be "good for the Jews." In Russia, Tsar Nicholas I instituted a series of reforms, culminating in an 1840 law that turned Enlightenment ideals against the Jews, noting that "the best among the Jews feel that one of the chief causes of their humiliation lies in the perverted interpretation of their religious traditions" and that the influence of the Talmud "can be counteracted only by enlightenment, and it remains for the government to act in the spirit of the handful of the best among the Jews. The reeducation of the learned section among the Jews involved at the same time the purification of their religious conceptions."[31] The law made plain the intentions of the tsar to use Enlightenment ideals to pressure Jews to shed, rather than retain, their distinctive customs and become modern Russian subjects.

Throughout the twentieth century, advocates of Jewish education largely followed the pathways laid down in the eighteenth and nineteenth centuries. Jewish education could, they imagined, adapt the model of Enlightenment education in the service of Jewish communal vitality. By the late twentieth century, this logic had funneled elements of Bildung through the surge in interest in ethnic origins that took root in the late 1960s to create an approach to education that historian Jonathan Krasner has called the "Jewish identity industry."[32] Though the term has roots stretching back decades, Jewish identity emerged in the 1960s and 1970s as a primary outcome for Jewish education. Only a strong Jewish identity, the logic went, could equip young American Jews with the cultural and social capital with which to resist the allure of American assimilation.[33] Whether Jewish education was up to the task is a different story, but the logic of Jewish identity burrowed deep in the enterprise as both a central logic and a desired outcome. Jewish identity was good for the Jews.

By the early 1990s, concerns about Jewish identity had begun to make their way from the United States to Israel, as Israeli educators began to reflect on the repercussions of the country's approach to education and what it portended for the Jewishness of the nation and its citizens.[34] In 1991, the Israeli minister of education, Zevulun Hammer, commissioned professor Aliza Shenhar to investigate Israeli state schools and offer recommendations that might bolster students' Jewish knowledge and sense of commitment to Jewish peoplehood. Historian of Israel Ilan Troen described it like this: "The central problem for Zionist educators in the twentieth century was how to provide Jewish children in an avowedly Jewish state with a secular 'Jewish' education. Immigrants and native-born had to be loyal citizens, committed to the new state and deeply rooted in the land. At the same time, they had to see themselves as responsible members of the Jewish people, maintaining ties to a common culture which, increasingly, they did not share. Israeli educators were acutely aware of the contradictions inherent in their endeavors."[35] Released in 1994, the Shenhar Report presented a portrait of education in Israel that was caught between commitments to secular nationalist ideals and a desire for greater affinity toward the country's distinctly Jewish roots.[36] Though specific to Israeli education, the Shenhar Report emerged from the paradox that has long defined Jewish education and could be traced back to earlier debates about the nature of education in the Yishuv, or the role of education in Zionism.

On this score, the Shenhar Report added an additional layer of concerns: the cultivation of connections between Israeli Jews and those who lived in the Diaspora, and the sense that they shared a common history and destiny as members of a singular community. Outside of Israel, concerns about commitments to "the Jewish People" had long dominated research on American Jewish education and had been advanced as a desirable outcome for decades.[37] In a sense, it underwrote approaches to Jewish education that foregrounded a commitment to "survival" and, later, to "continuity" and "engagement." The underlying idea, carried through any number of research papers and books, was that more education would lead inexorably to a stronger commitment to things Jewish, including a stronger sense of membership in the Jewish People.

Such a feeling of connection could, many people imagined, even make up for the shortcomings of family life or neighborhood, serving as a kind of communal cultural supplement for Jews unable to sustain their Jewishness on their own. Perhaps more importantly, such a feeling could—and should—be taught. Yet, as the Shenhar Report indicated, and as many Enlightenment-era leaders felt, education also contained the potential to lead Jews astray. If education was to be good for the Jews, it had to both capitalize on the universalism of the Enlightenment and foster the particular concerns that would not attenuate connections to the Jewish people. This is the paradox of Jewish education that has become the most popular candidate for combating a weakened sense of membership in the Jewish people and thus, the sine qua non of what is thought to be good for the Jews.

Kaf—Keneged Kulam

The opening of Mishna Peah (1:1) equates "Talmud Torah" with a number of acts of kindness, whose reward will not be felt until the "world to come." The list includes visiting the sick and honoring one's parents, among others. "Talmud Torah," or study of the Torah, is equal to them all (*keneged kulam*); according to some interpretive traditions, "study leads to them all."[38] In this formulation, the value of study lies not in its own rewards but in its ability to propel people to act positively or ethically toward others. One can study all day, the Mishna suggests, but study rises to the level of these other actions and merits a posthumous reward only if it drives a person toward action. Who cares, asks the Mishna, if you have a transcendent moment of understanding if you are not turning those moments of transcendence into ethical or moral action? The logic of keneged kulam advances a rationale for Jewish knowledge that defers the value of learning on to practice.

But the Mishna offers another perspective, courtesy of Rabbi Meir, who is quoted as saying that the value of study lies not in the rewards one reaps from it but only in study "for its own sake."[39] For Rabbi Meir, to study with the intention that study will yield some other outcome is to undermine the value and beauty of learning as its own reward. Rabbi Meir's emphasis on the purity of study stands in opposition to the concerns for application suggested by the formulation of Torah study as keneged kulam. The tension between learning for the sake of learning and learning for right action lies at the heart of the Neusnerian Fallacy as well as the paradox of Jewish education because it also runs through many historical debates about how and what to learn and whether the transmission and production of Jewish knowledge ought to be for its own sake or for some other purpose. Meanwhile, it imagines that the difference is clear.

Anthropologist Jonathan Boyarin, in his account of his time studying in a *kollel* (a *beit midrash* for married men), ties himself in ethnographic knots in an extended meditation on precisely this tension. "What if this ethnography," he muses, "were the 'payment' for my time at the yeshiva—in two senses of the term, that is, the recompense that is owing to me, and the product that I owe to the academy that supports me? If I truly were intent on proving that my own study was leshma, that might dictate that I fail to present this book, to both my colleagues at the university and to my friends at the yeshiva. And yet here it is."[40] The tension induces some generative introspection and some keen observations about what scholars of education characterize neatly as "intrinsic motivation" and "extrinsic motivation." But Boyarin can't get out of the bind, ultimately conceding to the paradox and begging of his reader, "enough already with leshma" (Rabbi Meir's term for "for its own sake").

The tension between scholarship and sentiment discussed above can also figure in here, as producers and transmitters of Jewish knowledge tried to conceive of their efforts as both lishma and keneged kulam. On some measures, the answer was clear: Jewish learning should be oriented around a concern for practical knowledge. But the definition of what this meant proved to be quite negotiable and often meant drawing on sources that were not only Jewish in origin. Hai Gaon (d. 1038) ruled that "it is permitted to teach Arabic calligraphy and arithmetic in the synagogue together with the Sacred Law. Non-Jewish children may also study in the synagogue for the sake of good relationship with the neighbors, although this is not desirable."[41] Joseph Ibn Ankin (ca. 1150–ca. 1220) left a will that outlined his vision of a proper curriculum that included "reading, writing, Bible, Mishna, Hebrew Grammar, Talmud, philosophy of religion, philosophy, logic, mathematics, arithmetic, optics, astronomy, music, mechanics, nature study, medicine and metaphysics."[42] A Spanish syllabus from the Middle Ages included a similarly broad array of topics: "Bible, Hebrew Poetry, Talmud, the relation of philosophy and relation, the logic of Aristotle, the elements of Euclid, arithmetic, the mathematical works of Nicomachus, Theodosius, Menelaus, Archimedes, and others; optics, astronomy, music, mechanics, medicine, natural science and finally metaphysics."[43] Judah Ibn Tibbon's ethical will (France, ca. 1160) admonished his son for keeping his distance from the books that Judah had collected and encouraged him to "devote yourself to the study of the Torah and to the science of medicine. But chiefly occupy yourself with the Torah."[44] Admonitions like this one emphasized the study of Torah (perhaps lishma) but in partnership with science and medicine (keneged kulam).

Under conditions of modernity, the lishma–keneged kulam tension recurred over and over again. During the first part of the twentieth century, Orthodox leaders in Poland advocated the liberalization of attitudes toward the education of girls as part of a larger strategy to preserve their way of life in the face of internal weakness. This strategy created space for Sarah Schenirer to establish her Bais Yaakov school for girls in interwar Krakow, which fueled a global movement in Jewish study for Orthodox women that both adheres to Orthodox tradition and communal structure but has proven empowering for many women in Orthodox communities.[45]

The belief that study could spark desire emerged as a central feature in Jewish education beyond the Orthodox world as well, with the adoption of "Jewish identity" as a desired educational outcome.[46] It also underwrote the Neusnerian Fallacy, which imagined that study could be separated entirely from the people doing the studying. Literary scholar and translator Robert Alter recapitulated this perspective in a potent 1974 article in *Commentary* called "What Jewish Studies Can Do."[47] In the article, Alter tried to dispel myths about Jewish Studies as an effort to bolster "consciousness raising" for Jewish students. Instead, he argued, "Jewish studies integrated into the American university can no longer be a matter of confessional concern or ethnic loyalty; by entering the academy, Judaica entered the public domain. Jewish Studies courses clearly must be open to students of all backgrounds, and cannot be designed to meet the special religious, ethnic, or national needs of Jewish students."[48] In this, Alter aligned the burgeoning field (only some five or six years after the creation of the Association for Jewish Studies)[49] behind the logic of Jacob Neusner, who had choice words for scholars whose pursuit of Jewish Studies was motivated by something less than intellectual inquiry. Or, as we might think of it in this context, Alter, in this respect like Neusner, argued for less keneged kulam and for more lishma.

The tension extends to other arenas of Jewish study as well. Sam Heilman's ethnography of Jewish study circles in Jerusalem and New York emphasizes the "spiritual meditation on and lifelong review of Jewish books" that he calls "lernen."[50] In his ethnography of learning circles, Heilman notes that the books and their content are not the point. "Nothing less [than the actual experience of lernen] can genuinely inform one of what it means to sit in a circles, to hear the sounds of lernen, play by its rules, fall into the Talmud page and work one's way back out again, join in fellowship and become touched by the cultural sense of one's Jewishness and the religious spirit of one's Judaism."[51] The beauty of lernen, Heilman argues, can be found not in the text but in the secondary effects of the study. Torah Lishma, for Heilman, lies in the benefits that study bears beyond an increased knowledge of the text at hand.

This approach to learning "off book" is part of what educational theorist Phillip Jackson has called the "hidden curriculum."[52] With this concept, Jackson referred to the unwritten and often unstated dimensions of a learning environment or experience. In addition to learning math, English, or music, students learn how to take turns, how to sit still, how to show up to class on time, how to raise their hand, and other dimensions of contextually appropriate behavior.[53] Or, as educational anthropologists Zvi Bekerman and Adina Segal have put it, "What is being learned in Talmud class: Is it class or is it Talmud?"[54] Of course, the answer is "both." If the study of Torah is equal to a bunch of other actions, then those actions are also equal to the study of Torah. One can learn as much by action as by study.

Qualities

Nun—Narishkeit

Narishkeit, the Yiddish term for "silliness," has a bad reputation. In so many historical instances, rabbis or other teachers wielded knowledge with the intention of keeping people from wasting their time on whatever was considered narishkeit: idle chatter, gambling, secular literature, popular music. Narishkeit is often cast as the opposite of whatever is thought to be worthwhile. It is a derivation of the German word for "fool," though it sounds like the Hebrew *na'ar*, meaning "male youth" (a female would be a *na'arah*), employing homophony to imply not simply foolishness but youthful foolishness. In Yiddish, *narishkeit* suggests something that is not worth the time spent on it. The beauty of the term is that it could be just as easily applied to both childish ephemera and the overburdened contortions of hyperintellectualization. Although they seem to occupy different realms of cultural life (one "high" and one "low"), they can both be dismissed as narishkeit for their apparent loss of connection to some other referent known as the "real world."

Teachers always seem to be holding back a tide of narishkeit. Throughout the history of Jewish knowledge production and transmission, people have written seriously about all of the things that might lure people's attention away from sustained study: coffee houses, gambling, sex, secular leisure, sports, baths, beaches, bubble gum, fashion, and so much more. Whatever is not deemed "serious" enough to deserve a person's attention is deemed narishkeit, and to give in to the temptation of narishkeit is to neglect an opportunity to do something more serious with one's time or energy. But to be called narishkeit, something has to pose a serious enough threat to deserve the appellation. To call something narishkeit is not to place it beyond the pale but to locate it on the low end of a hierarchy of value.

There is much that has been tarred as narishkeit that has given us glimpses into much deeper cultural phenomena: comic books, rock and roll, folktales, folk rituals, food, and so on.[55] All of these were dismissed as narishkeit by various self-described "serious" people, and all have persisted and eventually have come to be appreciated for their contributions to culture, knowledge, and understanding. What seems like narishkeit in one setting might hold the keys to unlocking powerful new modes for learning about Jewishness in another. This is not to argue that narishkeit can be redeemed only if it is exposed to be far more serious than it initially appeared to be. Instead, I want to highlight the conceptual value of narishkeit and the role it plays in the organization of knowledge, arrayed as it often is from "significant" to "ephemeral." It is narishkeit that gives gravitas its weight and makes things worth knowing in the first place.

Sometimes silliness is serious, like in the commandment to celebrate with a marrying couple, or in the customs associated with the Jewish holiday of Purim that include carnivalesque practices like dressing up in costume and drinking so much alcohol that one no longer knows the difference between the hero of the Purim narrative and the villain. Conversely, some things seem silly even when they're trying to be serious. Take the following discussion about *yeridat hadorot* ("the decline of the generations"), an implicit theory of history and knowledge that imagines each successive generation growing further and further from the truth and thus worse off than the one that came before. In a series of hyperbolic accounts of yeridat hadorot retold in the Gemara, R. Zera said in the name of Rava bar Zimuna, "If the earlier [scholars] were sons of angels, we are sons of men; and if the earlier [scholars] were sons of men, we are like asses."[56] Not satisfied with the comparison, the text recorded the response of Rava bar Zimuna, who was quoted by Rabbi Zera as saying, "If the early generations are characterized as sons of angels, we are the sons of men. And if the early generations are characterized as the sons of men, we are akin to donkeys. And I do not mean that we are akin to either the donkey of Rabbi Ḥanina ben Dosa or the donkey of Rabbi Pinḥas ben Yair, who were both extraordinarily intelligent donkeys; rather, we are akin to other typical donkeys."[57] Not satisfied with a comparison to donkeys, the rabbis had to up the discursive ante to clarify that they were not talking about the *really smart* donkeys either, lest this generation believe themselves to be better than they are. But more significantly than the precise kind of donkey that humans resemble is the logic of the argument that leads one to conclude that if generational decline is a fact of history and time, then there is no way to resist it or change its course.

Somehow, this particular episode made it into the Talmud and is not, by and large, considered narishkeit. Thus codified, narishkeit becomes canon. We see this elsewhere, from comic book superheroes to rock and roll, and from serialized fiction in the Yiddish press to seemingly ephemeral viral videos. What initially seemed disposable, trifling, silly, childish can become foundational, influential, eternal. Silliness can be serious business, and one generation's asses can be the next generation's scholars.

Zayin—Zitsfleysh

Literally, this Yiddish term refers to the flesh of a person's backside, but in this case *zitsfleysh* refers to a person's capacity, either real or imagined, to sit still and focus. It is something like perseverance but with an undercurrent of commitment to the task at hand. Some define it as "patience," though that seems to imply the ability to wait, which is too passive. It is not exactly what yeshiva students call *hasmodeh*, which means diligence, because that emphasizes plain old hard work. Instead, zitsfleysh refers more directly to a person's inner state and capacity to sit with both patience and diligence to work through a particular issue or problem. Zitsfleysh is a quality that a person has or does not have, though it can be acquired through practice. Any kind of learning in nearly any kind of setting requires a certain level of zitsfleysh, whether we are talking about the study of texts, solving a problem in engineering, learning scales on the piano, dancing, cooking, or whatever. Given the peculiar pressures of the "attention economy" that characterizes life in the twenty-first century, zitsfleysh is a rare commodity.[58]

Distraction, however, is nothing new, though the particularly alluring aspects of social media or the ease of online shopping have, perhaps, amplified its power. It could fairly be said that the emphasis on study in Jewish life derived from a concern for what might be distracting some people from what other people (rabbis, parents, communities) thought they *ought* to be doing. Whether people thought that ideas of the Haskalah were a distraction from Jewish life or thought that study of scripture was a distraction from training for modernity, both could be understood as efforts to counter whatever they might have considered a distraction from the important knowledge at hand. Distraction, after all, is just what people call the process of turning one's attention away from whatever it is that one *ought* to paying attention to in the first place. It is a term of judgment, of power, and of context, whether that judgment comes from oneself or another person.

Historically, claims about what is distracting and what is worthwhile have underwritten a great deal regarding the education of women and girls. The question regarding the education of women was not whether or not they had zitsfleysh but what the men in their lives thought they needed to know in order to maintain a Jewish home and family. Often this was limited to the oral transmission of ritual performances, the preparation of food according to Jewish law (*kashrut*), general ethical principles, and matters of family and menstrual purity.[59] Some influential instructional texts from medieval Europe, like the *Sefer Hasidim*, state that girls should learn neither Hebrew nor Bible and should not study with male teachers, lest their interaction lead to suspicions of improper conduct or contact. Consequently, *Sefer Hasidim* instructed fathers to teach their daughters the laws of domestic Jewish life but to be careful not to teach them from books.[60] Books, the *Sefer Hasidim* concluded, would be distractions.

Jewish approaches to learning and study brim with concerns about distractions and with valorizations of sustained, careful attention to matters at hand. Isaac Farhi (1779–1853), a Palestinian author of numerous books about *musar* in both Hebrew and Ladino, complained about how difficult it is to draw people toward study and away from their leisure time activities. Farhi complained that were he to try to convince someone to study Torah, "he will say mockingly: I will gain nothing by studying except for anxiety and distress of the heart. It is better to go amuse oneself in the coffeehouse or the comedy, for there one finds amusement, laughter and pleasure."[61] Farhi's frustrations were not uncommon and reflect an understanding that students are easily distracted, not serious, and hard to inspire. Though for linguistic reasons he would not have used the term *zitsfleysh*, he worried about laziness and the implications of the lack of attention to serious, sustained study.

He was not alone in this concern during either his time or others. The French commentator Rashi (the acronym for Rabbi Shlomo Yitzchaki [1040–1105]) wrote his commentaries on the Bible and the Mishna and Gemara with an eye toward revealing the plain and direct meaning of the text to those he believed to be average readers. He aimed for clarity of content in context. "Let Scripture be explained in its literal sense so that each statement fits into its proper setting," he wrote.[62] Yet he also worried that too much attention to textual literalism could cloud people's ability to wrest the meaning from the text. "Don't train children in scripture more than is necessary," he warned, "lest they be drawn into it."[63] What constituted "necessary" drew a line between what was important and what was distracting, what demanded attention and what diminished it. In so doing, he helped define worthy knowledge from the distractions that so closely resembled it and take a little pressure off those people who did not have the zitsfleysh necessary to probe the texts by providing them with a more accessible way into them. The relationship between textual complexity and human distractability is dynamic, and many others shared Rashi's concern that average people did not or could not penetrate the sometimes dense or meandering sources of Jewish knowledge. Rabbi Isaac ben Jacob Alfasi ha-Cohen (1013–1103) was among the first to compile a volume that tried to streamline and categorize the knowledge in the Mishna and the Gemara into a more accessible code. His *Sefer Hahalachot* (Book of Laws), published in Fez in 1088, compiled the legal rulings of the Mishna and Gemara so that the books' more narrative or theoretical flights would not distract readers from rendering the wisdom immediately useful to them in their daily lives. Rabbi Moses ben Maimon (1135–1204, better known as Maimonides or the Rambam), took a similar approach in his *Mishne Torah*, which offered a readily accessible, practice-focused, systematically organized account of Jewish law by stripping the Talmud of its more discursive dimensions and systematically reorganizing its contents for easy reference. By organizing knowledge into an accessible code, he reconfigured the Mishna and the Gemara (together known as the Oral Torah) around a primary concern for what he thought important and necessary for the Jews of his time. This was, for the Rambam, a response to conditions that threatened to weaken Jewish life, in general. "At the present time," he wrote in the introduction to the *Mishne Torah*, "when several disasters keep following one another and the needs of the moment brush aside all things, our wise men lose their wits and the understanding of our clever people is hidden. Hence the commentaries, the codes of law and the response, which were written by the Geonim [rabbis trained by an earlier generation of rabbinic academies] who regarded them as easily intelligible, have presented difficulties in our days, so that a mere few are capable of understanding the subject matter properly."[64] Maimonides wanted to bring the qualities of his "clever people" back to the surface, to translate the wisdom of previous generations for his generation, and to explain anew the beauty and insights of Jewish law and custom by presenting only what he thought necessary for that purpose. But the deeper problem he was trying to solve was that people had a hard time paying attention.

The *Mishne Torah* inspired additional efforts to streamline the Oral Torah. Following Rambam, Spanish rabbi Yaakov ben Asher (1270–1340) compiled the *Tur*, which, unlike the *Mishne Torah*, omitted commandments that were no longer actively performed (like the rites of sacrifice in the Temple in Jerusalem) in order to further focus attention on what Jewish people needed to know for their own ritual and communal lives. Centuries later, Spanish scholar Josef Karo (1488–1575) authored commentaries on both the *Mishne Torah* and the *Tur*, which he brought to bear on his commentary *Beit Yosef* ("House of Josef"), which served as the basis for his masterpiece, *Shulkhan Arukh* ("The Set Table"). Karo, whose family fled Inquisitions in Spain and Portugal before finally settling in Safed, organized the *Shulkhan Arukh* as a more streamlined version of Jewish legal codes, and it has since become an authoritative source of rabbinic law. Each of the examples in this succession of codes was designed to focus readers' attention only on what they needed to know, largely because the audiences imagined for the work did not have the zitsfleysh necessary to conduct study at the level the texts demanded. Each of these works represents both a tacit acknowledgment of that fact and an effort to compensate for it by making knowledge more accessible and more available.

Ayin—Osek

When the Gemara presented a dispute about what blessing to say in advance of engaging in the study of sacred texts, it quoted Rabbi Yehuda, who quoted Rabbi Shmuel, who said, "The formula of this blessing is like the standard formula for blessings recited over other mitzvot: 'Blessed are You, Lord our God, King of the universe, Who sanctified us with his mitzvot and commanded us to engage in matters of Torah.'"[65] *Osek* is the verb used for "to engage," though it might also be understood to mean "work" or "occupy," as it relates to the word for "occupation" and "profession," hence the term's colloquial usage in modern Hebrew to refer to things business- or job-related. And yet the Gemara does not refer to the study of sacred texts as *an* occupation or profession, and in some cases it explicitly prohibits earning an income from teaching.[66] Nevertheless, the implication of the term in this context is that one occupies oneself fully with study.

The text's formulation of the blessing for study appears in the middle of a longer discussion about what kinds of texts and what kinds of study require blessings and which do not. The Gemara implies that one can read any number of texts, but only some are sacred enough to require a blessing. Similarly, one can study any number of things, including how to behave in the world, but the rabbis of the ancient world conclude that only some forms of study require a blessing. For example, the Torah commands parents to teach their children, but only those engaged in the study of sacred materials are expected to be "occupied" by them.

This sense of study as a full and nearly total engagement is reflected in one of the most popular formulations about the nature and power of study, akin to what learning scientists have called "flow." Psychologist Mihaly Csikszentmihalyi, who pioneered the term, defined flow as "a state in which people are so involved in an activity that nothing else seems to matter; the experience is so enjoyable that people will continue to do it even at great cost, for the sheer sake of doing it."[67] Flow is an optimal state of immersion in which other considerations evaporate and the activity and the actor fuse. For Rabbi Meir, the formulator of Torah lishma, at least, study was always supposed to be like this. For most of the rest of us, most of the time, this has not been the case. Flow remains an aspiration. It is possible to read the blessing as an intention, recited to prepare oneself for or remind oneself of the ideal version of the task at hand: to unite knower, knowing, and knowledge.

Ironically, this more closely echoes some of Jacob Neusner's writing than it does the more instrumental approaches that have defined Jewish education. The Neusnerian Fallacy held that this was not what was happening or, at least, was not the aim of higher education. But as we found in chapter 1, this was very much a part of his orientation toward study in the first place and why he valued it. Jewish education, by contrast, has been defined largely by its desired outcomes. Whatever students experienced along the way has received less attention than have the intentions of those who put Jewish educational programs into motion. In this way, Neusner's approach to Jewish Studies is a better fit for the blessing than many of the endeavors that have emerged under the rubric of Jewish education.

Yet, this dynamic also informs the paradox of Jewish education, which has always been imagined as an extension of and in some cases a replacement for the transmission and production of Jewish knowledge that people have associated with old neighborhoods, Jewish towns, batei midrash, yeshivot, and other sites of Jewish study thought to be "authentically" Jewish.[68] Immersively Jewish. Holistically Jewish. Romantically Jewish. *Fiddler on the Roof* Jewish. *Yentl* Jewish. The paradox of Jewish education reminds us that people embraced modernity to supplement what people thought had been lost to modernity and through the passage of the generations. What was imagined to have been second nature to family and communal life now had to be taught in school. Of course, this was never the case. Jewish communities have long engaged in the transmission and production of knowledge in order to ensure the continuation of Jewish life even before they called it "education." People have always tried to learn what they did not know. Similarly, people have always tried to teach other people what they thought other people needed to know.

The question in modernity was how to do so at scale. In the late eighteenth century, textbooks represented a new technology suited for this purpose. Historian Jakob Petuchowski identified 160 such books that were published between 1782 and 1884 and were designed to optimize students' time and attention within the emerging framework of a standardized school day.[69] But the textbooks and their authors were not yet ready to take the Neusnerian plunge and divide knowledge-how from knowledge-that. Petuchowski noted that despite the adoption of the modern form of the textbook, most began with treatments of Judaism's religious dimensions, specifically its "ethical duties and its credal affirmations," intended to bolster students' sense of belonging to and engagement with Jewish communal life and culture.[70]

Jewish schools of all stripes from Ben Gamla to now, share a common concern: that Jewish life, culture, and knowledge had attenuated over the generations and stood in need of systematic, learned intervention. The question has always been: how? Over time, different communities developed different strategies and approaches to respond to this question.

In the United States, the most popular response has been the supplementary school, designed to work in tandem with compulsory public schools, holding classes on Sundays, or weekday afternoons. Also known as "Hebrew schools" or "religious schools," they were meant to supplement the perceived lack of thick, deep, or otherwise holistic Jewish life. Though modeled after American public schools, they were really supplemental to family or communal life. But, it quickly became clear, supplementary schools could not shoulder the responsibility with which they were charged, and even Samson Benderly, their chief advocate, pivoted toward overnight camps that promised a more immersive learning environment. Jonathan Krasner cites two of Benderly's students who outlined the vision of Jewish summer camping. For "educational camping pioneer Albert Schoolman, the camps were conceived as an 'experience in the art of Jewish living.' Elaborating on this point, Isaac Berkson, co-owner of Camp Modin, the first private Jewish educational camp, asserted that these camps were built on the premise that 'all genuine education implies a form of living as well as knowing, that learning and living are parts of the same process. The basic aim and method of education therefore becomes participation in Jewish life in all its aspects—cultural social and communal.'"[71] Camps were supposed to re-create the immersive experience of "Jewish living" at a holistic level. Regular ritual, the use of Hebrew, the celebration of Shabbat and other holidays were intended to teach children what their home lives and communities could not. Immersion had to be re-created where it did not exist.[72]

A similar impulse inspired Rabbi Aaron Kotler to establish an institute for advanced religious study, known as a yeshiva, that he called the Beth Medrash Govoha in Lakewood, New Jersey, in 1941. Kotler believed that the only way to advance serious Torah study in the United States was to ensure that it was kept as far away as possible from the influences of secular society. As Kotler said, "The raison d'être of Lakewood is 'limud ha Torah lishmo'—to learn Torah for its own value."[73] To do so, he adapted the approach of the Lithuanian yeshivot to the American suburban context.[74] To keep study vibrant, he operated the Beth Medrash Govoha as a kollel, which paid young, married men stipends to support their ongoing studies. Putting the yeshiva outside of a large city established a natural barrier between the yeshiva and the world it was trying to keep at bay. As the yeshiva grew in both prominence and influence, so too did Lakewood, attracting other young families wishing to live at a distance from the larger world.[75] At the center, though, remained the yeshiva and its vision of focused, immersive learning.

The desire for the "flow" version of learning also infused some young Jewish revolutionaries who, in 1969, staged a sit-in and protest at the annual meeting of the largest Jewish charity groups in the United States. Inspired by their campus peers, this group protested what they saw as the sorry state of Jewish education and made a case for renewed investment in the area, with deeper attention to profound content that they believed could provide the deep, immersive learning they felt necessary for reviving American Jewish life. In an impassioned speech on behalf of the youthful protesters, Hillel Levine took the assembled leaders of American Jewry to task for investing in "the recreation oriented center of low Jewish content over Jewish education of substance."[76] Two years later, James Sleeper, another outspoken member of this group, extended this argument, which promised that education could not only save Jews from America but save them from an American Judaism that, he lamented, had become little more than "a collection of mimeograph machines and pooled nostalgia."[77] These members of the Jewish counterculture saw Jewish education as both the problem and the solution. It was weak, detached, arid. But if undertaken with greater passion, engagement, and investment, it could inspire a renewed engagement in Jewish life. Jewish education, they argued, held the key, and deeper Jewish learning would lead to deeper Jewish lives.

If Lakewood represents an approach to Jewish study that tried to be fully osek, Sleeper and Levine critiqued Jewish education that was not osek enough. A powerful similarity, however, can be found in the ways that each imagined the relationship between knowledge and knower. While Sleeper and Levine were not advocating for a Lakewood approach to their own Jewish education or that of their peers, they understood that their experiences left them wanting a sense of connection to the Judaism they were studying. Kotler, too, imagined his yeshiva as a place of study wholly for its own sake, undertaken by people who were also entirely immersed in a world of learning. All of them believed that modernity and the paradox of Jewish education left the experience of study feeling like it fell short of the mark.

Tet—Ta'am

Literally, "flavor" or "taste" as in the taste of an apple or a pear. But *ta'am* is also used to refer to experience, sense, or even sensibility of a phenomenon or a concept. A popular Yiddish idiom describes delicacies as *tam gan eden*, or having the flavor of the Garden of Eden. It is probably closer to something like "resonance," in that its application is not limited to the term's literal meanings, but it refers to instances when a person encounters the essence or core element of something previously foreign to them. Ta'am is to food what sense is to an argument. Along this line of thinking, the first part of Psalm 34:9 uses a synesthetic metaphor that exhorts readers to "taste and see how good the LORD is." There is little in the context that suggests "taste" in the literal sense of the term. In this respect, the term is probably closer to something like know, but know intimately, sensuously, on a gut level.[78]

Ta'am is most vividly represented in the tender ritual that marked the beginning of formal schooling in Eastern European Jewish communities. According to memoirs, legend, and folklore regarding a male child's first day of school, around age three, his teacher would put honey on a tablet containing either the whole aleph-bet or just the shape of aleph, the first letter, and invite the child to lick it off. The ostensible motivation for this practice is for the child to develop an association between the letters of the Torah and the sweetness of honey.[79] In his sprawling ethnographic survey, Yiddish writer and folklorist Shai An-Ski asked about the practice. "Do people smear the alefbeys [alphabet] tablet with honey so that the child will lick it? What is the reason for this?"[80] An-Ski's survey was never administered in full, but the question itself is an indication of this practice as one among many designed to initiate the student into a life of learning, but also more than that: a life alive with the sweetness of learning. Like the verse from Psalms quoted above, this approach is synesthetic, intended to stoke interest by building a sensuous connection between learning, letters, and the taste of honey. One day of eating honey may begin to sow the sweetness intended, but it cannot sustain. More pragmatically, it may have been a cheap trick, a bait and switch before the real work of school begins.[81] Still, the romantic connection persists, between taste and learning, and between taste as a quality of learning and taste as the thing being learned. It works as a metonym for all of the sensual ways in which knowledge takes shape and the dimensions of sense perception can lead to deep insights and even to knowledge that is unattainable through straightforward cognitive work.

For young boys in Eastern Europe, this meant tasting the letters, but ta'am has another meaning as well, pertaining to other sensorial dimensions of meaning. The text of a Torah scroll is traditionally written without punctuation, orthography, or diacritical markings, and the Hebrew alphabet contains no vowels. In other versions of the text—medieval parchment, printed versions of the Five Books of Moses, and so on—the text often appears with two sets of markings that indicate both vowel sounds and syllabic emphasis. One set represents the vowel sounds, and the other symbolizes short tonal or melodic phrases meant to instruct readers in vocalization. The latter set is known as the *ta'amei hamikra*. Talmudist Daniel Boyarin defines *mikra* as "that which is read aloud and in public."[82] Both sets of symbols were developed and codified around the turn of the first millennium.[83] In order to chant Torah, people typically learn both the proper pronunciation of the passage and the ta'amei hamikra from a printed volume and then read it from the scroll, recalling the manner of reading that they had practiced. Mastering this process can be exacting and is often a central feature of training for b-mitzvah and thus a major part of many people's Jewish education.

The tradition of reading the text aloud traces back to Ezra the Scribe, whom the Book of Nehemiah described as having "brought the *teaching* [Hebrew: *Torah*] before the congregation, men and women and all who could listen with understanding. He read from it."[84] Nehemiah continues, "They read from the scroll the Teaching of God [Hebrew: *sefer Torat ha'elohim*], translating it [Hebrew: *meforash*] and giving it the sense, so they understood the reading."[85] Ezra's practice of declaiming the text in public emphasized not only his faithful reproduction of the words for an audience who may or may not have been able to read them on their own but also "translating" or interpreting it so that they could understand. Understanding speech or words relies on all kinds of extratextual or supralinguistic modalities like gesture, intonation, inflection, and accent. For someone reading a scroll, this may also have included a tonal dimension that, for nonliterate people, may not have been experienced or understood as distinct from the words that Ezra read.

In Nehemiah's account of Ezra, most people who encountered the performed text of the Torah likely did so aurally, as listeners, which would have placed significant interpretive weight on the proper recitation of the text as it was either memorized or chanted. The creation of a system of tonality within a world in which texts were often experienced aurally thus would have figured significantly in how and what people would have understood, and the authoring of such a system was likely informed by a concern for what the authors wanted people to hear and to know. As the historian David Stern has written, aurality shaped how the rabbis of the Mishna and the Gemara knew their sources. Stern traces the prevalence of rhymes and other aural modalities in rabbinic interpretive logic to claim that the rabbis both read and heard text but that "it was not, however, from such reading [alone] that a rabbi acquired his primary knowledge of Torah but from the continuous experience of hearing the text, and that auditory experience determined the way in which he 'knew' Torah."[86]

Stern argues that the ancient rabbis placed significant emphasis on the proper recitation of the text and great responsibility on the determination of what constituted "proper." Such concerns led Aaron ben Asher in the early tenth century to publish his *Sefer Dikduke Te'amim*, "a book of rules concerning vocalization and accentuation . . . with the goal of describing a more general grammar of the language."[87] Ben Asher is often credited with systematizing the ta'amei hamikra, though his book suggests that he approached the grammar and the sound of the text as component features of meaning making, performance, interpretation, and meaning.[88]

In his ethnography of chanting Torah in the lives of American Jews, musicologist Jeffrey Summit noted that it is possible to observe the practice from two "keys," which straddle the line between textual fidelity and personal meaning, between accurate representation and subjective experience.

> When viewed in the key of religious obligation, the Torah service is about the correct and accurate performance of a required act. From this perspective chanting Torah is an exacting performance of the text with important theological and ritual implications in regard to practice and daily life. However, when viewed in the key of the individual's personal agency and desire to express one's identity and connection to peoplehood, chanting Torah becomes about self-actualization as a Jew, the desire for intensified experience, an intimate connection to place and community.[89]

This tension is further elaborated by the fact that the performances of ta'amei hamikra differ widely by region and tradition, even when the assignment of the notation is fairly standard. Musicologists have identified eight such traditions.[90] When pioneering musicologist Moshe Idelsohn first heard the sounds of cantillation of Jewish communities from Arab countries, particularly those of Yemenite Jews, he concluded that they were closer representations of the musical modes of ancient Israel than were those from Eastern Europe, with which he was more familiar. Idelsohn's conclusion smacks of Orientalism, and he mistook the presence of the ta'amei hamikra for evidence of the persistence and continuity of an oral/aural culture that he heard to be purer than his own European one.[91]

Idelsohn's romanticization of Yemenite cantillation notwithstanding, differences in cantillation indicate more than just a "flavor" of what distinguishes different Jewish communities from one another. Rather, the ta'amei hamikra constitute those differences. How else could one distinguish the taste of an apple from a pear? It is hard to know about ta'am without experiencing it firsthand. It is possible to explain taste or tune, but descriptions of a pineapple, for example, or the presentation of ta'amei hamikra are not equivalent to the experience of eating, hearing, or singing. The melody may, in fact, be inseparable from the meanings of the words. Rather than a simple embellishment or mnemonic device, ta'am suggests a modality of knowing that blurs the lines between what is possible to know about and what is possible to know from experience. The Neusnerian Fallacy hangs on the proposition that it is possible to know about, but ta'am's place in making meaning implies that the distinction is harder than it seems. It may be impossible to separate the two.

Frameworks

Mem—Maser

The opening verse of Pirke Avot (I:I) posits a grand genealogy of Jewish learning as something that is passed from generation to generation. Using the Hebrew word *maser*, the verse tracks the transmission of Torah from the Revelation at Sinai to the rest of us: "Moses received the Torah at Sinai and transmitted it to Joshua, Joshua to the elders, and the elders to the prophets, and the prophets to the Men of the Great Assembly. They said three things: Be patient in [the administration of] justice, raise many disciples and make a fence around the Torah." This brief encapsulation of transmission also tracks the transformation of knowledge from something possessed by an individual to something supported by an institution. Moses had direct knowledge of God and the Prophets had conversations with the divine and carried those messages to the people. The Great Assembly was something of a combination of a house of learning, an administrative unit, a court, and a center for textual explication; its members and their teachings live in Mishna and the Gemara. The rest of us are tasked with carrying on the knowledge that has traveled down that chain of transmission at some distance from the direct encounter that instigated it. Whatever Moses knew of God did not move, unchanged, to Joshua and so on down the line. According to the text, Moses "knew God," and although Moses taught Joshua what he knew, the transmission—like all transmissions—could only ever be partial. Joshua is described not as someone who "knew God," only as someone who listened carefully to Moses's teachings. He absorbed some of what Moses had taught him and passed it along, but it could not have been precisely what Moses had known. Thus, whatever Joshua transmitted to the elders had to have been a variation on a theme.

The straightforward reading (*pshat*) is that the story reinforces the authority of rabbis of the Great Assembly, who can trace their knowledge directly back to Moses. What better way to establish one's authority than to claim they got it directly from the source? Sherira Gaon, a tenth-century teacher and rabbi in the academy and Pumbedita, put his own spin on this narrative in a letter explaining the formation of the Mishna. Sherira wrote the letter in response to a query from the Jewish community in Kairouan, in what is now Tunisia. That community was largely Karaite, a subpopulation of Jews who have historically rejected Rabbinic Judaism, so their inquiry can be understood as something of a provocation to the center of rabbinic thought to explain itself.[92] Sherira's reply provided one of the first accounts of the formation of the Mishna revolving around the heroic character of Yehuda HaNasi and his efforts to collect, compile, and transcribe rabbinic wisdom after the failure of the Bar Kochba Rebellion (132–135 CE). "And in the days of Rabbi [Yehuda HaNasi], matters were aided such that the words of our Mishna were as if they had been said from the mouth of the Almighty. And they seemed like a sign and a wonder. And Rabbi did not compose these from his heart."[93] Without a Moses to convey prophesy and absent an Ezra to write and read the Torah in the marketplace, Sherira narrativized the chain of transmission such that it that ran straight through the rabbis of the Talmud to those of Sura and Pumbedita. His description of the Mishna represented the next link in the chain, as Talmud scholar Talya Fishman explained: "Though not the first chronology of the rabbinic generations, the Epistle [of Sherira] almost single-handedly shaped rabbinic culture's subsequent understanding of its own literary foundations."[94]

The term also appears in the designation "masoretic," which refers to the dominant version of a text included in the Hebrew Bible. The Masoretes were a group of scribes who reproduced and taught the texts as they were passed on to them and which they, in turn, transcribed, edited, taught, and passed on.[95] The oldest source of the masoretic texts dates from the tenth century and is typically referred to as the Aleppo Codex, which included vowelization, the ta'amei hamikra (see "Tet—Ta'am," above), and notes, referred to as the "masorah," which refers to instructions left by and for scribes in the margins of the text. The terms "masorah" and "maserete" refer to their role as transmitters, organs, or agents of textual fidelity. They also refer to their place in the process of transmission and the claim that they held a position that allowed them to faithfully transmit their knowledge. Of course, the question of what made such an act "faithful" and to what (or whom) remained something of an open question. Claiming fidelity to both the process of transmission and the product being transmitted was crucial to establishing one's authority over both.

This tension is evident in the name of the body of rabbinic writing known as musar literature, whose title also draws on this concept. Historian Immanuel Etkes explained that "in contemporary Hebrew, the term Mussar is used in a sense more or less synonymous with the Western concept of 'ethics.' In biblical wisdom literature, the word refers to a punishment or verbal rebuke directed against a negative act, while in medieval Hebrew literature it refers to proper interpersonal behavior."[96] Musar literature emerged as a way for rabbis and scholars to translate innovations in rabbinic thought into practical advice.[97] As a result, the tradition of musar took on the cultural contours and folk conventions of the communities in which it flourished.

Etkes's study of musar draws heavily on the work of Rabbi Israel Salanter (1809–1883), a Lithuanian rabbi who advocated for musar as the primary purpose for study. "The focus of education in a musar yeshiva was not the next world . . . but rather on developing a moral attitude toward this world. The emphasis was on man, rather than on God—Just as in the approach of the Haskalah the goal of full realization of ethical potential was seen as the pinnacle of achievement. However, in contrast to the Haskalah, the ultimate goal of musar remained the service of God."[98] Salanter landed strongly on the "keneged kulam" side of things, with an approach to study that connects what one *knows* to what one *does*. But the purpose of study in the musar tradition was not only to be able to act ethically at any given moment, but also to cultivate one's own character so that ethical action derived from the knowledge that doing the right thing indicated one's connection to the divine. Etkes explains that the study of musar was to arouse the emotions of the student, cultivating in him (Salanter, at least, imagined men as the students of his vision) intense feelings of fear of Divine retribution, feelings that would accompany him constantly and affect his actions. Thus, musar to transform the "fear of punishment" from an abstract theological principle, present on the conscious level, to a quality residing within the soul.[99] The logic of musar, as Etkes explained, is steeped in both formal study (Torah) and the felt or imagined fear or awe of God [Hebrew: *yir'ah*].

Historian Matthias Lehmann's study of Judeo-Spanish musar literature takes a different approach that focuses less on its logic of inner transformation and more on its role in "the construction and maintenance of the symbolic and social order of Ottoman Sephardic tradition."[100] He argues that it played this role in a variety of ways, one of which was the provision of an opportunity to study as a tool for sacralizing socializing, serving as a kind of rationale for semistructured and rabbinically sanctioned social activity. Gatherings to study musar literature were called *meldados*, which Lehmann observed were both "the most important forum of the new Judeo-Spanish reading public" as well as a "rabbinic response to the appearance of secular forms of sociality."[101] Restricted to men but possible only because of the domestic labor of women, meldados emerged in response to fears that the coffeehouse and other modes of secular sociability would take up leisure time and distract people from study. Concerned about alcohol, "idle talk," and other pursuits that did not enhance people's spiritual or ethical selves, rabbis institutionalized meldados to carry out their belief that "socializing itself should always be 'sanctified' through learning."[102] Thus configured, musar takes a more expansive role in Jewish knowledge production. Study could serve both social and sacred ends, at least as far as rabbis were concerned.

Whatever one might think about musar literature and its contents, its institutionalization both in Salanter's Lithuania and across Ottoman-Sephardic culture represented a significant instance of the social qualities of Jewish teaching and learning. Central to cultural forms, as historian Jacob Katz argued, lay a strategy that mobilized tradition in the name of innovation. Whatever was being taught in Salanter's yeshiva or in the meldados, their leaders and teachers rooted their teachings, like Sherira Gaon, in their unique access to the tradition that they were passing along to their students. The linguistic similarity between *maser* as a verb and *musar* as a noun allowed them to frame the significance of the knowledge they were transmitting in terms of its relationship to the process of transmission itself.

Reysh—Rabbi

Rabbi is the title of some Jewish clergy who serve as the primary ritual functionary in contemporary Jewish life.[103] Throughout the Mishna and the Gemara, people are referred to as both *rabbi* and *rav*. Moses's nickname is *Moshe rabeinu*, which is usually translated as "Moses our teacher." The term derives from the Hebrew word for "grow" or "increase." It shares etymology with the words for great quantity, as in the commandment to "be fruitful and multiply" and the description of the generation of the Exodus from Egypt as a "mixed multitude."[104] The same word becomes an honorific when turned into the word *rabon*, or master, as in *rebono shel olam*, or "Master of the Universe."

The title *rabbi* was either adopted by or assigned to scholars and teachers that followed; a distinction between scholar and teacher would have been lost on the ancients. Yet, as historian Shaye Cohen has observed, "The term 'rabbi' is ambiguous. It may be either a popular designation for anyone of high position, notably—but not exclusively—a teacher, or it may be a technical term for someone who has been 'ordained' and has achieved status and power within that society which produced the Mishna, the Talmudim, and related works."[105] In other words, he noted, "even in antiquity not all rabbis were Rabbis."[106]

The informality of the title carried through the Middle Ages and into modernity, when, as sociologist Max Weber explained, systems, institutions, and organizations tried to assign order to rapidly changing societies. A key feature of modernity was its approach to organizing the production and transmission of knowledge: Science birthed taxonomies of all kinds, universities expanded, and the emergence of scholarly disciplines tried to organize knowledge into discreet and meaningful fields. New institutions emerged to train and credential a new professional class, including Jewish seminaries, which proliferated in the nineteenth century. In 1854, Zacharias Frankel established the first Jewish Theological Seminary of Breslau, to be followed nineteen years later by Israel Hildesheimer's Rabbinical Seminary for Orthodox Judaism in Berlin.[107] The Pressburg Yeshiva, an influential force in emerging Orthodoxy, was founded in the first decade of the nineteenth century but was recognized by Emperor Franz Joseph I only in 1855.[108] Meanwhile, across the Atlantic, Rabbi Isaac Mayer Wise established the Hebrew Union College (HUC) in Cincinnati in 1875. Only a decade later, in 1886, the Jewish Theological Seminary of America (JTSA) began training more traditionally oriented rabbis, and a decade after its founding, in 1897, the Rabbi Isaac Elchanan Theological Seminary emerged out of a growing sense that neither HUC nor JTSA provided adequate instruction in Jewish tradition.[109]

The emergence of seminaries represented a shift not only in the formalization of rabbinical training but in the landscape of Jewish life. Each of the three American seminaries established in the late nineteenth century began ordaining rabbis according to their respective perspectives on Jewish knowledge, practice, and custom. The rabbis, in turn, sought employment from congregations who may or may not have been formally affiliated with one of the movements, but the selection of one rabbi over another indicated something about their orientation toward the kind of Judaism they wished to embody. Early on the associations between rabbi, congregation, and movement were quite fluid, though as the movements became more institutionalized, the distinctions grew increasingly rigid.[110] By establishing institutions for credentialing rabbis, the seminaries effectively helped segment and organize American Jewish life according to the familiar tripartite structure of Reform, Conservative, and Orthodox, and for much of the twentieth century this structure dominated American Judaism.

The seeds of a more diverse religious structure, however, began to take root in the years after World War II, with the establishment of new rabbinical seminaries. The Academy of Jewish Religion opened its doors in Los Angeles in 1956, and the Seminario Rabínico Latinoamericano in Buenos Aires followed some six years later. The Aleph Ordination Program operates largely virtually and ordained its first students sometime in the mid-1970s, New York's Yeshivat Chovevei Torah, a liberal orthodox seminary, opened its doors in 2000, and the nondenominational Hebrew College was founded in 2003 in Boston. Hadar, which began in the late 1990s as a small independent *minyan* (prayer community) on the Upper West Side, has grown into a major center of study with an ordination program as well. The establishment in 1999 of the Abraham Geiger Kolleg gave Germany its first seminary since the Holocaust, and in Israel the Shechter Rabbinical Seminary launched a "post-denominational" ordination program in 1984. Even more recently, the Rimmon Rabbinical School launched a fully online ordination program in 2020. There are others, of course, but even this short list captures the range and diversity, in terms of geography, orientation, and mission, of these approaches that are changing the nature of Judaism by expanding the range of institutions empowered to ordain rabbis.

The emergence of new ordination programs reflects a desire for clergy who embody and practice alternatives to the legacy religious movements. But by creating the concept of a "nondenominational" rabbi, the new wave of ordination programs also establishes an institution and a credential that both clergy and communities can recognize. Expanding understandings of what rabbis do and who they are accompanied the expansion of professional opportunities for rabbis outside of the synagogue: in schools and summer camps, campus Hillels, hospitals, and even federations and foundations. Thus, changes at the institutional level both drive and are driven by changes at the communal level regarding what rabbis do, what they know, how they teach, and what they represent.

But perhaps the largest and most significant change in the rabbinate has not been the diversification of training programs or professional opportunities but the ordination of women rabbis, beginning with Sally Priesand, who was ordained by HUC in 1972.[111] The Reconstructionist Rabbinical College began ordaining women shortly thereafter, and the JTSA followed more than a decade later.[112] Priesand was not the first female rabbi (that would be Ray Frank), but she was the first to be ordained by a seminary in what amounted to a formal, institutional response to feminism.[113] More recently still, institutions like Yeshivat Maharat (established in 2009) have launched ordination programs for Orthodox women, further expanding and advancing the leadership roles of women across the range of Jewish communal life. Although the movement to ordain women as rabbis began in the United States, it has spread rapidly as female rabbis have assumed leadership positions in institutions and communities around the world.

Other changes in the composition of the rabbinate have further shaped understandings of who rabbis are and what they do. Increasing numbers of LGBTQ rabbis and of rabbis who identify as Jews of Color have enriched the clergy by bringing their experiences to their teaching, preaching, pastoral work, and practice. The issue is not simply that there are people who hold these identities—as women, as queer, as African American, and so on—but rather that they bring their experiences and those identities to the work of being a rabbi. The diversification of the rabbinate from an exclusively male and normatively heterosexual profession to one that is represented by a variety of people with a range of experiences, backgrounds, communities, and commitments vastly expands the body of knowledge that can be recognized as rabbinic. Thus, as rabbis increasingly represent the range of identities in their communities, so too do their contributions to the production and transmission of knowledge.

These developments in the rabbinate are the result of both the institutionalization of knowledge, through the development of seminaries and formal training programs, and the acknowledgment of the value of diverse perspectives on Jewish life, practice, and experience. Together, they represent an expansion of awareness regarding the diverse needs of Jewish communities and the desire for clergy that can meet them. Tacitly, too, the increasingly diverse rabbinate reflects an understanding that rabbis can serve communities in a variety of ways, and not only through their embodiment of a particular ideological or denominational perspective. Thus, we return to the term *rabbi* and what it means. On the surface, it signals the possession of a credential as a response to the issue that Shaye Cohen noted in ancient Israel. But, drawing on its root meaning "great" or "increase," we might understand its application as "teacher" as indicating someone whose efforts add to the community by producing and transmitting knowledge. The more diverse the rabbinate, the more diverse the knowledge available to the community and the greater it might become.

Yod—Yeda

The Hebrew root *yod-dalet-ayin* indicates knowledge and knowing. The Bible contains more than nine hundred words that derive from this single root, suggesting that it signifies a concept of some import, if only by its ubiquity. The Bible does not regard knowledge as something special, and the word applies to knowing all kinds of things in all kinds of ways: other people, God, skills, proper comportment, and self, to name a few. Knowing in the biblical sense can refer to sex, but that is not definitive of how the word was used in Scripture.

Both epistemologists and learning scientists understand that, just as in the Bible, there are many different forms of knowledge and many ways of knowing. Muscle memory born of repetitive action is one kind, rational argument is another. The knowledge born of firsthand experience affords one type of knowledge, while empirical data provide another. Whether or not knowledge reflects truth is, as Michel Foucault reminds us, complicated by differential power, and so is the ascription of value to knowledge more generally.[114] Some educational theorists argue that knowledge is passed along via direct instruction or rote repetition, while others claim that knowledge is only ever produced or constructed by learners who access both their own cultural resources and those presented to them in classes or clubs or elsewhere.

The Bible treats knowledge as a problem from the very beginning.[115] With some encouragement, Adam and Eve eat fruit from the tree of knowledge, which initiates their expulsion from the Garden of Eden and, in some theological accounts, leads directly to the present situation facing human civilization. It is worth emphasizing that the tree was not a tree of good and evil but a tree of *knowledge* of good and evil. The story's power derives from its acknowledgment not that God created good and evil as forces in the world but that *knowing* about good and evil poses its own challenges. Following philosopher Michel Foucault, good and evil are not static categories, rather power lies in the ability to make something known to be good or evil. In the biblical narrative, good and evil are not the cause of the trouble: knowledge is.

Consequently, the Bible does not regard knowledge as a universal good. Cain lies about knowing the whereabouts of his brother, whom he recently killed. When Noah wakes, hungover, the text says that he knew what had happened the night before. Generations later, when God reappears to Abram to make promises about his legacy and his land, Abram "put his trust" in God but still wonders, "how shall I know that I am to possess it?"[116] After a night wrestling with an angel, Jacob remarks with some measure of wonder that he did not know God was in that place.[117] The whole narrative of slavery and the Exodus for Egypt begins with the rise to power of a Pharaoh who is described as not having known Joseph, and the text explains the struggle between God and Pharaoh in terms of an effort to ensure that the Egyptians know "that I am the Lord."[118]

The use of this term in the Bible typically refers to a kind of knowing that is deep and sometimes profound. It might be more like "understanding" or, to borrow from popular culture, "grok," than simply to recall a fact or reproduce a series of steps to complete a task.[119] Or, to borrow from Jewish terminology, it might land more closely to someone who is a "maven," which derives from the Hebrew for "understand" and may originally have been the term for an interpreter or translator of Torah chanting. As a result, the status of knowledge in the Bible is not entirely cognitive. It indicates a relationship to understanding that can be intellectual as well as sensual. To feel that one knows something is not the same as knowing it, but it seems hard to know something without feeling that one knows it. Recent research into neuroscience has revealed what many people have known intuitively for a very long time, that "emotions are not add-ons that are distinct from cognitive skills. Instead emotions, such as interest, anxiety, frustration, excitement, or a sense of awe in beholding beauty, become a dimension of the skill itself."[120]

This approach to knowing has been both central to and at odds with historical engagements with Jewish knowledge which have, for some time, revolved around the study of text. People disagreed about what texts ought to be studied and by whom, but in the main, the commitment to the importance of texts and its centrality in schools and for teachers cannot be underestimated. Textual knowledge was understood as the basis for action, and its impact on action was thought to be causal: knowing the right sources would lead to the right actions. As the Rambam concluded in the section of his *Mishne Torah* titled *madda* ("knowledge," also a derivation of the root *yod-dalet-ayin*), "in every instance study precedes practice."[121]

But Jewish practice has long been rife with other modalities of knowing. The *havdalah* ("differentiation") ritual marking the end of the Sabbath engages the senses through blessings over seeing candlelight, smelling spices or fragrant leaves, and drinking wine. Food in general is a particularly powerful vector for the production and transmission of knowledge from generation to generation and within communities, through family recipes, the laws of kashrut, or communal meals. The choreography of synagogue worship—standing, sitting, singing, listening—invites the sensual and embodied into communal practices, and they can become avenues through which people learn how to participate in communal activities or how to pray. Even the physicality of the Torah scroll—retained even after the invention of the printing press and the ready availability of other forms of textuality that were more compact, more readable, and easier to transport and access—speaks to the significance of what scholars of religion sometimes call "material religion" to elicit certain ways of knowing that are not limited to cognition alone.[122] Even the power of Jewish museums is embedded in their ability to present material, visual, and sonic aspects of Jewish life that can and do teach not just about what Jews thought or did, but about how they lived as sensual beings.[123]

The classic if oversimplified division in Jewish life between cognition and feeling has even translated into a clumsy distinction between two influential approaches to piety and practice. Hasidism is often understood as having rejected the tenets of Enlightenment-based education, which they felt were antithetical to Jewish modes of study and practice, most notably the knowledge of Jewish mysticism.[124] Their critics, known as Mitnagdim ("the opposition"), thought that Hasidism had strayed too far from the expectations of serious text study and wrote strong, occasionally caustic critiques of Hasidic thought, characterizing them as joyous fools or naifs. However, even Rabbi Hayim of Volozhin, one of the most vaunted mitnagdic educational leaders and the founder of the venerable Yeshiva of Volozhin, engaged with mystical concepts in some of his work.[125] And Hasidic communities also value scholarship and study. The point is not whether or not Hasidim or Mitnagdim actually live up to their caricatures (who does?), but that the caricatures represent some of the conventional ways in which people divide knowing from feeling and project those distinctions on practices and people.

The upshot is that the lines people draw around where knowledge is held or how it is or ought to be produced are far blurrier than they appear. For all of the significance that has been placed on ideas and texts, bodies bear a great deal of responsibility for absorbing, retaining, and transmitting massive amounts of knowledge. The not quite logical or the not entirely scholarly dimensions of knowledge and its sources thus found their way into so many formulations of education as a core principle of the undertaking. Philosopher Franz Rosenzweig believed this to be central to his vision for a revitalized adult Jewish educational program. "The task of Jewish religious instruction is to re-create that *emotional* tie between the institutions of public worship and the individual, that is, the very tie which he has lost."[126] Samson Benderly, architect of the supplementary school approach to Jewish education that dominated American Jewish life during the twentieth century and a strong believer in the tenets and structures of modern American education, advanced a similar vision, but for American Jewish children: "Above all it is necessary to bring home to the children the grandeur of Jewish history, the heroic struggle and the unparalleled martyrdom of the Jewish People for the sake of its ideals, to arouse their pride in our great past, and to stir enthusiasm for the endeavors marking the Jewish revival of our own days."[127] Even those who opposed Benderly's approach and advocated for the creation of Jewish private schools shared his belief that the central concern was that of American Jewish youth who felt the disjuncture between their Jewish and American selves and suffered as a result. Judah Pilch, a midcentury scholar of and advocate for day schools, wrote that "the progressive day school, in which stress is laid upon an integrated program of general and Jewish studies, [is] where the child learns of the *'spiritual kinship between Judaism and Americanism.'*"[128]

The affective turn in Jewish education has gained purchase as Jewish education has embraced "informal" or "experiential" education as a powerful modality for the production and transmission of knowledge.[129] One of the pioneers in the field was Shlomo Bardin, who established new, immersive educational experiences that catered to adults in what Deborah Dash Moore has called "spiritual recreation."[130] Bardin, she writes, focused on the affective dimension of Judaism, constructing an educational experience that emphasized the senses and sensibilities of Jewish life over its formal, doctrinal forms. As Bardin explained in 1958, his intention was "to give the young a feeling of belonging; to make him feel at ease as a Jew in an American environment."[131] Inspired in part by the Zionist vision of Louis Brandeis (Bardin called his undertaking the Brandeis Camp Institute), Bardin envisioned an educational approach that could salve the tensions of American Jewish life by making people feel better about it and, at the same time, serve the collective enterprise of the Jewish people. As Moore observed, "Bardin deliberately set out to arouse emotions: to awaken interest in the Jewish people, to stimulate a desire to pursue Jewish knowledge, and to instill a sense of responsibility for the Jewish future."[132] Central to this vision, she noted, was the "centrality of experience to knowing."[133]

Bardin's logic has only grown more influential in the decades since he began his work in Southern California. Jewish museums, book clubs, film festivals, and, of course, overnight summer camps have capitalized on a similar set of affective investments in learning to make good on the romantic underpinnings of Jewish educational visions in modernity. The largest recent undertaking in this regard has been Birthright Israel, which employs heritage tourism as its basic curricular approach, bringing thousands of Jews ages eighteen to twenty-six to Israel for ten-day tours.[134] Erik Cohen, a scholar of heritage tourism, observed that "Jewish travel may be seen" as a modality in which "tourists seek, to varying degrees, emotional connection with their own roots, exploration of the self through encounter with the exotic 'other,' intellectual stimulation, and an enjoyable break from daily routine."[135] What people might learn on vacation, at museums, or at film festivals varies greatly, but the status of knowledge in Jewish life reveals a few long-running traditions that engage with it as a product of both study and sentiment. The multimodal nature of knowledge and the twin emphasis on cognition and affect suggest that the knowledge one produces and the means of its production are ultimately inextricable. The trouble with knowledge, suggested in the Garden of

Eden story, is really a problem with people, what they do with knowledge and how they make distinctions between its different forms.

Lamed—Lomed

The Hebrew terms for both teaching and learning derive from the same root: lamed-mem-dalet. The verb form does not appear in the first four books of the Pentateuch, but it shows up four times in Deuteronomy. Most famously, Deuteronomy 11:19 instructs its readers to "teach (ulemadtem) them [these words] to your children—reciting them when you stay at home and when you are away, when you lie down and when you get up" (see "vav—veshinantam," above). This verse appears within a longer section that is also recited in the collection of three biblical passages that follow the recitation of the Shema, and it is a near verbatim repetition of the veshinantam verse, but with a different verb.

Veshinantam is not a form of a root that is in wide use, in either biblical or colloquial Hebrew, but lomed is. Both teaching and learning are active forms of the same conjugated verb, indicating that learning is neither the passive nor the reflexive (as in "I taught myself") form of teaching. Rather, they are symbiotic concepts, related by practice and context. From lomed also derive the word for student (talmid) and the title of the Talmud, as well as lomdus, a nickname for a method of Talmud study known as the Brisker Method, which originated with Rabbi Hayim Soloveitchik of Brisk.[136]

The term also appears tucked into the word melamed, which was the informal title applied to men who were hired by families and communities to teach youngsters either as tutors or as instructors in the heder. In modern Hebrew, the term for teacher (gendered female: morah; gendered male: moreh) derives from a separate root entirely (see the entry on "Torah," below). To be a melamed, one did not have to be particularly learned (such a person would probably have been called a lamdan; same root, different form). Melamdim (the plural form) were not trained pedagogues and often worked with substandard materials for substandard pay, and how much they earned and how they were paid was a source of ongoing uncertainty. Where parents had the means, they would hire melamdim as tutors for their children, but sometimes students boarded in the melamed's home, an arrangement that increased the financial benefits of teaching children.[137] Sometimes parents would band together to hire a melamed, or, in cases where families could not afford to hire a melamed, the community would collect funds to support them.

In Eastern Europe, a female melamed took the female-gendered version of the term, melamedke, though they were also known by other terms like rebitsin or rabbanit.[138] Melamedkes taught both boys and girls, though they were a less regular and stable presence. The best available evidence suggests that rather than a low status, if consistent profession, women taught in formal settings for shorter periods than did their male counterparts, in order to bring in income that would supplement their husbands'. When the family no longer needed the income, they would usually stop teaching.[139] This made melamedkes a presence, albeit an inconsistent one.

Parents who had the financial means strove to ensure that their children studied with tutors. Elazar of Mayence (Germany, ca. 1357) addressed his ethical will to both his sons and his daughters, writing, "If they can by any means contrive it, my sons and daughters should live in communities, and not isolated from other Jews, so that their sons and daughters may learn the ways of Judaism. Even if compelled to solicit from others the money to pay a teacher, they must not let the young of both sexes go without instruction in the Torah."[140] Similarly, in a will found in the Cairo Geniza, Wusha al-Dallala, a successful eleventh-century businesswoman, outlined her expectations for the education of her son, upon her death. "The melammed [sic] Rabbi Moses shall be taken to him and teach him the Bible and the prayerbook to the degree it is appropriate that he should know them."[141] She goes on to stipulate that "the teacher should be given a blanket and a sleeping carpet so that he can stay with him," in addition to a salary. Other wills and documents from the period contain similar charges, demonstrating parental concern both for their children's learning and for the centrality of the melamed within it.

According to historian Ephraim Kanarfogel, this resulted in a widespread but generally uncoordinated approach to education in Europe during the Middle Ages: "While there was . . . ample educational opportunity for a boy growing up in Ashkenaz, his taking advantage of these opportunities depended on where he lived, what his parents could afford, and the interest they displayed in his education. . . . There was no system of elementary education in Ashkenaz."[142] Yet he also observed that the melamed was "the central figure in the educational process."[143] Shaul Stampfer described the role of the melamed in the *heder*, a kind of Jewish one-room schoolhouse: "Most heder teachers entered the profession because they had no alternative and not from a desire to be an educator or because of personal qualifications. Heder teaching was, in a sense, a safety net for the unemployable who in other societies would be welfare recipients. Many heder teachers were highly unqualified and were neither learned nor creative."[144] There were, of course, exceptional melamdim who prepared their students for higher learning, but they could not raise the status of the melamed in general.

Teaching and learning, however, were not limited to the work of melamdim, and neither were they limited to children. And they were not limited to males, either. As historians Elisheva Baumgarten and Judith Baskin have found, a handful of women engaged in advanced learning. Baumgarten found that in at least one case, midwives were required to be literate.[145] One notable and learned woman, Dulcea of Worms (d. 1196), was described by her husband both as learned and as a teacher of other women including their daughter. "In all the cities she taught women, enabling their 'pleasant' intoning of songs."[146] Leon Modena's aunt, Fioretta, was known to be very learned in Talmud and Torah.[147] Historian Howard Adelman noted that in late medieval Italy "women who studied with male or female teachers attained a level of learning which included the ability to read the Bible, to participate in the three traditional daily services, and to teach others, albeit young children."[148]

Documents from the Cairo Geniza contain numerous references to learned women and even to women who served as teachers. S. D. Goitein, the scholar of the Cairo Geniza, noted one document from Yemen in which a copyist named Miriam asked forgiveness for any errors she made in her work while she was nursing. Another document from the twelfth century told of the daughter of one of the leaders of the Baghdad Jewish academy who was "so learned that she was able to teach her father's students not only the Bible, but also the Talmud."[149] Still another told of a Cairene woman who had been abandoned by her husband and opened a school with her brother.[150] Although these women were exceptions to a more general rule, the presence of female teachers or leaders was not such a rarity. Eleventh-century Cairo had a Synagogue of the Women Teachers, which suggested that there were enough female teachers that they came to be the distinguishing feature of the synagogue.[151]

In scholarship on education, the term *lomed* has turned into the Hebrew version of the catchall disciplinary suffix "-studies," as in religious studies, cultural studies, gender studies, or Jewish Studies. Jewish private schools construct their school days to distinguish between *limmudei kodesh* (religious studies) and *limmudei chol* (general studies like math, social studies, and the like). The World Union of Jewish Studies, the largest learned society committed to Jewish Studies, uses the term *limmudei yahadut* to signal its scholarly focus and to distinguish it from other forms of Jewish study. The appearance of the term in the administrative vernacular of higher education emphasizes the quality of the term that implies an empirical relationship to the object of study: "Jewish Studies" refers to the study of things Jewish: people, ideas, communities, texts, and so on. But the term also reveals that the object of study bears knowledge sought by the student, to be extracted, refracted, and otherwise transformed. In this way, the subject of the study also teaches, echoing the linguistic core of lomed and the complex interdependency between "study of" and "study about," and between teaching and learning.

Pay—Pilpul

Deriving from a verb meaning "to search," *pilpul* has most often been used in reference to what might generally be called "talmudic debate," the long, sometimes circuitous, sometimes arcane, and sometimes penetrating engagements with the meanings of sacred texts. Shaul Stampfer wrote, "Pilpul is very hard to define . . . and one scholar's peshat (simple interpretation) is seen as pilpul by others. The concept can be roughly described as an attitude or approach that focuses on forcing texts into agreement (or disagreement) with each other rather than focusing on what was most likely the original intent of the statement, though the term is not suited to a formal and explicit definition."[152] The term is hard to define in part because the practices to which it refers are themselves hard to identify and because the knowledge pursued through pilpul is also difficult to locate.

Scholar of the Talmud Daniel Boyarin outlined two qualities of pilpul, one that emphasizes the "relentless insistence of wresting meaning from every word and every letter of the text" and another that advances "seemingly endless dialectics involving the setting up of false interpretations only to disprove them at the end."[153] The first corresponds to a meticulous concern for the "contribution to meaning on the part of every word" and the second with a "string of logical arguments to the text in order to surface its larger meaning."[154] Thus, Boyarin concludes, pilpul can be called "a logic of commentary." It is, for him, an exegetical method.

Boyarin traces the history of pilpul to the work of Rabbi Yitzchak Canpanton (d. 1463), a Spanish rabbi whose book *Darkhe HaTalmud* ("The Ways of the Talmud") advanced a streamlined style of textual study called *iyun* ("the direct approach").[155] Boyarin explained that Canpanton's approach was an effort to reconcile the written language of the text with the mental language of meaning. Interpretation, therefore, played a crucial mediating role. But how much interpretation? For Canpanton, the answer was minimal: no more than was absolutely necessary to bridge the gap between text and meaning, provided it was supported from within Jewish sacred writings. Canpanton and his followers treated the entire corpus of rabbinic writings as a single entity in which each text, and thus each word, acquired the same status.

As pilpul migrated across Europe and proliferated as a practice, students and teachers began relishing the flights of logic and wordplay that came to characterize the practice. Interpreters could read any term or text against or alongside any another. Students and teachers relished the interpretive possibilities that the approach allowed, and their efforts drew them further away from questions of practice, application, and legal rabbinic rulings and toward an appreciation of the hidden web of connections that they found beneath the surface of the texts. Prefiguring the insights of philosopher Jacques Derrida, there was nothing outside of the text, but the text provided a vast and varied playground of meaning and connection.[156]

But as scholarly logic and argumentative flair gained more attention, pilpul began acquiring something of a bad reputation as the provenance of highly literate elites who had lost touch with the needs of people who sought guidance from the Mishna about how to live their lives. At its best, it revealed new connections and insights. At its worst, it had become a kind of highly literate entertainment, relishing high-flying intertextual connection but otherwise utterly removed from anything resembling the real lives of people outside the practice of pilpul. Among its most prominent critics were Judah Loew of Prague, known as the Maharal (1525–1609), who wrote passionate critiques of pilpul for being full of vanity and "dishonesty."[137] By pandering to pilpul and the intellectually frivolous and increasingly intricate rhetorical efforts it required, Loew feared that people would miss the meaning of the Oral Torah, which he believed contained the knowledge necessary for Israel to fulfill its divinely appointed mission.[158] Another prominent critic was Rabbi Elijah of Vilna (1720–1797), known as the Vilna Gaon ("the Genius of Vilna"). For the Vilna Gaon, the creative but sometimes tenuous logical contradictions that characterized typical pilpulist inquiry unnecessarily distracted people from the straightforward meaning of the text.[159]

Trying to frame these debates, historian Elchanan Reiner traced them to the disagreement between the functionalist trends of the Ashkenazi Yeshiva during the Middle Ages and the interpretive character of pilpul as unrelated and perhaps opposed to the usage of canonical texts in the service of rabbinic jurisprudence.[160] The distinction between functionalist and interpretivist approaches bore not only the study of Jewish sources but also their circulation beyond the yeshiva and the beit midrash. For Reiner, the question of pilpul amounted to a disagreement about the purpose of study: Was it supposed to serve practical ends, or was it a matter of interpretive inquiry for the sake of the scholars and their texts? Pilpul emerged at the center of the debate because it offered an identifiable set of interpretive practices that appeared to elicit strong opinions about the purpose of study.

But pilpul was, at its core, an approach to study. It was a method, and the disputes that Reiner identified or that the Maharal of Prague or the Gaon of Vilna participated in were, at their core, animated by a concern about *how* one studied Torah. Method mattered. Studying text the "wrong" way would lead to the wrong lessons being learned. Thus, concerns about methods are never only about the tools of scholarship or study, but they are also about what kinds of meaning people wrest from text, and for what purpose. Pilpul and its controversies cracked open the relationship between how one studied, what one studied, for what purpose, and what that relationship meant in ways that predicted the paradox of Jewish education. They also shed light on the Neusnerian Fallacy, which draws such strength from the fantasy of pure scholarship.

3   Modes of Transmission

CATALYSTS AND TECHNOLOGIES

This chapter continues the out-of-order alphabetical primer in the production and transmission of Jewish knowledge that began in chapter 2. The previous chapter examined the logics of production, exploring the values, qualities, and frameworks that inform how Jews and their communities have thought about making knowledge. This chapter focuses on transmission—how people structured what they knew in order to share it with others. It is organized into two sections. The first focuses on catalysts or devices used to advance knowledge and its transmission. The second section targets technologies or specific cultural forms that have been employed in the service of Jewish knowledge work.

A note about the organization of this chapter bears repeating here: Production and transmission are intimates. They are symbiotically related to each other, and their separation across these two chapters or in the chapters' subsections should be taken with this caveat in mind.

Catalysts

Hey—Haskalah

Haskalah refers to the Jewish Enlightenment, the historical period in which Jews began participating more actively in the broader flows of scientific and humanistic discovery that played a central role in the global transition out of the Middle Ages. Like its English counterpart, the Hebrew or Yiddish term (differentiated by accent or inflection, but spelled the same) implies a concern for wisdom or understanding; in Modern Hebrew to have *sechel* (same linguistic root) is to have common sense. Intertwined as the Enlightenment is with the weakening of religious authority, the emergence of humanistic and scientific thought, political emancipation, the rise of nation states in Europe, and the establishment of modern research universities, it also brought with it a redoubled emphasis on the power and significance of ideas as the drivers of history. Though the Enlightenment has become its own proper noun, it referred to a process by which people became *enlightened* (or at least claimed to be), and that almost always signaled a change in both what they knew and how they related to the knowledge they now possessed.

Though the Haskalah is sometimes understood as a radical break with prior practices and beliefs, recent scholarship has surfaced a more dynamic relationship between the Haskalah and what came before. Historian Olga Lit-vak advanced a reading of the Haskalah that locates it more closely in line with European romanticism, a framing that highlights the ways in which its adher-ents were less scrupulously scientific in their pursuit of knowledge than they were passionately trying to capture the spirit of Judaism and Jewishness and reconfigure it for modernity.[1] Litvak's interpretation emphasizes spirit over sci-ence, casting the Enlightenment as more enchanted than its champions wished to admit.[2] Historian Jacob Katz argued that the Haskalah was not a sequential break from what came before it, but a moment whose concepts helped shape ideas about both what was happening then and what preceded it. Katz argued that the word "tradition," which suggests a kind of timelessness and even irra-tionality, gained traction and significance under the conditions of the Haskalah. "Future generations—and sometimes the one immediately to come—became bearers of this hope for the renewal of society. It was vital to involve the next generation in the effort to reform the future—paradoxically, through main-taining the tradition."[3] Together, Katz and Litvak remind us that the Haskalah both drew on emerging changes in knowledge production and helped generate new ways of thinking about knowledge and its role in the service of sustaining Jewish life.

Jewish communities differed on how to meet the changes brought on by the Enlightenment, but each attempt can best be understood as *part of* the Haska-lah, not as *responses to* the Haskalah. The Haskalah can thus be understood as a period in which the self-conscious production and transmission of knowledge emerged as a feature of Jewish life, mobilized in the service of maintaining a shared Jewish identity. Historian Dan A. Porat has examined representations of Jewish history in late nineteenth-century European textbooks and found that they reveal orientations to history that reflect this sense of self-awareness, spe-cifically regarding Zionism.[4] With this self-consciousness came a rush of cre-ative responses for how best to produce and transmit knowledge that could serve this end.

One response to the pressures and opportunities of the Enlightenment was the creation of schools that sought to balance general studies with Jewish Stud-ies under the auspices of the Jewish community. We can call this the "synthetic" approach. Historian Marcin Wodziński noted that education became a central feature of *maskilic* (the adjectival form of Haskalah) thinking in Poland where "supporters of the Haskalah recognized the fact that education, interpreted as the entire educational process, was basic tool for change."[5] Education, wagered champions of the Haskalah, could serve the needs of the Jewish community by carving out a route by which Jews could learn their way into the broader soci-ety while also retaining elements of their distinctive culture.

In one of the most famous and controversial examples of the synthetic approach, Moses Mendelssohn (1729–1786) translated the Bible into German, a feat that he believed could address two pressing concerns at once. First, he thought it would make the text more accessible to German Jews and thus give them access to Jewish knowledge. Second, he believed it would represent an example of the value of Jewish culture to a German non-Jewish audience as well. A foundational event of the Haskalah, Mendelssohn's translation presages some of Neusner's concerns in the twentieth century. Yet Mendelssohn was explicit about his intention to provide a benefit to Germany's Jews "by giving into their hands a better translation and explanation of the holy scriptures than they had before. This is the first step toward culture, from which, alas, my nation is kept at such a distance that one might almost despair of the possibility of an improvement."[6] As historian Jonathan Sheehan observed, "Mendelssohn sought, at one and the same time, to train the Jews in German culture, to produce a German-Jewish literary monument, and to persuade Germans that the wisdom of the ancient Hebrews lived on in meaningful poetry and philosophical terms."[7] Following Sheehan, we can understand Mendelssohn's effort as essentially educational, insofar as his efforts to produce knowledge were also attempts to transmit it, and his approach drew together a high level of scholarship with a concern for benefitting his Jewish community.

His student, Naphtali Herz Wessely (1725–1805), turned Mendelssohn's impulses toward refashioning the formal education of European Jews.[8] Wessely's vision of Jewish education held that "secular knowledge should precede the teaching of the higher laws of God," since a greater understanding of the world at large, including science, would provide the basis for more serious study of Torah.[9] Wessely is a pivotal figure in this story for two reasons. First, his book, *Words of Peace and Truth*, was among the first in Jewish thought to lay out a systematic approach to the schooling of Jewish youth that drew on secular studies. Hayim Nahman Bialik called it the "educational manifesto of the Haskalah."[10] Wessely formulated his vision for schooling in response to a decree by Joseph II, emperor of Austria, that advocated for the establishment of schools for Jews that taught in German. He recognized in the decree an opportunity to reformulate the production and transmission of knowledge for the Enlightenment. The second reason he figures in this account is that he was one of the first to use the term *chinuch* to refer to a systematic approach to teaching children. Though he used the term in the subtitle of his book, he employed it sparingly throughout the document, indicating that it had resonance but that it was not yet widely embraced, even by *maskilim*.

While Wessely embraced the Enlightenment, other Jewish leaders built institutions designed to resist it. One such response is epitomized by the Yeshiva in Volozhin, established by Rabbi Hayim ben Yitshok (1749–1821). Rabbi Hayim feared the study of Torah was in decline, that the Enlightenment was threatening Jewish life, and that the only way to sustain Jewish life was to encourage study free from the pressures of daily life and the limitations of communal politics: "The Torah is being forgotten . . . and is vanishing and disappearing . . . because they have ceased to maintain yeshivas . . . all those who seek God and seek His Torah . . . have been scattered."[11] He responded by establishing a center for study that was committed purely to study. His yeshiva did not train students for positions of communal leadership or for answering practical concerns regarding the application of Jewish law. The yeshiva was essentially "a place for study, rather than a framework for teaching."[12]

A parallel development emerged among the students of Israel ben Eliezer (also known as the Ba'al Shem Tov or "Master of the Good Name"), who died in 1760.[13] His followers, known generically as *hasidim*, distinguished themselves from the high intellectualism emerging from the Lithuanian yeshivot, like the one at Volozhin, and what they saw as the encroachment of the Enlightenment on Jewish culture. The Ba'al Shem Tov believed in making the teachings of Jewish mysticism (the domain of the Kabalah) accessible to nonscholars and everyday Jews. His commitment to transmission resulted in the production of new knowledge about Judaism and new ways of practicing it, in which knowledge could be found primarily not only in texts and their study but also in the cultivation of practices.

Dividing Hasidism from the scholarly approaches of the Lithuanian Yeshivot employs a too-neat division of thinking and study from feeling and experience. It imagines Jewish approaches to learning could be divided into head and heart, elite and populist, feeling and thinking, pure scholarship and embodied practice, and scholarly ideals and communal concerns. It also relies on stereotypes about both communities that paints them too monochromatically. There is ample evidence in the historiographies of both of these phenomena that demonstrates the significance of study and scholarship in Hasidism, as well as an engagement with mysticism in the Lithuanian scholarly tradition, even by Rabbi Hayim himself. While much has been made of the difference in their approaches, they both nevertheless represent different modalities in the production and transmission of knowledge in Jewish communal life that helped shape the contours of the Haskalah. In rejecting the terms of the Enlightenment, they also helped shape it by positing alternative understandings of the place of knowledge and how it could be acquired, transmitted, and possessed in the service of Jewish life.

The third set of responses came largely from Zionist quarters that rejected both the syncretism of the maskilim and efforts to buffer Jews from the Enlightenment. Zionists mobilized the ideologies of European nationalism to advance a conception of Jewish self-determination and eventually, they hoped, the creation of a Jewish state. For much of its existence, Zionism has served as an umbrella term for an internally diverse set of ideologies and politics, characterized more by fierce disagreement than internal coherence. What they shared, however, was a concern for Hebrew as the Jewish national language as a centerpiece for the revitalization of Jewish culture.[14] In the late nineteenth and early twentieth centuries, Hebrew had not yet been embraced as the vernacular of any community, so everyone had to learn to speak it as they would a second (or third) language. In Ottoman and British Mandate Palestine, Zionist education also had to serve the function of enculturating Jews immigrating from different backgrounds into a political and cultural vision for their shared future. Schools, curricula, and the language of instruction became sites of conflict as Zionist leaders negotiated the terms of their autonomy with representatives of the British Mandatory administration.

Each of these three approaches to the Haskalah—the synthetic, the resistant, and the nationalist—highlighted the production and transmission of knowledge in the service of a vision for the future of the Jewish people. They each also took great strength from positioning themselves in stark contrast to previous versions of Jewish schooling, especially the one-room schoolhouse known as the *heder* (literally "room"). To many, the heder represented all that was backward and stunted about Jewish knowledge and about Judaism more generally, and they took particular delight in savaging the quality of its teachers and its antiquated approach to teaching, study, and learning. They decried its poorly trained teachers, informal curricula, and depressing settings. Even worse, they complained about the fact that it did not seem to be teaching them anything worth knowing, anyhow. In his memoir, Solomon Maimon (1753–1800) described his time in heder with particular horror, as a place where "the children are doomed in the bloom of youth to such an infernal school."[15] Maimon, whose autobiography captures the fierce trajectory of someone quite enamored of the Enlightenment, described the dank, dusty room and the tyrannical "Jossel," who lorded over it violently. Though Maimon's own biography might have led him to embellish this aspect of his experience, he is a bit more reliable in his reporting on the curriculum, which he declared was primarily concerned with Hebrew and Bible, ignoring science or math. Modern writings on teaching and schooling treated the heder as a representation of all that was wrong, backward, old-fashioned, or plainly primitive regarding Jewish schooling before the Enlightenment. For many maskilic critics, the heder seemed like a school without education.

Though widely derided, the heder also fueled no small amount of romance, and around the turn of the twentieth century it also came to be seen as a bearer of Jewish cultural authenticity. Of those who sought to revive the heder, historian Steven Zipperstein observed, "I would suggest that it was anxiety that inspired them, an unease, sometimes expressed openly (though generally taken for granted), that Jewish youth were slipping away from things Jewish and that the disappearance of the heder would immeasurably worsen this situation."[16] Schools and schooling came to be seen as both the problem behind and the solution for whatever ailed Jewish life.

The ire directed by Zionists and maskilim toward the heder represented a rejection of previous practices of Jewish knowledge production and transmission in Jewish societies more generally. The heder loomed as something between a bad dream and a metonym for all that was wrong about Jewish communal life before the Enlightenment. It stood figuratively as an example of all that the Haskalah opposed, whether one advocated a synthetic, nationalist, or buffered approach to Jewish knowledge work. Drafted to serve this heuristic purpose, the heder helped to advance the cause of schools and education as sites for strategic communal and ideological reform. Calls to update the schooling options available to Jewish communities began appearing in Eastern Europe in the late eighteenth century and soon resulted in the formation of modern, so-called maskilic schools, like those that Wessely envisioned.

The Sephardic analog to the heder was the *meldar*, which was remembered with similar lack of fondness. Typically, the meldar, which was also known as the Talmud Torah, served as a school for children without means of their own that was underwritten by the community.[17] In his memoir of growing up in Ottoman Salonika, Saadi A-Levi (1820–1903) recalled his "cruel teachers" who taught him prayerbook Hebrew and Torah in Ladino.[18] A-Levi recalled one such teacher with particular terror:

> This teacher, whose name was H. M. S., was one of the most cruel tutors of the Talmud Tora; he was of medium size, heavy, and hairy like Esau. On summer mornings he would come to his office . . . with his naked feet stinking to high heaven. He would roll up his pants to his knees and his sleeves up to his elbows that were covered with hair and looked like a scorpion fish. . . . To those students who took a look at him, he seemed like the Angel of Death. He grabbed a dry beef tendon to use as a whip.[19]

A-Levi welcomed reforms in the mid-nineteenth century that, he hoped, would improve matters and better equip Jewish youth for participation in modern society, ultimately leading to the establishment of an Alliance Israelite Universelle school in 1873.

The poor quality of schooling in the heder and the meldar played a social role, as well. As so much scholarship on education has argued, the aim of organized education has more often been the maintenance of social hierarchies, and not the provision of skills for social mobility. This may have been the case in Jewish communities during the Haskalah, as well. Jacob Katz explained, "The heder was simply a reflection of the system of values upon which all of Jewish society was built. Even if only a minority could actually engage in it, study of the Talmud was a primary value for the entire society. The educational goals for the people as a whole, knowledge of the fundamentals of Judaism and the fulfillment of its precepts, were considered as no more than byproducts of an educational system directed at developing Talmudic scholars."[20]

Shaul Stampfer extended Katz's argument to claim that the "hederization" (his term) of Jewish learning reinforced a social order that both fortified the honor affixed to learnedness and sorted those who could advance through study from those who could not.[21] One outstanding success of this approach to schooling was in its teaching that "all students, successful or not, learned that it is very hard to understand the Talmud and even harder to master all of the rabbinic literature; anyone who did so was deserving of great respect and could not be argued with on his terms."[22] Social mobility, as Stampfer wrote, was accessible only to a few, and though becoming a scholar opened up some doors, the culture as a whole was not meritocratic. At best, Stampfer noted, "A poor but brilliant Talmud student could become the son-in-law of a rich merchant and thus rise instantly to the top of society."[23] The same basic relationship between study and the social order seemed to prevail in rural areas of nineteenth-century Jewish Morocco as well, with the more successful young students graduating from heder to the regional yeshiva.

The role of schooling in maintaining the social order was also apparent in its division of gender. In the main, the heder and its counterpart known as a Talmud Torah served male children, but not exclusively. Girls were mostly expected to grow up to run their households, so their studies—both formal and informal—tended to focus on the practical aspects of cooking and budgets, but also on the Jewish legal know-how that dictated how one ought to do so in line with Jewish law and traditions. There were handbooks for women and girls, often written by men but whose presence suggests a level of literacy among women, at least with regard to ritual and Jewish legal concerns.[24] Even where girls received formal education, they were not expected to progress to advanced levels of study.[25]

Given social norms that dictated gender segregation, "boys' heders" and "girls' heders" were most typical. But some heders taught boys alongside girls. According to historian Avraham Greenbaum, "The girls in these institutions were a minority but not a negligible one, and in the mixed heder the girls almost always attended the lower level and not longer than two years."[26] Sometimes, the girls were brought by their brothers who came with tuition in hand, which basically forced the melamed to accept girls into the heder, whether he wanted them or not.[27] An early mention of a girls heder comes from the memoir of writer Paulina Wengeroff, who prior to 1850 attended one that served the daughters of middle-class and wealthy families.[28] This arrangement was by convention, if not design, intended to reinforce hierarchies between genders and within gendered populations. Stampfer extended his analysis of the class-reproduction purposes of the heder to the gendered access to learning as well. "Lack of a 'school education' was part of a system that functioned to condition women to accept their role in the family and society with a minimum of conflict—just as the fact that most men were unlearned (and knew it!) was one of the ways that led them to accept communal authority."[29]

Girls who attended heder learned to read Hebrew, but given that the boys' curriculum favored prayerbook literacy while girls were neither expected nor permitted to participate in communal prayer, reading Hebrew was usually not emphasized.[30] Memoirs of girls' heders note that they were taught by untrained teachers who instructed mostly by rote and repetition. Women who had attended heder as children called their teachers *shraybers* ("writers") or, as Zionist educator Purah Rakovsky recalled, a *kotev* ("writer").[31] If they were especially learned, teachers would be called *Rabbit* or *Rabbanit* (two female-gendered versions of *rabbi*) or *melamedke* or *rebetsin*. The terms differed by region.[32] If girls read anything in heder, they likely read *tkhines*, a collection of women's prayers written in Yiddish, or the *Tsena Urena*, a Yiddish rendering of the Pentateuch, the five scrolls (Ruth, Esther, Ecclesiastes, Song of Songs, and Lamentations—all found in the "writings" section of the Hebrew Bible), and the *haftaroth* (supplemental readings from the Prophets).[33] The *Tsena Urena*, compiled by Jacob ben Isaac Ashkenazi, was intended to make the classical texts useful, accessible, and lively. Instead of a dry, word-by-word, literal translation, which was often the pedagogy for teachers in heder, the *Tsena Urena* reanimated biblical stories and adapted them in the vernacular to a broader audience that included women.[34] As Ashkenazi explained on the title page, "The advantage of this work is that . . . it is intended for men and women to find rest in their souls in understanding the words of the living God in simple language."[35] The text is less a literal translation than an attempt to engage a variety of sources and to refashion them into sources that anyone could read and from which anyone could learn. Written to widen access to classical sources, the *Tsena Urena* spoke to broad audiences of both men and women, within and beyond the heder. In fact, the sheer popularity of the *Tsena Urena* suggests one indicator of just how widespread women's reading practices were. By one estimate, the work was reprinted some 210 times between 1765 and 1850, evidencing just how widespread women's literacy in Yiddish probably was.[36]

Considering the prevalence of literacy among women during this period, taken together with the analyses of Katz and Litvak, the Haskalah begins to take on a more subtle set of overtones. Despite the tendency to pit the Haskalah against religion and tradition, the conceptualization of those spheres grew out of the same cultural soil and a similar set of concerns about the future of the Jewish people as much as the past. While pre-Enlightenment thinkers certainly advanced visions for Jewish knowledge production that emphasized its role in keeping people committed to Jewish life more generally, the influence of the Enlightenment and its ideas (and ideals) about education caught the imagination and fear of Jewish leaders who recast older ideas about learning into modern forms ready to teach Jews who they were and who they could be in modern Europe and beyond. And, as schooling became a feature of nation states throughout Europe, so, too, it became a feature of Jewish communal life that mobilized education in a variety of forms to help cultivate Jewish knowledge for communal survival in modernity.

Did these efforts emphasize scholarly detachment or communal engagement? The answer is "both." Under the conditions of modernity, the Haskalah fostered ideas about the scientific study of Judaism, and Jewish communities could employ education to advance the ends of political and cultural emancipation. The production and transmission of Jewish knowledge emerged sometimes as a form of resistance to and sometimes as a synthesis of these two currents. But they are not as far apart as they might seem, as Litvak suggests. The scientific impulse to study Judaism and the desire to contribute to it have always been closely intertwined.

Kof—Kemach

"Im eyn kemach, eyn torah. Im eyn torah, eyn kemach."[37] Without flour, there is no Torah; without Torah, there is no flour. In this context, kemach refers to resources. Or money. The phrase's reciprocal nature suggests that study cannot survive without material support but that material support alone cannot sustain the pursuit of knowledge. It is the Talmudic recapitulation of the biblical verse that "humans cannot live by bread alone."[38] Jewish education, in almost any form or fashion throughout history and around the world, has relied on the financial support of supporters and partners, general charity, tzedakah, pushkes, schnorrers, appointed fundraising emissaries, philanthropies, informal systems of mutual aid and support, drives, donor-directed funds, tuition, scholarships, and fundraisers.[39] The relationship between education and charity is so obvious as to be almost a punchline to a joke, with buildings and programs, lectures and book series, endowed chairs, and synagogue libraries bearing the names of partners whose generosity made all of those things possible.[40] Traditions of charitable giving to support students, teachers, and schools extend back centuries from community-supported talmudei Torah to the tradition of providing housing or food for young yeshiva students and the support necessary to keep the shelves of batei midrash full and the candles burning. Even the plans for the biblical Tabernacle began with a commandment that people should make contributions to the effort. Historian Lila Corwin Berman opens her American Jewish Philanthropic Complex by enumerating a number of ways in which she has benefited from philanthropic contributions, before observing, "Almost any person who affiliates with an American Jewish community could make a similar accounting of the benefits they have reaped from Jewish philanthropy."[41] Berman actually understates the matter. The entirety of the collective enterprises of American Jewry, including its various educational and scholarly manifestations, is underwritten by philanthropy.

But philanthropy is only one dimension of the larger concern of *kemach*, whose relationship to education has a long and complicated history. Ben Gamla, who is credited in the Mishna with sanctioning teachers to replace parents as the primary instructors of children, did not stipulate how those teachers should be paid. Pirke Avot forbids teachers of Torah to be paid at all, asserting that "anyone who derives worldly benefit from the words of the Torah, removes his life from the world."[42] This dictate vexed commentators and scholars for generations who sought ways to engage quality teachers without violating these terms. As if Pirke Avot was not stringent enough, centuries later Maimonides reiterated the prohibition on paying teachers and tried to close an available loophole by opposing even the acceptance of charity by teachers, extending the prohibition to instances when it was not directly tied to their work as teachers.[43] Centuries later, Josef Karo tried to nuance Maimonides by arguing that teachers should be paid, but they should strive not to become wealthy. Rabbi Judah Loew (known as the Maharal of Prague) also weighed in, arguing that teachers of Torah should not take money for their work, lest they become indebted to their patrons and let their influence sway their teaching. The possibilities for corruption raised by Rabbi Loew shaped how Jacob Neusner thought about the relationship between kemach and Torah in scholarly research.

Historically, questions of kemach tended to revolve around the issue of who was responsible for it.[44] In Europe during the Middle Ages, families with the means to do so hired private tutors for their children. Tutors were not always paid particularly well, and many supplemented their teaching income by offering boarding to their students. This arrangement did not always benefit the students. Children from less fortunate families either did not attend school or attended heder or a Talmud Torah, a communally funded school for students whose families could not afford tuition or tutors.[45] Historian Ephraim Kanarfogel noted that during the Middle Ages different communities responded to schooling concerns differently and that in the main "Ashkenazic communities were much less active than their Spanish counterparts in providing formal support for education and in fostering the careers of scholars, young and old."[46] Under some circumstances, communities developed informal means for supporting their teachers. Such was the case in Yemen, where parents paid teachers directly and gave their teachers food, which the teachers sold if there was any left over.[47]

Arrangements like these typified the kinds of financial investments in teaching youth until and into modernity. They sparked no small measure of innovation, too, in how best to organize the relationship between kemach and Torah. Tired of relying on his local community for financial support of his yeshiva, Rabbi Hayim of Volozhin developed new approaches to fundraising that expanded his base of financial support and provided independence and financial stability for his school.[48] Similarly, the creation of the *kollel* in the late nineteenth century represented a response to this concern by creating a new institution that, according to Stampfer, "regularly distributes money to a defined group of married men, usually young, who devote all their time to Torah study."[49] Unlike a yeshiva, a kollel was usually not a specific place. Instead, it can be thought of as a financial instrument that raised funds and dispersed them to students who studied wherever and with whomever they wished. Though on paper the kollel model promoted the fact that it trained rabbis, in practice students did not receive instruction in matters that would have prepared them for positions as practicing community functionaries. Thus, according to Stampfer, the kollel could be best understood for being "innovative in its system for financial support, not in the education it offered."[50]

The emergence of new financial arrangements like the kollel model continued into the twentieth century. Jewish Federations established in American cities helped to centralize the collection and distribution of charitable funds including those dedicated to educational programming, though how much they would give and what role they would play in directing educational efforts have long remained active points of debate.[51] Wealthy individual members of communities have also, on their own, supported the construction of schools, provided scholarships, and donated time and expertise. In higher education, they have named chairs in Jewish Studies, maintained archives, libraries, and museums, established fellowships for research, and so on.[52] With the rise of "mega-donors" during the late twentieth century and the increased power of independent foundations, Jewish education has seen investments at levels previously unimagined, most notably in Birthright Israel, which leveraged commitments from a number of large donors to secure a contribution from the State of Israel that helped establish and sustain the program.[53] In fact, it is almost impossible to think of a single instance of the production or transmission of Jewish knowledge for the past one or two hundred years, no matter how large or small, that has not somehow benefited from the attention and investment of supporters who were willing and able to contribute to the cause.

The narrative of charity and philanthropy spelled out here accounts for the first half of the aphorism. But what about its latter half, which insists that without Torah there is no kemach? It is empirically untrue; Torah is not a prerequisite for either wealth or generosity. It is, however, possible to read the second half for its insight into the appeal of education to donors. Perhaps one could read it to say that Torah does not generate wealth on its own but instead functions, in Jewish communities, like a magnet that will attract charitable support in a way that other concerns may not. Without Torah, the aphorism warns, it might be difficult to attract kemach. This relationship fed Neusner's suspicion of Jewish Studies. He worried about the tie between kemach and Torah and about the real possibility that ideologically driven funding sources might undermine the pure pursuit of Torah in the university. Torah, he argued, should not be bait for fundraising, and any concern for fundraising should not direct the activities of scholarship. Still, someone had to pay Neusner's salary and support the private universities where he worked.[54]

Lila Corwin Berman has argued that Jewish philanthropists capitalized on (and sometimes helped to craft) law that infused their investments with a spirit of doing "good by simply existing" and by echoing the "language of Jewish survival and continuity."[55] Meanwhile, those less critical of philanthropic largesse can sometimes appear to be little more than smooth talkers whose ability to whisper the right things in the right ears has managed to convince wealthy donors of the propriety of their programs and their paychecks.

Crudely, the balance of kemach and Torah can be understood as a matter of how much of each is required for the other to exist. The relationship cannot be reduced to a calculation of how much Torah costs, exactly, because cost is not the right measure in a system wholly underwritten by charity. Similarly, it is not an issue of deriving a Torah-per-dollar formula, again because the inputs and outcomes, the incentives, values, costs, and benefits, cannot be easily calculated by applying standard economic models, even if we include those from behavioral economics.[56] Take, for example, low or no-cost efforts to attract Jewish college students. Part of the programmatic model of Hillel International, Birthright Israel, and Chabad's campus efforts is to give their programming away for free, in order to make it as accessible as possible to as many people as possible. There is merit in that approach, but "free" has a price, and the open doors of those institutions mask the substantial investments that make them possible in the first place. This is not to suggest that these institutions are merely doing the bidding of their sponsors, though that is sometimes the case for funders who leverage their commitments to ensure that an organization maintains a particular ideological stance. Rather, it is to observe that the production and transmission of knowledge in Jewish life is the result of sometimes complex and often opaque and hard-to-calculate financial arrangements that ensure its accessibility.

So how, then, do we understand the relationship between kemach and Torah? Is it a question for economists who can measure the whole economic world of the Jewish community and develop a formula? Is it a question for philosophers who can inquire about ethics and values? Is it a question for historians? Sociologists? Anthropologists? For scholars of Jewish Studies? I am not sure how best to consider, as Elizabeth Popp Berman has established in her history of economic thinking in American public policy, what "style of reasoning" ought to be brought to understand the economics of Jewish education.[57] Perhaps there is no single style of reasoning except to say that the relationship between kemach and Torah is both one of the most fundamental and one of the most threatening to the production and transmission of knowledge, so the aphorism might stand as a description as well as a warning.

Tzadee—Tziyon

Biblical and rabbinic texts do not have much to say about *tziyon*, other than its use as a synonym for Jerusalem. The entry for "Zion" in the 1906 Jewish Encyclopedia reads, simply, "see Jerusalem." Two pages later, though, it introduces an entry for the term "Zionism," which it describes as "dominating Jewish history," although Nathan Birnbaum had neologized it less than two decades before the encyclopedia was published. It would be easy enough to echo the observation of the encyclopedia's authors and say, simply, that it has nearly "dominated Jewish education" since then too. Concerns with the education of Jewish youth toward an engagement with Zion and various forms of Zionism has been a prevailing concern of the majority—though certainly not all—youth-oriented Jewish educational undertakings in the twentieth century.[58] Some of the biggest disagreements in Jewish education have revolved around questions like: What should people know about Israel and how should they be taught, and what role should Israel play in the educational efforts of Jewish communities around the word?

Though modern, these questions evoke the ancient term *tziyen*, which gives Zion and Zionism their linguistic root. The term, a verb, means "to mark a place on earth" usually with stones or some other element. Tziyon became the name for *the* place where ancient Israelites organized their ritual practices, providing an Axis Mundi, orienting ancient practices and cosmologies around this particular place on earth.[59] The modern educational questions echo with concerns for how to orient Jewish knowledge work, and how much or how little of Jewish education ought to guide people toward Zion. There is a host of secondary questions that ask how best to do that.

The Prophet Micah identifies Zion as the spring of the collected knowledge of the Jewish people and the word of God, which he imagines as a central gathering point for people from "many nations" to come and learn from it.[60] The wisdom of Zion, the text says, is not exclusively the provenance of Jewish people; anyone can come and learn. Centuries later, the transformation of Zion into Zionism, through circuitous political, metaphysical, metaphoric, and eschatological routes, has become both a focal point and a flashpoint for Jewish life around the world. The awareness of tensions in American Jewish communities around how to talk about Israel has become part of the lexicon of American Jewish communal life, while approaches to teaching about Israel have coalesced into a loose collection of programs and approaches collectively called "Israel education."[61] The suite of approaches seems to reverse the directionality of Micah's formulation by trying to orient Jews who live far from Zion toward Zion, and not the other way around.[62]

The Jewish educational organization Makom is a great example of this approach. Its website describes the organization's founding in the following way: "Makom was established in 2006 as a partnership between the Jewish Agency for Israel and twelve Jewish Community Federations in North America. Together they recognized that traditional Israel education had neither adapted to a complex unfolding Israel, nor to emerging Jewish identities. Young adults in particular were losing touch with Israel and Jewish Peoplehood."[63] A transnational partnership that operates in six countries around the world, the initiative emerged in response to concerns about attenuating relationships between younger Jews and the State of Israel. Makom, which describes itself as "the place for challenging Israel education," invites discussion and challenging questions about the relationship between Jews and Israel, offering "peoplehood" as a mediating term.[64] Makom aims to increase knowledge of and engagement with the State of Israel—its website hosts a lot of discussion guides for groups of all ages, as captured in its signature "hugging and wrestling" approach.[65] Its central pedagogical tool is organized around "four Hatikvah questions" that take their name from the Israeli national anthem. The four questions, modeled on the four questions of the Passover Seder, are designed to provide "clarity and affirmation as to the wonder of the State of Israel, while at the same time offering a shared conceptual space within which to address key questions of Jewish existence that take on Jewish Peoplehood on the one hand, and the centrality of Israel on the other."[66] Makom studiously avoids language that might give the impression that it is trying to be coercive with its approach, offering questions instead of a slate of answers as the "way to connect between our differences." Nevertheless, as the language of the four Hatikvah questions implies, the aim is to affirm the State of Israel as the center of Jewish life globally. The iCenter, another organization dedicated to Israel education, explained its mission in similar terms: it "continually moves Israel education to the heart of Jewish life."[67]

An orientation toward Zion has defined Israel education, especially as a corrective to fears that Jewish education was not sufficiently successful in cultivating a strong affective connection to Israel on the part of American Jews.[68] Philosopher Barry Chazan, one of the architects of Israel education, explained its mission in terms of "educating people to think, feel, and integrate Israel into their overall character as Jews and as human beings."[69] Chazan was instrumental in the establishment of Birthright Israel, which explains its own educational philosophy in precisely those terms: "Helping today's Jewish young adults in the Diaspora feel strongly connected to their Jewish heritage starts with helping them experience the land of Israel—its people, culture, religion, history, and more."[70]

Placing Israel at the center of Jewish life or as the impetus for Jewish living is both an extension of and a departure from earlier generations of Zionist education. Those earlier generations, including efforts based in the diaspora, largely tried to prepare American Jews for future immigration to Israel and promoted the power of Hebrew and the creation of a national home as the strongest pathways to a vibrant future for Jews and Jewish culture.[71] In this respect, the historical continuities are clear. But as sociologist Shaul Kelner found in his study of Birthright Israel participants, the program's most powerful educational outcome was its development of a population of Jews who identify with and support the State of Israel *from the diaspora*.[72] The program measured its impact, in part, not in the number of American Jews who eventually moved to Israel, but in the growing strength of American Jews' commitments to and sense of connection with Israel.[73] Israel education can be understood as both promoting a strong diasporic Jewish identity and reinforcing the centrality of Israel in Jewish life. In this way, it draws on the orienting power of tziyon's etymological roots.

Programs like Birthright Israel and organizations like Makom draw no small measure of criticism based on concerns that they are too prescriptive and not critical enough in their educational approaches to teaching American Jews about Israel. Worse, they have been called emotionally manipulative and even accused of engaging in indoctrination more than education (as if that distinction is sharp enough to be meaningful). Birthright Israel has even been the subject of at least one popular cultural parody on the show *Broad City* and at one point earned the moniker "Birthrate Israel," for its emphasis on hetero-hookup culture and its promotion of Jewish endogamy.[74] These jabs at the politics of Israel education highlight the tensions inherent in the enterprise that situate it squarely within the paradox of Jewish education, wherein the educators' desired outcomes can undermine any other overtures toward a more Enlightenment-informed understanding of education's many possible outcomes.[75]

A different set of concerns and tensions characterizes Israel's place among scholars of Jewish Studies, where teaching about Israel is probably the most hotly contested and terrifyingly political of topics. For a field of study so comfortable with heresies of all kinds, Jewish Studies remains fraught with regard to how to teach or talk about Israel and its politics. Pressure from the political right has led to scholars being sanctioned for taking political stands outside of the classroom and the formation of watchdog groups who police the activities of Jewish Studies scholars who have expressed criticism of Israel. On the political left, some Jewish Studies scholars have found themselves under pressure to be more vocally critical of Israel, lest people assume that they support the country's governments, policies, and actions. Professors, students, and researchers have been tarred for being either too complicit in Israeli politics or not supportive enough of them. The most aggressive of these come in the form of threats or, in more pronounced cases, when unhappy donors ask for their money back.[76] Debates around Israel in Jewish Studies should put the

Neusnerian Fallacy to rest, as throughout the field people are struggling to properly understand and act on their personal, political, and scholarly commitments.

In earlier generations, during the middle of the twentieth century, support of and engagement with Israel had been the consensus position among American Jewry. There were always anti-Zionist groups, but Israel's ability to galvanize the majority of American Jewish life has now inverted. There is no more fractious issue, and no other concern in either Jewish Studies or Jewish education that generates poignant debates, divisions, and disagreements. This trend shows little sign of reversing.[77] The divisions that have surfaced are amplified in educational contexts, informing concerns about research agendas, syllabuses, which programs receive funding, the establishment of new research or educational centers, and what might constitute a desirable educational outcome. Questions about Israel's place in educational matters and how strongly they ought to orient themselves toward Israel illustrate just how tightly scholarship and education are tied to broader issues in the world, and the ferocity of political perspective illustrates just how difficult—if not impossible—it is to keep them separated. Recalling its initial definition, tziyon might no longer mark a particular place on earth, but it has come to signify an axis around which many of the most challenging educational and political debates continue to take shape.

Shin—Shayla

Shayla means question, and questions hold a special status in Jewish learning as well. Stories about questions abound in fiction and memoir, and there is some joke about Jews answering questions with questions. Sherira Gaon composed his response to the Kairouan community because they asked him a question about the provenance of the Mishna as part of a format of exchange between people and rabbis in which authoritative rabbinic responses are called *teshuvot*, or "answers." Shaul Stampfer dedicated an entire essay to examining the status of questions in Eastern European approaches to Jewish learning, observing that in yeshivot the practice of asking had been elevated to "an art form—a form of mock battle."[78] Anthropologist Jonathan Boyarin raised the stakes further by appointing questioning as one of the fundamental characteristics of Jewish study. "Interrogation of the authoritative text is the essential pattern of Jewish study. It is traditional constantly to dispute and recreate what Judaism is." Still, questioning was not a given, leading Boyarin to warn that "the loss of that capacity reflects in turn a weakening of Jewish tradition."[79] Inasmuch as any tradition is reliant on the people who breathe life into it, Boyarin's comment implies that the power of questioning lies both with the questions themselves and with people who know how to pose them. Jewish life might thrive on questions, but it needs people who know how to ask them.

The question-answer structure also serves as the classical vision of teaching and learning. How was the world created? Why do people die? Where do rainbows come from? How did language develop? What is Judaism? Where is the closest grocery store? How do I get there? The whole of the book of Genesis can be read as a series of stories that, once upon a time, acted as answers to implicit questions about why the world is as it is and where the people who call themselves Jews came from. Socrates was famous for his questions, which gave us, among other things, a pedagogy based on inquiry. Science upped the ante on questioning and the terms on which answers could be considered reliable. Still, the technology of the question has retained its basic power and utility. Questions remain among the best tools for exposing knowledge, inviting conversation, revealing something that one does not know. Both researchers and teachers prize good questions. The Nobel Prize–winning physicist Isidor Rabi credited his mother with making him a scientist by encouraging him to ask questions. "Every other Jewish mother in Brooklyn would ask her child after school: So? Did you learn anything today? But not my mother. 'Izzy,' she would say, 'did you ask a good question today?' That difference—asking good questions—made me become a scientist."[80]

Though ubiquitous, questions are cultural constructs, and they are built on three kinds of knowledge already held by the person doing the asking. First, they know enough about a subject to ask a question that can be answered. Second, they know that they do not know what they wish to know. Third, they know that questions are a good way to find things out. So, the questioner asks their questions to someone else who either knows more than they do or can help them figure out the answer. If I want to know where rainbows come from, the person I'm asking should probably know what rainbows are, if not the physics behind them. Similarly, if I ask directions to the nearest grocery store, it might help if the person I'm asking is familiar with the neighborhood. For a question to be meaningful, it has to emerge from a context in which a good deal, but not everything, is known already. Questions are statements of partial knowledge and invitations to collaborate. They serve as the basis for scholarly research, for conversations with children, for examinations, and for legal proceedings. Questions can also be rhetorical, Socratic, pointed, probing, leading, rude, or practical. A question will set the stage for a reply, occupying the space between what is known and what is not yet known. When used well, they are a powerful technology for the production and transmission of knowledge.

Questions hold a special place in the Passover Seder, the festive meal celebrating the biblical exodus from Egyptian slavery. On the first and second nights of the holiday, people who celebrate use the Haggadah (plural: *haggadot*), an anthology of rabbinic sources that address the Israelite exodus from Egypt, as a kind of script for the evening's ritual meal. The heart of the Seder—the retelling of the exodus story—opens with a question, conventionally posed by the youngest person at the table: Why is this night different from all others? A prominent passage from the Haggadah describes four children, each of whom poses a question to their proverbial parent and embodies a distinct human quality; the first three children, from oldest to youngest, are called wise, wicked, and simple. The youngest child is described as "she eyno yodel lishol," which means "who does not know how to ask." The text of the Haggadah tells parents how to respond to each of the inquiries by employing a specific verse from the Torah chosen for its suitability to the child's character. For the youngest child, parents are told to "open the discussion" for the child and, referring to a verse from Exodus, are instructed to explain, "It is because of what God did for me when I went free from Egypt."[81]

The "it" refers specifically to the Passover sacrifice, but it might refer to the entire apparatus of the Passover Seder itself. The structure of the Seder is such that one does not have to be particularly literate or learned to find a way into the event: participants eat specific foods, observe symbols, sign and listen to songs, read texts, recline their bodies, drink wine, and so on. Passover Seders are also multisensory affairs, layering different ways of entering the ritual atop one another. The structure embeds the answers to questions within a constellation of symbols, sounds, and textual sources to provide the maximum possible entry points into the celebration and recitation of the story. Even the Haggadah, which can be overwhelming in its totality, can be approached as an anthology of sources from which people can pick and choose elements to include. For those unfamiliar with the ritual of the Seder and the practices of the holiday, there are lots of questions worth asking, even for those who do not yet know how to ask.

As a set of embodied practices, the Seder and the holiday can be understood as examples of Jewish practice that emerged at the intersection of procedural and propositional knowledge and from the interplay between scholarly study and lived practice. Because of the richness and diversity of practices associated with it, the Passover Seder offers a vibrant site for understanding Jewish life as folklore, as fine art, as an instance of the evolution of rabbinic law, as food, as family, as theology, as liturgy. But the ritual also serves an educational role. It works like an elaborate, multisensory, immersive framework that can engage participants in discovering the meaning of the Exodus and their relationship to ancient narratives about freedom and slavery, about revelation, or about the pressures and pleasures of family. Passover and its Seder, like schools, books, and other material objects, serve as an engine for knowledge production and transmission, a cultural form that makes it possible to think about such things, to engage people in narratives about Jewish life through the performance of the ritual. The knowledge of the experience of liberation is difficult to retain and a challenge to transmit on its own. So the very structure of the holiday becomes an occasion for asking questions and answering them, whether or not people can formulate them yet.

Technologies

Aleph—Alliance Israelite Universelle

Although neither its French name nor its Hebrew version begins with the letter "aleph," the Alliance Israelite Universelle (AIU) begins with the first letter of the French alphabet, so consider the switch from Aleph to "A" something of an indication of the complexities of writing about the multilingual, transnational, diasporic, multiethnic communities that compose global phenomena like Jewish education or Jewish Studies. Created by a group of French Jews in 1860, the AIU committed itself to "work everywhere for the emancipation and moral progress of the Jews, give effectual support to those who are suffering persecution because they are Jews, [and] encourage all publications calculated to promote these ends."[82] Its founders envisioned that it could be a "center of moral progress, of religious solidarity and of protection for all those who suffer for being Jewish."[83] The AIU was initiated in response to newly visible threats to Jewish communities around the Mediterranean, most notably the 1840 Damascus Blood Libel and the 1859 kidnapping and conversion of an Italian child, Edgardo Mortara.[84] In line with its tripartite program, the AIU developed political and philanthropic programs alongside a publication promoting its activities and ideas, but perhaps the AIU's biggest effort and most long-lasting impact has been its belief that the organization could achieve its goals through educational means.[85]

The AIU's vision was wholly in line with the ideals of French Enlightenment ideals about the power of schools and schooling, and the group committed to establishing schools for Jews (and sometimes non-Jews) that could serve as the vehicles for a complex set of goals including training for citizenship, integration into the broader society, and the modernization and uplift of the "primitive" Jews of the French colonies.[86] The term they used was "regeneration." A historian of the AIU, Aron Rodrigue, wrote, "The obtaining by the Jews of legal equality and their 'regeneration,' integrating them into Western civilization, had emerged as its cornerstones. This was motivated by defensive reasons over the embarrassment caused by 'backward' Jews to the acculturated elite, as well as by a strong sense of solidarity with fellow Jews in political and social distress."[87] "The symmetry between emancipation and 'regeneration,'" he continued, "summarizes the essence of the ideology that guided the work of the Alliance."[88] The logic cut both ways. The AIU advocated for an approach to education that was steeped in the French colonial perspective, yet the organization also acted upon a legitimate and sincere desire to assist Jewish communities that appeared less stable and often under threat. The group's efforts often smacked of paternalism in the ways that projects so deeply tied to Enlightenment ideals can be.

Nevertheless, the AIU worked quickly and established its first school in Tetouan, Morocco, followed two years later by schools in Tangiers (1864), Edirne

(1867), and Baghdad (1868) as well as two schools in Paris (1867), one for men and one for women, that trained teachers for work in AIU schools.[89] The Paris school, the Ecole Normale Israélite Orientale, reflected Enlightenment ideals, right down to the notion that teachers ought to be trained. The AIU recruited the brightest students from its schools and offered them a curriculum steeped in Enlightenment ideals and modern notions of pedagogy. As historian Michael Laskier noted, these teachers "aimed at educating rather than instructing which meant that burdening the youth with an overabundance of facts for the sake of memorization, a method popular in the rabbinical schools, was ruled out. Instead, these teachers sought to promote intellectual stimulation and analytical interpretation, facts being essential for the comprehension of their own significance."[90] By contrasting "rabbinical schools" (by which Laskier meant schools led by rabbis, not schools for rabbis) with AIU schools, Laskier emphasized the shift proposed by the AIU in both content and approach. It was not enough to change the facts students memorized; the AIU also tried to develop in their students modern dispositions toward independent thought and critical analysis. They also worked to update the teaching of Jewish sub-jects and often emphasized elements of Jewish knowledge that they felt might better amplify similarities rather than divisions both among Jews and between Jews and non-Jews. Part of this also meant training students to be productive members of society, and many AIU schools provided training in vocational skills, from carpentry to agriculture to bookkeeping. By 1913, the AIU had established 183 schools, supporting 43,700 children, boys and girls, Jewish and non-Jewish.[91]

The relationship between the AIU, which emphasized instruction in French as a feature of its overall educational vision, and the communities in which they established schools was not always easy. Most of the communities in which the AIU established schools already had schools, although, as Rodrigue noted about the Jewish community of Thrace, "very little is known about the traditional mode of education, except for the fact that as elsewhere in the Otto-man Empire it consisted of the learning of Hebrew prayers and the reading and writing of Judeo-Spanish, the mother tongue of all the Jews of Demotica."[92] Local religious leaders who often led those schools resisted the AIU's desire to reform them. In Morocco, for example, rabbis often felt that the AIU was "de-judaizing" the youth, presenting, as Rodrigue described it, a "highly abstract and rather aseptic" approach to Judaism that was "far removed from the popular religiosity that has been all important" to preexisting schools.[93] Elsewhere, like Egypt and Tunisia, local leaders were more welcoming of the AIU's promises of modernization. Struggles over schooling were also struggles over authority, but more to the point they were struggles over what adults believed children should know if they were to become adult Jewish members of their various societies. AIU teachers wrote regularly and with some disdain about the quality of instruction in the schools led by local rabbis, and they saw their mission very much as one geared toward either reforming or replacing those schools. One AIU teacher wrote that education in the rabbinically led schools meant poring over "interminable and incomprehensible texts," and posed "field trips, physical education and vocational pursuits" as a proper alternative.[94] Their critiques often combined a sense that both the schools' content and their approaches were outdated and were reinforcing students' marginal position and low social status. At issue was not only what students were learning but how and, more to the point, how approaches to the production and transmission of Jewish knowledge contributed to individuals' ability to contribute to society and their sense of self and self-worth. The AIU thought it had the solution.

Institutionally, then, the AIU can be understood alongside other advances in mass education that featured in many nineteenth-century European national and colonial movements. Recall Herder's comment about education as a tool of colonialism and France's relationship with Morocco and Tunisia. Even if the AIU did not quote Herder, it ascribed generally to the ideals of Bildung that he helped shape, responding to the call that Jews learn to be citizens of their host nations. "In the ideal world of the Alliance, the virtues enshrined in Judaism were the same that characterized the model modern citizen."[95] This same ideal echoed in the writings of Rebecca Gratz, the pioneering American founder of the first American Jewish supplementary school in 1838, who feared that "the want of education shuts the door of advancement into private or public nations."[96] This approach echoed throughout much later writings regarding the power of Jewish day schools to provide a Jewish antidote to what their champion Alvin Schiff called "Democracy's dual effect on Jewish living."[97] In all of those cases, too, Jewish schools promised a solution to social and political problems.

In this way, the AIU provides a lens onto the paradox of Jewish education. By trying to apply modern ideals and practices of mass schooling to Jewish communal concerns, it bought into some of the more paternalistic qualities of Enlightenment thinking and reproduced aspects of the colonial mentalities of European states. It positioned itself as both the savior and the chief antagonist of established, religiously run schools and approaches to both what and how Jewish subjects were taught. The AIU embodied commitments to both the broadest ideals of the Enlightenment and ethnically grounded concerns for Jewish people and their communities. And it positioned education as the programmatic response to these issues, placing it and all of its contradictions at the heart of a transnational vision of modern Jewry.

Bet—Beit Midrash

Bet is the second letter of the alphabet and the first letter of the Pentateuch. It is also the first letter of the word bayit, or "house," a word used to convey places both real and conceptual. Both Temples in ancient Jerusalem (the first was destroyed in 586 BCE, the second was built some decades later on the same spot and later renovated by King Herod, before being destroyed again in 70 CE) were known as the *beit hamikdash*, or "house of holiness." In Hebrew and Yiddish, they are referred to as the First House and the Second House, no further modifiers or descriptors necessary. Bayit is also used in a variety of other settings, most typically in its plain meaning of house, as a place where people live. The generic modern Hebrew term for school is *beit sefer*, meaning "house of books," and the term is also used more generally to refer to schools of thought, as well. *Beit knesset* is a common term for synagogue, which translates more directly as "house of gathering" rather than "house of prayer" and suggesting a traditionally Jewish understanding of synagogues as serving a number of communal functions.

The general term for a place of study is *beit midrash*, and it usually refers to a study hall in which people learn together, though, often enough, synagogues functioned as places of study in addition to places of worship.[98] Anthropologist of Moroccan Jewry Shlomo Deshen noted that "specialized study groups were, however sometimes located in synagogues. In eighteenth-century Fez we hear of a *hevrat hesger*, literally 'association of the enclosed' (more probably, 'the sedentary'). This was a group of men who devoted time to Torah studies and obtained material support from others."[99] But, generally, *beit midrash* is the generic term for a space set aside for study, though it can refer both to a particular room within a larger building or to a stand-alone institution that is dedicated to learning. It is a classroom, but it usually has neither the structure nor the comportment of a typical Western classroom, with neat rows of desks and a teacher and chalkboard at the front, focusing everyone's attention. In his ethnography of a New York yeshiva, Jonathan Boyarin called it "the big room," and it provided the setting for much of the action he described. "Those who animate the room," he wrote, "sit at several rows of metal tables, laid out along the axis between East Broadway and the interior courtyard, with seats facing in both directions to facilitate face-to-face study in pairs or slightly larger groups."[100] As Boyarin described, the main activity of the beit midrash—or as Boyarin calls it, using a transliteration of the Yiddish pronunciation, the *beis medresh*—is largely study, but not the quiet study of a library or a high school study hall. Not at all.

Typically, a beit midrash is an exceptionally loud and chaotic place. Learning in the beit midrash tends to be directed by the students. People get up and walk around as they need, grab books from shelves when required, and sometimes have their studies intruded on by others in the room. There is little formal, frontal instruction, few chalkboards, and no apparent curriculum guiding all of the students' learning. When full, it looks about as far from your typical chairs-in-rows, teacher-at-the-front, curricular-oriented classroom as possible. Rather, pairs or small groups of learners pore over piles of books on their own, while teachers circulate around the room, offering pointers or direction or insight. Philosopher Israel Scheffler recalled his early years in a beit midrash in precisely these terms: "'Study' did not imply silence; one had to articulate the issues aloud, respond to questions and answer the arguments of one's fellows, all within earshot of other small groups engaged in the same activity. The idea of a silent study hall in which each student simply peered at the page and cogitated soundlessly would have seemed to us in that context simply absurd."[101] In a beit midrash, learners are usually self-paced and often self-directed, though that depends on the orientation of the institution within which they are studying. Anthropologist Shlomo Guzmen-Carmeli has explored this nexus in depth, arguing that *batei midrash* (the Hebrew plural) provide places for encounters between people and their Judaisms that are mediated by text.[102]

The beit midrash is also an intensely social place. Because beit midrash study is not organized around discreet class periods, people come and go and discussions often veer into and out of the subject immediately at hand. Historically, too, the bit midrash provided a homosocial space for men to congregate outside of their homes under religious auspices but not necessarily involved directly in prayer or practice. As opposed to other places for gathering, like taverns, the beit midrash offered a socially sanctioned arena where men could gather to study, but also to socialize, catch up on gossip, or just avoid their families.

The informality and sociability of beit midrash–style learning is part of its charm and part of its appeal; it emphasizes the connections between the study of Jewish sacred texts and the social life of a larger community. Study is the ostensible pretext, and it may occupy a great deal of participants' energy, but it is intertwined with the relationships formed in, around, and through the act of studying. The theory of learning in the beit midrash, therefore, is about not only extracting knowledge from books but also building knowledge in relationship around those books.[103] It models a kind of intimacy between knowledge and people that can be readily romanticized but nevertheless captures a version of ideal learning that is about knowledge not only in the abstract but in the cultural, the concrete, the interpersonal realms as well.

A beit midrash, therefore, is better understood as Jewish educational technology. It makes possible certain ways of knowing that are distinct from those enforced by the neat organization of subjects according to discipline that characterizes much of Western public schooling and scholarship.[104] If modern, scientific structures of knowledge management rely on taxonomies and the orderly presentation of information *about* certain topics, the approach characterized by beit midrash learning is anything but.[105] What one learns and how one learns it—and how one learns to learn it—are brought together in the relationship between the text, the relationships, and the larger context that makes it possible.

The term *beit midrash* dates back to the rabbinic era, around the destruction of the Second Temple, and throughout the centuries that followed the term was used to refer to any space dedicated to study.[106] Historian Gershon Hundert pointedly noted that batei midrash typically "had two indispensable elements: males and books for them to study."[107] Historian Simha Assaf found that these institutions were usually supported by charity and open to the male public twenty-four hours per day.[108] Some contained thousands of volumes for study but largely lacked a set curriculum or instructional method, which meant that they functioned more like a public library than a school, only louder. They were also found in almost every community in Eastern Europe and provided study opportunities for young men, though rarely on a full-time basis.[109] As Stampfer has argued, this was not always the case: some batei midrash were open only to those adult males who demonstrated the capacity for rigorous learning and had effectively proven themselves capable of independent study.[110] In modern times, the beit midrash has become nearly synonymous with the practice of learning characteristic of the yeshiva (plural: *yeshivot*), the term for academies for the advanced study of Jewish sacred texts including scripture but more typically focused on the Talmud and its commentaries.

The beit midrash was also a feature of Jewish communities around the world. Salonika boasted one of the longest-running and most influential houses of study in the Jewish world.[111] Established in 1520, the Talmud Tora Agadol (English: Great Talmud Torah) persisted through a handful of fires, until the end of World War I. Historically, the Talmud Tora served as a combination beit midrash and communal organization, housing a publishing house, rabbinical courts, and schools for children as well as serving as a centralized collection and distribution point for charity.[112] In this capacity, its role and stature extended well beyond the city of Salonika. By the nineteenth century, its stature as an academy of higher learning had diminished, though it continued to serve as a school for the youth of Salonika.

The beit midrash served not just as a site for study but as an implicit method too. As a result, it is easy to grow romantic about beit midrash–style learning (see the depiction in Barbara Streisand's film *Yentl*, which juxtaposes the love of learning with the romantic love between the title character and Anshel, played by Mandy Patinkin). Scholars and teachers are not immune to this tendency either. Ethnographer Sam Heilman rhapsodized over communal adult text study, calling it a "devotional" practice.[113] Therefore, it is worth recalling that the chaos and cacophony of beit midrash does not serve all learners equally, and that its male homosociality has long excluded women, though there are now many batei midrash for all genders and gender-queer people as well.[114] Additionally, a handful of "secular batei midrash" have opened in Israel, dedicated to the study of classical Jewish texts in a secular setting.[115] These efforts seek to undo some of the masculinist power of the historical approach and redeploy it in the service of expanded access. Yet the retention and adaptation of the model speak to its continued resonance and its unique position as a Jewish educational technology informed by a fundamental proposition about the social nature of knowledge, and its relationship to study as something more than just the mastery of content.

Dalet—Drasha

Drasha is a term that can be modified to refer to a kind of school, a pedagogy, a body of literature, or a key to mystical understanding. Its ability to signify in these four contexts speaks to the complex ways in which the production and transmission of Jewish knowledge have been understood as the result of inquiry, exegesis, explication, investigation, and teaching. It is helpful for understanding the state of the question because it offers a linguistic route through a variety of examples of relationships to knowledge in historical Jewish contexts. What connects its different incarnations is a preoccupation with the relationship between method of inquiry and emergent knowledge, between the form that makes knowledge shareable and the process of its production.

The first character in Jewish literature to take an action referred to as "drasha" was Rebecca, the beloved wife of Isaac and mother of Jacob and Esau. The book of Genesis explains that "she went to inquire (lidrosh) of the Lord" about the twins in her womb who struggled with one another.[116] She was asking out of some combination of curiosity and frustration, implying that the meaning of the term lies somewhere between "to seek" and "to demand." For Rebecca, it was almost certainly neither an open-ended inquiry nor a rhetorical question. God answers her in the very next verse, making her one of the first people in Jewish history to have a conversation directly with God.

Rebecca's approach models the term's contemporary colloquial usage in which drasha (plural: drashot) is a synonym for "sermon." Education scholar Lee Shulman identified it as one of the "signature pedagogies" of Jewish education, and based on its featured slot in Saturday synagogue services and b-mitzvah, he is correct.[117] It is an opportunity for a member of the community (often a rabbi but not always) to teach the congregation something by expounding on or offering an interpretation of the weekly Torah portion, which they likely just heard chanted aloud from the Torah scroll in the original Hebrew. A drasha can take many forms—homily, close textual analysis, philosophical rumination, poem, cheeky reflection on popular culture, exposition on current events—but the essential concern of a drasha is usually the same: to pursue and explain some insight into the meaning of a text that is not entirely apparent upon first read.

Historically, the centrality of the synagogue in Jewish life made sermons seem like a practical and efficient way of teaching the entire congregation at once, regardless of how often or how infrequently they happened. Logistically, it made sense: If most men were in attendance, then why not capitalize on the captive audience and try to teach? Deshen observed that in nineteenth-century Morocco "the main scholarly activity that did take place in synagogues was the frequent delivery of derashot-type lectures by sages. These were wide ranging discourses of biblical homiletics, practical halakha, and general rabbinic learning. . . . The audience was normally passive at the derashot, and books were not used."[118] During the Middle Ages, rabbis began thinking about their own drashot in new ways, publishing compilations of their thoughts and sometimes even offering criticism or instruction manuals about how to deliver them even more effectively.[119] Jacob Anatoli (d. 1237), who lived most of his adult life in Naples, was among the first to publish his sermons as a book. Anatoli titled his collection *Goad for Students*, which he imagined as an answer to what he understood to be the state of the question in the early twelfth century. He did not hold back with either his criticism or his hope that knowledge could transform his community and their relationship to God:

> But we walk away from the truth which the Lord has handed down to us. This is because of our laziness, whereby we read the Torah in a weak way like youngsters, without investigation and interpretation, so much so that the teachers of our people rely on reading out the parashah in Hebrew twice and once in translation, as prescribed by our rabbis (see b. Ber. 8a). However, the latter's rule implies more than just recitation . . . [they wanted us] to consider the Torah each and every Shabbat and each and every yom tov [holiday], for everyone is free on those days to search, investigate, learn and teach, which is what those holy days are for. But we do not do so.[120]

He worried that the ritualistic weekly recitation of the Torah would not suffice in awakening his congregation. But a drasha could bridge the gap, turning community gatherings into opportunities for "investigation and interpretation" that could chart a path back to "the truth which the Lord has handed down to us." The drasha promised to make the knowledge in the Torah more accessible and hopefully encourage people to live lives of greater adherence to God's law.

Anatoli built his approach to drasha on his belief that people needed greater explanation of the texts they recited, a meaning that connects to the second form of the term: *midrash*, which is the name given to the body of sometimes fanciful stories and allegories that evolved alongside the Talmud and the Tanakh. Midrashic stories take literary liberties to provide fictionalized but now canonical interpretations of biblical characters' inner lives, thought processes, motivations, and interpretations of events. If you ever wanted to know what God or Moses or Sarah was thinking during a particular episode, check the midrash. The function of midrashic literature is to answer questions about biblical texts that cannot be answered without the addition of narrative insights that cannot be found within the text in question. Midrashic stories provide an explanatory apparatus around a specific text, scaffolding interpretive efforts by adding extratextual insight, narrative, and character development.

Third, the term also figures in the mystical four-layer interpretive method for studying text. According to this method, each layer of analysis reveals a deeper meaning hidden in the text. The most direct, surface-level reading of a text is called *pshat*, derived from the word for "simple," and it refers only to the surface meaning of a text. It engages with text at the level of its most direct and obvious meaning. A wink, at this level, is always just a wink.[121] The next level is *remez*, meaning "hint," and it refers to an allegorical or metaphorical reading of a text in which transposing the elements of a text can generate a deeper understanding. Think of a code key or George Orwell's *Animal Farm*. *Drash* refers to the third level, in which meaning is even more deeply hidden and requires further inquiry and analysis in order to surface it. At the level of the drash, meaning is present but requires investigation and exposition. The deepest of the four levels is *sod*, meaning "secret." Sod is the level at which the most esoteric, most obscure, and most powerful meaning lies, but remains a secret to all but the most committed initiates. Together, the initials of the four layers spell out the Hebrew word *pardes*, meaning "orchard."[122]

Finally, the term is also employed in *midrasha* (plural: *midrashot*), the name typically reserved for women's academies for advanced study of sacred texts, usually but not solely in Orthodox communities.[123] The first midrashot were established in the 1930s, and the number and variety have steadily increased to serve a growing sense of importance regarding the formal education of women. Usually, the term is reserved for postsecondary educational institutions. In Israel, many midrasha graduates study education in preparation for entering the Israeli teaching core, often in state-sponsored religious schools. Other midrashot emphasize the value of learning and offer rigorous courses of text-based study in academic settings. The midrasha at Bar-Ilan University in Israel explains that "its aim is to assist students in the development of their spiritual identities through the acquisition of a solid foundation of knowledge and experience in all areas of Torah study, and in the synthesis of all the areas of religious and academic studies."[124] In keeping with its other uses, midrasha refers to a place for the formal pursuit of knowledge within a community that had not historically dedicated resources to women's learning at scale.

Together, these four modalities of drasha indicate the variety of settings in which question and answer serve the production and transmission of knowledge. The case of midrashot is, in some ways, the most obvious as they often train teachers. But the others also indicate a connection between inquiry and exegesis that can be traced back to the biblical figure of Rebecca as the instigator of this form of knowledge seeking.

Samech—Sefer

The first people to engage with the technology of the book in a Jewish context were the scribes of ancient Israel. Ezra the Scribe was among the most famous, and he is attributed with being among the first to commit Jewish practice to text, which he then read aloud.[125] The Hebrew word for scribe, *sofer*, derives from the same root as the word for "book" (*sefer*; plural: *sefarim*, or as commonly rendered in transliteration from the Ashkenazi pronunciation, *seforim*), and also for the verb "to tell" (Hebrew: *lesaper*), as one does with stories (Hebrew: *sipur*). Sometimes in literature (Hebrew: *safrut*) from the ancient Near East, the word *sofer* is rendered directly as "teacher," inasmuch as teachers worked in both literary and oral (and aural) modalities. As a scribe, Ezra operated within the mandate of his profession in which the lines between writing, reading, and interpretation were more porous than they might seem from a more modern perspective.[126] Historian David Carr argued that scribes were not just literate functionaries but also speakers, storytellers, and teachers.[127] "There is more emphasis in the biblical tradition on 'hearing' than on the 'writing' and 'reading' of biblical texts, let alone the education of students in such texts."[128] Scribes transmitted knowledge that was sometimes written and sometimes oral, and it is not entirely clear that the cultures of the ancient Near East were as concerned or as aware of the distinctions as some more recent scholars have made them out to be.[129]

Yet books have come to hold a special place in Jewish vocabulary and culture, and not only because of the Jews' designation by Islam as a "people of the book." The term *sefer* appears in the contemporary Hebrew words for library (Hebrew: *sifriya*) and school, *beit sefer* (house of the book), whose usage can be traced back to the Middle Ages, but it did not refer to school as an independent institution. Rather, as Ephraim Kanarfogel has discovered, "it refers most often to either the home of the melammed or rooms rented by the melammed to which students came. This term also refers to the home of the student, where some melammedim lived."[130] Thus, the term served a more descriptive purpose, referring to the room or designated space in which books were stored and in which instruction took place. It seems the term served a descriptive function rather than a prescriptive one. Kanarfogel has written that there was no "system of education" in medieval Ashkenaz, but we might extend his insight to conclude that there was not yet a concept of schooling that could have been systematized.

Nevertheless, the emergence of the term *beit sefer* and its application suggest that some melamdim defined their efforts through this reference to books. The beit sefer was not a beit midrash (see the entries for both "Bet—Beit Midrash" and "Dalet—Drasha"), perhaps because the latter was primarily considered a setting for adult male study. But neither was it a *beit kneset* (English:

house of gathering), a term usually reserved for synagogues, where no small amount of teaching and instruction took place. Rather, the term highlights the prominence of books in the instruction of children, rather than oral recitation, debate, sermonizing, embodied practice, or aural immersion. Of course, those other dimensions of learning and instruction can be at play in the beit sefer too, but the designation of the book as the defining quality of this instructional approach highlights the power of the book as a locus and focus of study.

With the advent of the mass production of texts and later moveable type, the number and diversity of books proliferated, as did access to them. More books and more access ignited debates about which books deserved scholarly attention and which were distractions. In Eastern Europe the status of books was reflected in their categorization as either *sefarim* or *bikher* (the plural form of *bukh*, which borrows from the German). Sefer came to refer to a holy book, or a book pertaining to the study, teaching, or explication of religious texts and life. To call something a sefer was to endow it with significance and implicitly to set it apart from other books. Sefarim elicit a range of practices intended to distinguish them from other kinds of books—people will refrain from placing them on the floor or putting them upside down on a shelf. If a sefer falls to the ground, one is expected to kiss it, as a sign of respect, before replacing it on the table, cover side up. If a sefer falls into disrepair, it is supposed to be placed in a special temporary storage area called a *geniza*, before being buried in a cemetery; sefarim are not to be thrown away or recycled. Historian Talya Fishman has argued that the rise of the Talmud during the Middle Ages was reflected both in its emergence as a focus of study and in a change in its status as a sefer.[131] Calling something a "book" referred not to its physical properties but to its cultural meaning. Commenting on this period, historian Nahman Danzig observed that the Talmud came to be recognized as a "book" during the Middle Ages, which, as Fishman notes, was "a status that Jews had previously bestowed only on the Tanakh itself."[132] The emergence of the Talmud as a sefer marked a change in its cultural status as well as its material form.

A *bukh* in the Yiddish-speaking world, by contrast, was a secular volume. It could be maskilic literature or fiction, and regardless of its content it did not warrant the treatment of a sefer. Memoirs of the interwar period in Poland include references to *haskole-bikher* (Enlightenment books) and *treyfene bikhlekh* (forbidden books). One described "booksellers who had sforim [transliterated here with the Ashkenazi pronunciation intact], tefiln, taleysim, mezuzes, and other wares to sell] frequently came to [the town of] Strikov. Secretly they also sold *mayse-bikhlekh* [secular Yiddish story books], making sure that no hasid would see."[133] These memoirists not only distinguished between sefarim and *bikhelekh* but noted that the latter were hidden and forbidden.

In the late nineteenth and early twentieth centuries, a new generation of Yiddish writers embraced the bukh as a conceptual and practical vehicle for circulating their new ideas about Jewish culture. The literary review *Bikher-velt* ("Book World") launched in Kiev in 1919 as an organ of new, modernist Jewish culture, a central feature of which was the provision of Jewish literature for children as part of renewed attention to education in the service of Jewish cultural, not religious revival.[134] Reclaiming bikher as a vehicle for modernist Yiddish culture carried on the legacies of the Haskalah, channeling them into visions for cultural uplift that joined secularism and education.

The idea of what constitutes a "sacred text" has taken on new and expansive parameters, as people read both *Harry Potter* and the *Big Book* of Alcoholics Anonymous with devotional attention.[135] But sefarim do not exist without people who read and treat them differently than they do other books. The same is true of bikher. For those who know and care, the meaning of those books transcends their contents, suggesting that the range of things learned when attending to those texts extends far beyond the book itself.

Tav—Torah

Finally, we have arrived at the last letter of this quasi-alphabetical exploration and the final keyword of the keywords. The last letter is *tav*, which is the first letter of the word *Torah*. In some ways, Torah is the perfect place to end this exploration because it is also the beginning, the source for Jewish education and Jewish Studies because it has, in practice and in myth, been the foundational text for Jewish life in virtually all its forms. In the Jewish vernacular, Torah usually refers to the scroll that contains the Pentateuch, and it is ritually read portion by portion over the course of a year as part of weekly prayer services. Sometimes people refer to the scroll as "a Torah" or "the Torah." More precisely, the ornately dressed scroll, written on parchment and wound around two wooden staves, should be referred to as a *sefer Torah*, or a "book of the Torah." A sefer Torah, written by a *sofer* ("scribe"), contains the text of the Five Books of Moses, written in a specific calligraphic style and presented without punctuation or diacritics.[136]

The term appears a number of times in the Pentateuch, revealing a few different meanings, and although some interpreters wish to read the appearance of the term *Torah* as a literal reference to the contents of the Pentateuch, the immediate meaning could readily be understood to refer to something more general like "teachings," "wisdom" or "lessons." Twice the book of Exodus refers to Torah as something akin to what we might think of as law, and both instances insist that the same laws apply to Jews and non-Jews alike.[137] Elsewhere in Exodus the term suggests a more general notion of teaching or instruction, as in the book's account of the Revelation at Sinai. "God said to Moses, 'Come up to Me on the mountain and wait there, and I will give you the stone tablets with the teachings (torah) and commandments which I have inscribed to instruct them.'"[138] When it appears in Leviticus and Numbers, the term usually refers to specific directions, as it pertains to ritual sacrifice or to processes of adjudication. But in Deuteronomy, the term echoes its appearance in Exodus, referring to a more generic sense, meaning instructions or teachings.[139]

To engage in "Torah study," however, does not necessarily mean that one is studying the Five Books of Moses. Despite the centrality of the word "Torah" in phrases like "Talmud Torah" or "Torah study," the Five Books of Moses have traditionally occupied a position at the bottom of the hierarchy of preferred subjects for serious study. Often, it has been relegated to children. In the section of his Mishna Torah called "Talmud Torah," or "Torah study," Rambam explained how adult males ought to regard the Pentateuch in their studies. "When they mature in wisdom and have no need either for further study of Holy Writ (Hebrew: *torah shebichtav*) or for continuous devotion to the study of Oral Torah (Hebrew: *torah shebe'al peh*), they should read Holy Writ and traditional matters at appointed times merely so as not to forget any matter pertaining to the laws of the Torah, and turn their attention to a continuous study of Gemara, of course, in proportion to the broadness of their heart and peacefulness of their mind."[140]

Although the Rambam considers the study of Torah to be a sacred act, he regards the study of the Five Books of Moses as necessary but not particularly sophisticated or challenging. In his vision of Torah Study, the Pentateuch serves as a reference text. Adult males should review it periodically, but the Rambam suggests that they focus their effort elsewhere. Women, he explained, are permitted to study Torah, but their "reward" will be less than men's because they are not obligated to study.[141] When the Rambam and others write about studying Torah, they use the term as a synecdoche, as a part that stands in for a larger conception of the whole corpus of sacred text worthy of study.

But Talmud Torah has meant different things in different contexts. Sometimes, as Matthias Lehmann has argued, the study of Torah in the form of musar literature emerged as a rabbinically sanctioned leisure time activity. The Rambam opened his *Mishne Torah* with a chapter on Talmud Torah. Rabbi Hayim of Volozhin understood his mandate was to teach students Torah, as did Rabbi Kotler of Lakewood, and Rabbi Salanter of the musar movement. Elsewhere still, as in the example of the kollel, the study of Torah became a full-time occupation. Regardless of the particularities of the study and its orientation, almost all of the instances of the production and transmission of Jewish knowledge can be understood as Talmud Torah, even when people study books and texts other than those included in the Torah itself.

So pervasive was the term *Talmud Torah* that it regularly served as a generic name for Jewish schools for children. Sometimes, congregations adopted the name as their own and sometimes the term referred to a non-maskilic Jewish school that might otherwise have been called a yeshiva.[142] Typically, Talmud Torahs were community-supported endeavors, unlike the private heder. As such, they provided a modicum of communal supervision, though they were still limited in range and scope, focusing on the study of Torah and Tanakh in the younger grades, and rabbinic literature as students matured.[143] As with the heder, Talmud Torahs oriented their students and their studies toward fundamental knowledge that would enable them to participate in public forms of Jewish communal and ritual life.[144] As Emanuel Gamoran concluded, the "Talmud Torah . . . was but a natural consequence of the social conditions under which the Jewish people lived in Russia and Poland, and, although they did not prepare the child for a vocation, they enabled him to participate effectively in the social and religious life of the Jewish community of the ghetto."[145]

So central has the practice of Talmud Torah been that for some it contends with prayer for primacy in Jewish life. Influential Orthodox Rabbi Joseph Soloveitchik explicitly connected the two: "Intellectual redemption through the study of Torah resembles, in its structure, the redemption through prayer. It was for a good reason that Moses and Ezra integrated keriat ha-Torah [the weekly reading of a portion of the Torah] into the framework of tefillah [English: "prayer"]. Without Talmud Torah it would be difficult for tefillah to assure man of total redemption."[146] For Soloveitchik, prayer cannot stand alone. It must be supported by the study of Torah, hence the inclusion of the weekly reading within normative Saturday morning prayer services to ensure at least a minimum of engagement with source texts. In a more general way, sociologist Sam Heilman's ethnography of adult study circles highlighted the "devotional" dimension of the practice he referred to as "lernen" (see "Lamed—Lomed"). Others, too, have argued that the study of Torah is a religious practice, an act of piety or meditation, and even a modality for communing with the divine presence. Sometimes it was just one of these. Sometimes it was all three together.

So what does it mean to study Torah? In modern Hebrew, the same root that gives us the word *Torah* refers to the act of aiming (as one does with an intention or a gun) and for teachers (male *moreh*, female *morah*; Hebrew does not yet have a nongendered term for such a person) and guides (Hebrew: *moreh derech*). All of these imply guidance, direction, and intention. As it applies to the scroll and its contents, the term refers not to what the book *is* but to what the book *does*: the book(s) of Torah are supposed to teach, guide, and direct. It is a book *of* teachings and a book *for* teaching.[147] But as a synecdoche of Jewish knowledge more generally, teaching the book is not the point.

The Torah refers to the accumulated wisdom and knowledge of the flexible, dispersed community known generically as "the Jewish people." Whatever Moses or Miriam or Joshua might have known was transmitted from generation to generation, expanding to include the Gemara and the Mishna, alongside the commentaries and contributions of later explicators of texts, and on and on. Torah is a vast, flexible, porous category, and how and where one decides what is Torah and what is not is, of course, where the debates begin.

What should people study? How should they study? Who should study? What kinds of changes are to be expected or encouraged as a result of their studies? Does Torah include the songs of Leonard Cohen or Ezra Furman or Shoshana Damari or Drake? The art of Wassily Kandinsky or Mark Rothko or Judy Chicago? The recipes of Michael Twitty, Joan Nathan, Yotam Ottolenghi, or Mollie Katzen? The poetry of Kasmuna, of Rachel, Celia Dropkin, of Marge Piercy, of Irena Klepfisz? The fiction of Cynthia Ozick, Dara Horn, A. B. Yehoshua? The scholarship of . . . ? And some would say that the debates over Torah are also part of Torah, provided they are for the sake of heaven.[148] The term Torah refers to the Five Books of Moses, but the knowledge it embraces is not limited to them. The study of Torah captures all of these elements, shaped by various methodological approaches, value propositions, schools, institutions, prohibitions, and other political, spiritual, and ideological commitments. So perhaps better than the "law" or "teachings," we might think of the Torah more immediately as "the instructions" or "the knowledge."

PART III
IN A NEW KEY

4   Learning in Jewish Education

Any musician can tell you that the key is the *key*, that songs in C have a different feel than songs in E flat, and that transposing songs can change their sound and their feeling. Altering the key does not change the relative distance between any two notes in a melody, but shifting a song's tonal center alters its whole gravitational pull. One of the oldest songwriting tricks in the book is to write the "bridge" of a song in a different key or to change keys for the final chorus, in order to emphasize the contrast between it and the song's other parts and amp up the piece's emotional tension.[1] Think about the final chorus of Whitney Houston's "I Will Always Love You" (1992) and you get a sense of the impact.

To tell the story of Jewish education in a new key means taking what is familiar and altering it such that it heightens the tension between what came before and what is new. This chapter still focuses on the production and transmission of knowledge, but in a slightly different way. The preceding chapters laid out case studies from Jewish communities stretching as far back as I could identify. Chapter 1 looked at one specific pair of cases—Jewish education and Jewish Studies—in order to highlight how their respective concerns regarding each other's approaches mask some significant similarities between the two efforts. The implicit argument connecting the case studies of chapters 2 and 3 was that in nearly every instance the study of Jews and Judaism intertwined with existential concerns about the present and future of Jews and Judaism. The modern cleavage of knowledge-that (the purported domain of Jewish Studies) and knowledge-how (that of Jewish education) can thus be understood as something of an historical anomaly.

Yet, Jewish Studies and Jewish education, like all of the case studies in the preceding chapters, do share one quality that has fundamentally shaped theory and practice: They have been primarily organized by an interest in how best to teach someone else what they ought to know. Although they represent a remarkably broad range of strategies and approaches for *what* to teach and *how* to teach, they scarcely acknowledge *how people learn*. Most historical actors have been preoccupied with the question of what people should know and how they should act, so they poured resources into writing books or creating institutions that they believed would likely generate the outcomes they desired. Codes of Jewish law, Sunday schools, maskilic schools, Zionist youth groups, children's bibles, fields of scholarship, summer camps, books of Hebrew grammar, new rituals, and inspiring trips all took shape in the shadow of someone figuring that someone else was missing something. So they created these innovations to fill whatever gaps they thought existed. Jewish education and Jewish Studies, too, have invested heavily in curricula and syllabuses, in philosophies and material, always asking "what do people need to know?" but never "how do people learn?"

Cue the Key Change

If we were to attempt to derive a theory of learning from the examples presented in the preceding chapters, it would be something like this: well-presented knowledge would be internalized and put into action. Someone wondering how to slaughter a chicken according to the laws of kashrut could consult the Shulchan Aruch and learn how. Someone who thought their children were missing out on some dimension of Jewish experience could send them to summer camp to experience it. If children didn't know the tenets of Judaism, a catechism could explain it. Though these are different examples, they share common roots in the theory that if people had access to the right knowledge appropriately presented, then they would acquire it and act accordingly.

The main problem with this theory is that it rarely happens in practice. Learning is not just the result of good teaching, clear instruction, or innovative programming, though those things help. Nor is it the same as "studying" Jewish texts, or what ethnographer Sam Heilman calls "lernen."[2] So, what is it? Is it the same as making meaning? As mastering content knowledge? As grasping propositional knowledge about Jewish life? Is it knowing how to bake challah or tell a bedtime story? Is it the process of internalizing the skills, habits, or dispositions that will enable "the capacity to describe, analyze, and interpret, in its own terms, . . . the inner life of 'Israel,' the Jewish people," as Jacob Neusner wrote?[3] Is it the process of developing a predetermined set of commitments, beliefs, orientations, or attitudes? Is it about acquiring knowledge of Jewish texts and practices, or is it about embodying them? Learning can be some of these things, but it is not the sum of them.

To hear Jewish education in a new key, then, is to attend to learning first. In a new key, the refrain is the same: learning also consists of the production and transmission of knowledge, but emphasizes the processes and practices of people often imagined to be on the receiving end of educational work. It will shift the gravitational center away from the prescriptive approaches that have characterized past efforts in this domain, and toward an understanding of how people produce knowledge, not because they think someone else needs to know it but because that is how they come to know it themselves. Attending to learning should provide insights into these processes by amplifying the tension between an understanding of Jewish education that has largely emphasized the provision of knowledge in the pursuit of a desired set of outcomes and an understanding of learning as a discreet phenomenon that makes it possible to know anything at all about Jewish life.

Drawing on insights from the Learning Sciences, a field of study that took shape in the 1980s and 1990s around the question of how people learn, this chapter lays out what learning might look like in Jewish contexts.[4] The Learning Sciences are great on defining learning in settings where knowledge is demonstrable and answers are often clearly correct or incorrect: math, physics, chemistry, computer science. They have been less fruitful for the humanities and related areas like civic or moral education, and they have had nothing to say about religion generally or Jewish education specifically. Still the Learning Sciences offer a vital source of insights that point to ways to reconfigure Jewish education and Jewish Studies around the ways people learn, and not just beliefs about what they are supposed to know. Without a consideration for how people learn, the greatest teachers in the world and the most innovative programs are hamstrung because they fundamentally do not understand their audience. Placing learning at the center of Jewish education inverts the conventional ways in which people have been thinking about Jewish education. It reverses the directionality of the enterprise as envisioned in books like *Visions of Jewish Education*, which begins with an imagined figure of "the educated Jew" and then reverse engineers curricular pathways that people might follow so that they, too, might be considerd "educated Jews." Instead, it puts learners and learning first, taking the traditional question of Jewish education, "what do people need to know?," and transposing it to ask "how do people learn?," and beginning there.

On Jewish Teaching

First, though, we should labor a moment over the use and misuse of the term "learning" and how it has often been used to signal Jewish *studying* or *teaching*. This is true even of philosopher Franz Rosenzweig's book, which, despite the title, *On Jewish Learning*, has little to say about learning. Rosenzweig's short collection of essays and letters exhibits a generalized concern for learners and how they might learn better and more deeply, but his inquiry leads him to formulate visions for a new approach to teaching, a new institution, and a theory of how to approach the presentation of Jewish knowledge. His name for this new institution, the *Lehrhaus*, loosely translates as a "house of teaching," as opposed to a *Lernhaus*, or house of learning. A better title for his book might have been "On Jewish Teaching" or "On Jewish Schooling." Still, his inquiry led him to formulate a version of the paradox of Jewish education that he calls "learning in reverse order." With a romantic historical glance backward, he imagines "a learning that no longer starts from the Torah and leads into life, but the other way round: from life, from a world that knows nothing of the Law, or pretends to know nothing, back to the torah. That is the sign of the time. . . . There is no one today who is not alienated, or who does not contain within himself some small fraction of alienation. . . . We know that in being Jews we must not give up anything, not renounce anything, but lead everything back to Judaism."[5] Rosenzweig's response to the pressures of modernity is to double down on the possibility that new educational institutions can ensure that Jews live lives "surrounded by an atmosphere Jewish to some degree, by a Jewish world."[6] As compelling as his vision might be and as stirring as his sentiment is, he ends up sounding like so many other efforts to employ a new school, an innovative curriculum, an inventive medium, or a new pedagogy in the service of salving the tensions of modern Jewish life. Rosenzweig's enthusiasm catches him in the logic of a classic educational trap: the belief that better teaching and better institutions are going to drive better learning because learning is what happens in schools and in the presence of inspirational teachers.

Rosenzweig is not alone among Jewish educational thinkers who use the language of learning when they mean teaching. A more recent example of this confusing terminological substitution can be found in Jonathan Woocher's 2012 article, "Reinventing Jewish Education for the 21st Century."[7] Woocher argues that the question facing Jewish education is "How can we help Jews find in their Jewishness resources that will help them live more meaningful, purposeful, and fulfilling human lives?"[8] For Woocher, the role of Jewish education is not to reproduce "educated Jews" but to provide people with the tools, conceptual and otherwise, for living happier, more fulfilled lives. He envisions Jewish knowledge as procedural knowledge. But his vision of Jewish education retains teaching at the center, reinforcing extant power relationships and well-established hierarchies of agency and authority, even if clad in the language of "learner centered education." "If Jewish education can deploy the rich resources of Jewish tradition and contemporary Jewish life to help learners answer their authentic questions and experience the mix of joy, purposefulness, wonder, invigoration, and peacefulness that most humans seek, *then it can thrive.*"[9] It is an odd claim, concluding as it does with a reflection on Jewish education, and not an insight into the learners or learning. With this flourish, Woocher imagines Jewish education as the beneficiary of the effort. But Jewish education for its own sake cannot be the point. I realize that Woocher was writing for Jewish educators, but still, shouldn't Jewish education aim to serve its intended students? What good is a Jewish education whose ultimate outcome is its own vitality? I doubt that even Rabbi Meir would agree. Further, Woocher's vision for Jewish education does not really change the balance of power as it still imagines Jewish education to be driven by people who can "deploy the rich resources of the Jewish tradition." Deploy is such a strong word in this context, at odds with a "learner-centered" approach in which other verbs—activate, engage, create— might be more appropriate. Indeed, the whole effort of the article focuses on improving the efficiency and impact of Jewish education, and it avoids talking about learning at all. It centers learners but it reveals little about what the learners do. Woocher's vision sheds precious little light on how people learn or what learning looks like when it happens. His educational call to arms can be understood as "learner-centered" only insofar as it sandwiches learners between educational inputs and desired outcomes.

Instrumentalizing Jewish Education

Woocher's concern for outcomes fits into a long-running trend in Jewish education that has mostly approached it as a means to an end. The lack of attention to learning has not, for the most part, troubled people committed to Jewish education because, in most circumstances, the value of Jewish education has been assessed in terms of its impact on people's lives, often in areas that bear no direct relationship to whatever it was that was supposed to have been learned in the first place. The emphasis on outcomes—whether or not people who, say, go to Jewish day school are more or less likely than their public school peers to light Shabbat candles or feel a connection to the State of Israel—undermines the educational process and effectively back-loads the value of education onto a secondary and sometimes tertiary effect. If outcomes matter most, then the most valued educational approaches are organized in the service of those outcomes, with little regard for what might be learned along the way or how people might learn it.

This framing of how to understand the importance of education is precisely what Jacob Neusner feared and why he argued so stridently against Jewish Studies. He feared that the scholarly study of Judaism would become a higher education version of an instrumentalized Jewish education. In trying to safeguard the work of professors, he also helped to reinscribe an outcomes-oriented understanding of Jewish education that was aimed largely at youngsters, and one that further segmented Jewish Studies from Jewish education. In this effort, he was aided by a raft of studies that reinforced this approach and supported his critique, albeit obliquely. Published by the pile beginning in the 1970s, they bore titles like "The Impact of Religious Schooling: The Effects of Jewish Education upon Adult Religious Involvement,"[10] "The Jewish Schooling of American Jews: A Study of Non-cognitive Educational Effects,"[11] "The Impact of Childhood Jewish Education on Adults' Jewish Identity: Schooling, Israel Travel, Camping and Youth Groups,"[12] "What Difference Does Day School Make? The Impact of Day School: A Comparative Analysis of Jewish College Students,"[13] and "When They Are Grown They Will Not Depart: Jewish Education and the Jewish Behavior of American Adults."[14] It seemed that most of the scholarship, and certainly the most influential examples of research in American Jewish education confirmed the instrumental model.

Perhaps the most popular iteration of this approach was formulated by Seymour Martin Lipset in an oft-quoted 1994 report, "The Power of Jewish

Education."[15] Lipset analyzed data from the 1990 National Jewish Population Survey and concluded that with regard to Jewish education, "the iron law of 'the more the more' prevails. The longer Jews have been exposed to Jewish education, the greater their commitment to the community, to some form of the religion, and to Israel. The relationships among type of school attended, attitudes, and behavior reiterate this conclusion again and again."[16] Lipset's "iron law" does not distinguish between types of education, nor does it attend to its qualities or modalities. It certainly does not account for the experiences of learners, or whether, how, and why they learned. Simply, he concluded that more is better than less. His formulation reduces education to the brute force of exposure in the service of a familiar refrain that has been so often repeated as to have become axiomatic. "The basic problem for the community is and will be to hold them, to keep them Jewish. The most important means to do this is education."[17]

If the impact of Jewish education could be summed up by Lipset's "iron law of 'the more the more,'" then the whole enterprise could be reduced to a kind of brutal behaviorism. If people were not attending synagogue or were failing to donate to Jewish causes, or their observance of the Sabbath was flagging or they began opting for soccer practice instead of Sunday school, then more education could provide the remedy. A similar logic could apply to much earlier efforts to teach people what they were supposed to know: if people cannot access the dense texts of Rabbinic Judaism, provide a legal code and once they have access to the knowledge they need to live more active Jewish lives, they will do so. All they need is knowledge, and the more, the more.

Channeled through the language of impact, Jewish education came to be meaningful largely in terms of its long-term effects, and not in terms of what or how people might learn along the way. Neusner's commitment to independence and objectivity, and the universalism of Bildung had almost completely disappeared beneath a desire and intention to prove education's ability to deliver experiences that would increase the probability of a young participant deepening their commitment to Jewish life as an adult. What people learned, to say nothing of how they learned, receded into the recesses of educational programming because the value of education is thought to be found largely in its impact well after the fact. Measured in terms of effect, a person who went on a heritage tour of Israel where they learned nothing about, say, Israeli history but reported feeling a strong attachment to the State of Israel would be considered a success, whereas someone who participated in the same program, but developed a more critical and thus more equivocal connection to the State of Israel might not be. This is a curious way of evaluating the success of Jewish education, unless, like Woocher, we find the programs at the center, not the learners.

In Woocher's model and Lipset's theory, educational programs set the terms of learning. In a model that centers learning, programmatic outcomes have to cede the focus to the participants. It means shifting the attention from the "impact" of a program to an appreciation of how learners go about producing and transmitting knowledge as a result of their participation in the program. The prevailing model of Jewish educational study emphasizes the role of the educational program or institution and seeks to measure that. An approach that emphasizes learning will emphasize the complex of processes—cognitive, affective, embodied, connected—that learners employ while they are doing what we might call "learning." Refocusing education around learning might even allow a return of Neusner's strong defense of scholarship in the service of a richer account of learners' experiences rather than just programmatic impact.

Understanding Jewish education solely (or even largely) in terms of its impact has diminished our understanding of what education is and the ability to imagine what it could be. Lipset's quantitative and instrumental approach to Jewish education has narrowed the definition of Jewish education to its ability to impact a few statistical variables. In the process, education came to be understood as an important driver, a force, an investment, and a producer of outcomes. Consequently, it became something of a universal solution to whatever ailed Jews and their communities, as in the foreboding rhetoric of the Mandel Foundation-funded 1990 Jewish educational call-to-arms, *A Time to Act*. "The responsibility for developing Jewish identity and instilling a commitment to Judaism for this population now rests primarily with education."[18] Emphasizing outcomes resulted in renewed investments in Jewish educational efforts but largely kept the orientation of those efforts intact: fund the providers and the learners will follow. But what about those learners? What are they learning? And how?

The Deficit Theory of Jewish Education

The educational logic of Lipset's "iron law" was effective in attracting philanthropic dollars and programmatic creativity that supported new initiatives, but it was reductive and simplistic in its conceptualization of how Jewish education worked. It figured things would work like this: the more funding, the more programs; the more programs, the more participants; the more participants, the more likelihood that people will engage in Jewish life as adults. At the core of this logic lay an implicit theory of learners and thus, of American Jewry. It was not flattering. The promise of rigorous analyses that could control for dimensions of learners' backgrounds and generate clean and clear portraits of the "impact" of Jewish education was underwritten by an implicit claim that only educational programming could produce and transmit the knowledge necessary to sustain the Jewish People. Here, again, is *A Time to Act*: "It is clear that there is a core of deeply committed Jews whose way of life ensures meaningful continuity from generation to generation. However, there is a much larger segment of the Jewish population which is finding it increasingly difficult to define its future in terms of Jewish values and behavior."[19] Tucked into this blanket assessment of American Jewish life was a pair of interwoven propositions. First was the claim that most Jewish families were incapable of sustaining themselves Jewishly. The second was that Jewish education could remedy their situation. Thus formulated, each proposition relied on the other: Jews who didn't know what to do needed education, and education could target the Jews who didn't know what to do. But underneath both of them lay a largely unsubstantiated but deeply held belief that American Jews were Jewishly deficient and that education could provide them what they lacked.

This approach to Jewish education has pervaded writing on the subject for decades across a range of approaches. Philosopher Israel Scheffler defined Jewish education in terms of its ability "to initiate the Jewish child in to the culture, history, and spiritual heritage of the Jewish people, to help the child to learn and face the truth about Jewish history, identity, and existence, to enhance his or her dignity as a Jewish person, and to enable the child to accept, and to be creative in, the Jewish dimension of its life."[20] Writing about Birthright Israel, Len Saxe and Barry Chazan explained, "The initial hope was that providing an educational trip to Israel, young Jewish adults from Diaspora communities would come to appreciate their Jewish identity more fully. That appreciation, in turn, would make Judaism a more important part of their social identities and lives."[21] Isa Aron added a negatively valanced perspective but retained the underlying logic. "Despite the extensive range of activities, Jewish education is not achieving its mission. Exposure to existing Jewish educational programs leaves many North American Jews indifferent to Judaism, and unwilling or unable to take an active part in Jewish communal living."[22] Sometimes, this rationale explicitly employed the language and logic of deficiency, deprivation, and deficit. Philosopher Barry Chazan explained, "Our Jewish children are culturally deprived, and the schools are not doing very much to help. It is a great tragedy that our children do not get a taste of Judaism's creative, exciting, and revolutionary ways of thinking and being. Our neglect of Jewish education threatens both the cultural lives of our young and the continued existence of our people."[23] Harold Himmelfarb offered a similar account in the title of his article, "Jewish Education for Naught: Educating the Culturally Deprived Jewish Child."[24] Framing learners as culturally deficient meant approaching Jewish education as a supplemental logic, filling in where families or some other imagined organic structure had previously failed.

The deficit model relied on a theory of learners that lacked the basic cultural tools for the construction, practice, or engagement of Jewish life on their own. Framed as culturally deficient, the approach subtly reinforces the power and centrality of Jewish educators while undermining the capacities of Jewish learners. The deficit model has little space in which to account for the capacities and cultural repertoires of learners. By placing the power to effect change in the hands of educators, the deficit model left almost no room for learning.

This theory of Jewish education, powerful though it was during the latter decades of the twentieth century, suffered from a highly selective theoretical and historical memory.

As chapters 2 and 3 laid out, people have been learning all along. When Ben Gamla advocated for hiring teachers for children, Jewish families did not stop passing their traditions, stories, habits, and celebrations down from generation to generation. Sherira Gaon's history of the Oral Torah did not necessarily shape the ways in which the majority of Jews, who lived in either Pumbedita or Kairouan, or who have lived in Paris, Essaouira, St. Louis, Recife, or elsewhere, saw, understood, or practiced their Jewishness. Parents learned from their children and children from their friends and grandparents. The compilation of the *Mishne Torah* did not stop Jews from breaking the law, identifying new loopholes, inventing new laws, or ignoring the law altogether. Each of these efforts represented a response to impressions that Jews were not living up to their Jewish potential and they had to be taught to do so. Many of these texts, often pointed to as evidence of the centrality of learning in Jewish life, can be better understood as aspirational visions for what their authors' ideal communities might look like than as descriptions of the communities in which they lived. Meanwhile, those communities were full of Jewish people who told stories, developed traditions, performed rituals, and continually produced and transmitted knowledge they needed to live the lives they wanted. Perhaps they benefited from an easy-access reference work for Jewish law, but perhaps they were happy—and fully Jewishly—to continue to reinvent their relationship to Jewishness by learning what they needed to do so.

The deficit theory provided a framework and a rationale for Jewish education, but it failed to appreciate the cultural resources that Jews possess. Despite the persistent fear that Jewish people did not know enough—or could not know enough on their own—to sustain Jewish life, they have always managed to do so. People have acquired the propositional knowledge of Jewish life and adapted procedural knowledge regarding how to put it into action. There is perhaps no better demonstration than learning of the interplay between the two modalities of thought that Jewish Studies and Jewish education have tried to distinguish. In Jewish life, knowledge-that and knowledge-how have a far more tangled, interdependent relationship than Jewish Studies and Jewish education often allow, and this history is most evident when we focus on learning, rather than teaching as the animating force. Seen in this light, Jewish education has been influenced less by a commitment to the production and transmission of knowledge than by a fear of ignorance and loss, and by claims of Jewish deficiencies. If the lachrymose conception of history lives, it lives, ironically, in Jewish education, which has long drawn on a portrait of Jews at risk of losing themselves, the thread of history, the responsibility, the covenant, the culture, and the knowledge. Although that portrait has underwritten a massive creative output of scholarship and schools, institutions, and ideas, it has nevertheless found its footing in a vision of Jewish people that sells short their cultural capacities, resources, and knowledge.

Learning from the Learning Sciences

How then to think about learning in this context? Neither Jewish education nor Jewish Studies have a history of studying learning as a discreet phenomenon that is related to but not coincident with teaching. Jewish Studies, for its part, has been preoccupied like so many of its counterparts with questions of methods. Organized primarily around research, Jewish Studies scholarship is evaluated on the basis of its scholarly rigor. Though most Jewish Studies practitioners teach, teaching is not the primary locus of action in the field. Reductively, we could say that Jewish Studies has been organized around a primary concern for the production of knowledge. Its reciprocal pair would be Jewish education, which has been organized primarily around the transmission of knowledge and how Jewishness should be taught. There are endless shelves of curriculum and instructional resources for teachers who focus less on scholarship and more on the practical day-in-and-day-out demands of classrooms, schools, camps and so on. Jewish educators have been preoccupied with teaching—or educating, if you prefer—with an eye toward outcomes. But neither Jewish Studies nor Jewish education has produced much that considers learning in any serious way.

Chapters 2 and 3 argue that the separation of powers between knowledge production and knowledge transmission, between knowledge-that and knowledge-how, is a fairly recent development. This chapter argues that this development, which divides the Jewish epistemological terrain between Jewish Studies and Jewish education, is not quite as clear or precise as it seems, and that the interplay between Jewish Studies and Jewish education can be observed if we examine them both from a perspective that places learning at the center.

So what is learning? The concept itself has a genealogy and it has gone through a few different revisions in its relatively brief history. There will undoubtedly be more revisions to come, especially in a field like Jewish education, which is just beginning this effort. At its core, I would argue that learning is fundamentally a process of changing one's mind. Change can be subtle or dramatic. It can result from a discreet and dedicated course of study or from a singular powerful experience. Both can and do change minds and leave learners knowing differently about their worlds. How that happens has been the subject of much scholarship, debate, research, and disagreement, which have led in part to the emergence of the Learning Studies.

Among the first to look into learning systematically was the psychologist Edward Thorndike, who defined it in terms of a person's ability to change. "Human learning," he wrote, "consists of changes in the nature and behavior of human beings. Changes in nature are known to us only by changes in behavior."[25] Thorndike's emphasis on behavior led to the school of research known as behaviorism, which primarily understood learning in terms of the process of establishing connections between stimuli and responses. These connections could be learned, and the aim of learning was to develop associations between stimuli and responses; the stronger the association the deeper the learning. A stimulus could be the ringing of a bell (think of Pavlov's dogs) or the presentation of an arithmetic problem. The response would be salivation or the calculation of an appropriate numerical answer. These both qualify as "learned behaviors." As Thorndike explained, "The word behavior as used here and later means anything which the human animal does. It includes thoughts and feelings as truly as movements and makes no assumptions concerning the deeper nature of any of these."[26] The power of Thorndike's approach drew both from its theory that learning manifest in behaviors and from its ability to track and measure behaviors through careful observation. Thorndike's approach made learning observable and measurable. The fusion of these two commitments allowed him and others to develop the first scientific theories of learning.

As a theory of learning, behaviorism reigned until advances in cognitive science during the 1950s revealed some of the weaknesses in the approach and introduced new ways of understanding the learning processes.[27] Cognitive science turned its focus away from the observation of learned behaviors and toward internal processes like attention and perception, memory, language, and the use of symbols.[28] Learning, this new approach argued, not only manifested in behavioral change that could be observed, but also found that it might take place within the domains of mind, attitude, understanding, meaning. Equipped with new and emerging tools both conceptual and scientific, researchers could explore how people learn without resorting to either the observation of behaviors or the theory that learning was largely a matter of stimulus-response training. Spurred by psychological studies by Jean Piaget and theorist Lev Vygotsky, among others, these approaches and their permutations have since gathered under the heading of the Learning Sciences.

The Learning Sciences paradigm has been brilliant in fostering theory building about learning across a variety of different domains as diverse as engineering, midwifery, air traffic control centers, chess playing, and computer-human interactions.[29] Strong traditions of research in the Learning Sciences have emerged in mathematics, physics, and computer science, where it is possible to observe and test learning theories by creating experimental conditions that can reveal how, for example, a novice chess player learns to read a chessboard by comparing their actions to the ways that expert chess players read the board. The field has excelled in arenas where it is possible to identify differences between experts and novices and then reverse engineer pathways in which the latter can become the former.[30] However, the Learning Sciences have been less interested in questions that have tended to fall in a more humanistic realm: How do people learn to appreciate poetry? How do people learn to adopt civic attitudes? How do people learn to evaluate reliable sources of news or information?[31] Though there have been efforts to account for different cultural bases for learning, the field has had practically nothing to say about religion; the word does not appear in either of the two volumes published by the National Research Council under the title *How People Learn*. Neither does it appear in the *Handbook of the Learning Sciences* or the volume titled *Handbook of the Cultural Foundations of Learning*. To be sure, Jewish education is not solely the domain of religious concerns, but religious texts, rituals, institutions, and concepts have long figured in Jewish culture, and it is hard to either teach or study Jewish life without running into religion and its vestiges in some form or fashion.

Still, there are some concepts from the Learning Sciences that can be usefully and productively applied to learning in this context. Specifically, we can look to constructivist and sociocultural approaches for directions about where we might identify learning in Jewish education.[32] Constructivism understands learning as the process by which learners construct knowledge and meaning. It rejects the model of learners as blank slates or empty vessels, which characterize what educational theorist Paulo Freire has called the "banking model" of education.[33] But it also goes a step further. In rejecting the banking model, constructivism also holds that learners play an active role in the learning process, combining and recombining what they know in the service of making sense of what they are coming to know. It is a matter not just of having preexisting knowledge but of actively mobilizing that knowledge in the service of new knowledge. According to the theory of constructivism, learners are active agents in the learning process, and learning can be defined as the process of constructing new knowledge, not just absorbing it or assimilating into existing substrata of experience or understanding. In this way, learning can be understood in terms of the production of knowledge, if only for a single user.

The constructivist approach also rejects the deficit model, insofar as it approaches learners as active agents who possess both the capacity and the tools to produce knowledge themselves. It could be said, following the scholar of museum education, John Falk, that learners can only be taught what they already know.[34] Or, put slightly differently, that learners can only learn what they *almost* already know. They have tools and skills that are poised to learn and, when faced with a new circumstance—a math test, an unfamiliar passage of a text, a strange city—they can put those skills to work to construct new knowledge and learn something.

For constructivists, knowledge is not just something one produces but something one also uses. Educational theorists John Seely Brown, Allan Collins, and Paul Duguid explain, "It may be more useful to consider conceptual knowledge as, in some ways, similar to a set of tools." Tools, however, are not generic. Rather, tools "reflect the cumulative wisdom of the culture in which they are used and the insights and experience of individuals. Their meaning is not invariant but a product of negotiation within the community."[35] To learn how to use a tool or apply an idea requires learning the tool in context and in conversation over the meaning of the tool. There are conceptual tools—like, say, knowledge of Ladino, an understanding of the difference between the Oral Torah and the Written Torah, an ambivalence toward the divine, an attachment to tradition—that appear to circulate widely in Jewish communities. How people construct knowledge out of new experiences depends a great deal on their ability to contextualize new experiences in light of prior knowledge.

Take, for example, someone lighting Chanukah candles for the first time. They might have no knowledge of the technicalities hashed out between the rabbis of the Talmud and whether one should light all eight candles on each night, when to light them, or whether one should begin lighting with the rightmost or leftmost candle. They might not even know that some Jewish communities consider these to be significant debates. But they might have candles and a Chanukah menorah, and they probably know that lighting candles is what one does as part of the celebration. Even if they are alone at the moment of lighting, they might call upon other cultural knowledge to do what they intend to: they have probably lit candles before, and they have a sense of how to do so safely. They might have seen photos of people lighting candles, or they might have a prayerbook on a distant shelf that contains instructions. They know it is dark outside and that darkness often calls for light. They know it is wintertime and cold, so fire might seem to be in order. They might Google "instructions for lighting Chanukah candles" and find an online recording of the blessings, and they might read them in transliteration or not at all. They might have nine candles or just one. But if they know it is Chanukah and they are lighting candles to honor that moment, they are putting knowledge into action while also producing new knowledge for themselves about the holiday by relying on what they know about the holiday.

Sociocultural approaches to learning, as advanced by scholars like Jean Lave and Barbara Rogoff, emphasize the role of cultural resources in learning.[36] Rather than emphasizing the construction of knowledge by individual learners, sociocultural theory situates learning in collective settings and tends to emphasize the ways in which learning relies on networks of people and resources both material and conceptual. To appreciate how people construct knowledge socioculturally is to understand that the individual ability to learn, though it often seems quite private, is infused by social concerns and other actors. For example Barbara Rogoff's study of Girl Scout cookie sellers argued that the sale of cookies lay at the heart of a network of knowledge held by a number of different actors, each of whom contributed to the act of the sale.[37] Parents knew how to map out a route for delivering the cookies. Siblings helped make change at the point of sale, and so on. Conceived as a collective effort, no single person "knew" how to sell cookies. Rather, the network learned how to undertake it by collectivizing the effort. Similarly, Jean Lave and Etienne Wenger argued for an understanding of learning that they called "situated."[38] Learning, they found, did not happen in the abstract or as the result of efforts of an individual agent. Instead, learning happened in cultural and social settings in which they could draw on the resources of others in addition to their own. Midwives, to take one of their examples, learned to be midwives by apprenticing with other midwives, both by observing but also by providing meaningful assistance. They learned the practices of midwifery and became midwives themselves by working with other midwives. For Lave and Wenger, learning was always "situated" in social and cultural contexts. As such, it was a collective effort.

In a related realm, sociologist Howard Becker argued that artists alone did not produce art. Instead, he coined the concept of "art worlds" to describe the social production of art. Art, he argued, resulted from the efforts of an array of actors including artists, but also critics, scholars, collectors, museums, and so on, all of whom contributed to the effort that made something "art."[39] Similarly, musicologist Tia DiNora's study of Beethoven emphasized his uncanny knack for composition but also traced his rise to fame through networks of cultural patronage, high society, and the worlds of European elite cultural production. He was brilliant, and perhaps a genius, but DiNora found that his ability to flourish could not be attributed to his efforts alone.[40] Another musicologist, Christopher Small, coined the term "musicking" to refer to the array of cultural practices—from strumming guitars to selling tickets—that share in the production of musical culture.[41] So, too, we might think of Judaism or Jewishness as fueled by individuals but enabled in collaboration with others, embedded in social contexts, and not solely the domain of individual cognitive effort.

The sociocultural approach to learning emerged alongside the formulation of the "extended mind," which understands cognition as interactive, social, and reliant upon more than pure brain power. From philosophy, Andy Clark and David Chalmers asked, "Where does the mind stop and the rest of the world begin?"[42] It is a good question, meant to provoke consideration of how people think about the parameters of their minds and their selves. When I write down a grocery list or look up the answer to a question on Wikipedia, is my thinking confined to my mind? Does Wikipedia or a grocery list enable my mind to work, or is it a necessary part of how I think and thus part of my mind? This is quite an abstract question, of course, but it is a provocative one for people who think about learning because it invites a critical reconsideration about the array of tools that we use to make the world known and knowable. It is possible to think of grocery lists or Wikipedia as crutches or cheats for people who cannot remember things "on their own." Or, it is possible to think of them as elements of an "extended mind" that questions the very premise of knowing something "on one's own."

In an effort to explain this in terms of learning, Learning scientist Roy Pea developed the concept of "distributed cognition," which anthropologist Edwin Hutchins refers to as "distributed intelligence."[43] Both of these terms and concepts, however, refer to the fact that knowledge is achieved through collective efforts, both coordinated and uncoordinated, between people and things in order to achieve understandings that enable people to solve problems or reach new insights. Hutchins made his discovery while watching a team of sailors steer a navy ship. He found that no single person or instrument could manage the complete task on its own, but by working together and sharing information, the sailors could achieve the task. We do not need to answer Clark and Chalmers's question with precision to appreciate the potency of their provocation. If we don't know where our mind stops and where the world begins, then we have to reconsider what and how we think about what learning is, but also about the people called "learners." If they are not individual, stand-alone agents responsible for their own learning, who are they and how do we understand what they are doing?

Ironically, Jewish life overflows with examples of the sociocultural qualities of learning, from the requirement that ten adults serve as a quorum for public prayer to the cacophonous nature of learning in a beit midrash. The pages of the Talmud offer a graphic and visual textual example of precisely this dimension of the social dimension of knowledge, as they present a variety of interwoven voices and commentary presented as a dialogue among people who may have lived hundreds of years apart. A sefer Torah, too, could be considered an example of an "extended mind," insofar as it orchestrates people's movement within the context of a synagogue prayer service. When it rises, people rise. As explained in chapter 3, a sefer Torah is more than a book, and its meaning is larger than the sum of the words on its parchment. Its materiality plays a significant role in how people behave while it is in the room, but it also allows people to think and to learn about their connection to its contents, its form, and one another.

But we could take a more quotidian example as well: Consider a young woman who is studying for her bat mitzvah. She has been in Hebrew school for years, as per the arrangement with her synagogue.[44] In addition to her ongoing studies in Hebrew school, she has also been studying with a tutor and meeting with her synagogue's rabbi. She has also been going to her friend's b'nai mitzvah with a keen eye for what aspects of the ceremony and party she would like to adopt and which she would not. She meets with her parents regularly to discuss everything from invitations to different ways they might want to honor various members of the family. Meanwhile her parents have been exploring caterers and party venues and talking to DJs and photographers about their roles in the party. Though it is the young woman who becomes a bat mitzvah on a particular date, there are any number of other agents—both human and nonhuman—that facilitate the event: parents and siblings, family and friends, technical experts (tutors, DJs, photographers, florists), the synagogue building, the Hebrew school, the sefer Torah from which she will read, and so on. Although she is the person marking the beginning of her adulthood in the Jewish community through this ritual, she does not learn to become an adult on her own. She does so in context and through collaboration with both people and things.[45]

Together, sociocultural and constructivist approaches introduce some new frameworks for conceptualizing Jewish learning and placing it at the center of the production and transmission of Jewish knowledge. Approaching learning as both socially constructed and culturally contextual removes it from whatever might happen within particular programmatic or institutional frameworks and opens new avenues for understanding learning not just as the domain of teachers or schools but as central to the fabric and practice of Jewish life. Learning is not merely a matter of acquiring the appropriate responses to stimuli, and neither is it wholly internal to individuals and their minds or brains. Rather, learning is tied to the qualities of social life. It refers to the processes by which people construct knowledge and the practices that enable people to learn from and with other people and phenomena. Learning is what learners do, whether or not their teachers are pulling their own weight. And it happens everywhere: on the street, in synagogue, at home around the dinner table, on sports fields and smartphones, on social media platforms, and in whispered secrets. It even happens in classrooms. Learning makes it possible to ask questions about what people know and how they know it. It invites opportunities to consider the nature of ritual, the dynamics of community, or the practices that might embolden creativity of expression or interpretation.

The Power to Know

As is always the case with matters of knowledge, this book's effort to center learning is also laden with questions of power. The deficit theory predetermined that what people knew was not sufficient, while the instrumental approach to Jewish education held that what people learned did not matter as long as they assumed behaviors preferred by educators. The construction of Jewish education around the concept of an "educated Jew" began with three assertions. First, that such a figure existed if only as an ideal case, and second that becoming an "educated Jew" was broadly desirable. But the third assertion is most troubling with regard to the question of power: that the people who constructed the figure of an "educated Jew" imposed their concepts of who that figure was and what they knew on Jewish education, broadly envisioned. All three of these approaches proved influential in the development of Jewish education but none acknowledged the power at play in their efforts.

As philosopher Michel Foucault explained, someone with significant facts at their disposal has limited access to power by virtue of their mastery of a domain of content knowledge. But he argued that a deeper power lies in the ability to construct what he called a "discursive regime" or an "episteme."[46] Epistemes are bodies of knowledge discreetly bound like disciplines. The term also refers to the ways in which things become knowable in the first place. For example, the concept of kashrut categorizes food and foodways into permissible and forbidden groups. It organizes what, how, and when people eat, but also what constitutes the very category of "food" and how to eat it. Similarly, the structure of time divides days of the week or months of the year into discreet entitles, and so on.[47] The power of Talmud scholar Max Strassfeld's book exploring gender in the Talmud rests not just in its recovery of more categories of gender than were previously known but in its rediscovery of an episteme that acknowledged a range of genders and gender expressions and not just the typical two.[48] Having knowledge is akin to the ability to play a game according to the rules; creating an episteme is like having the power to write and rewrite the rules of the game to direct play.[49] For Foucault, power resides not in one's ability to access an objective truth but in the ability to establish the rules of an episteme that make it possible for things to be known or to be true. Even truth, Foucault wrote, "isn't outside power."[50]

Jewish Studies is an episteme. So is Jewish education. So is the deficit theory. So are musical genres and styles of art or fashion. So are science and religion and law. People studied Judaism and Jewish culture for centuries before the invention of the field known as Jewish Studies. People taught and learned and wrote long before the invention of Jewish education. But the emergence of these terms to refer to particular ways of organizing the production and transmission of knowledge has proven powerful because they shape our understanding of how knowledge work occurs or ought to happen. Investments in Jewish education and Jewish Studies as two distinct epistemes are investments in certain relationships between power and knowledge. Specifically, they employ the power to determine what is knowable, what kinds of knowledge are valuable, who is a reliable bearer of that knowledge, and who is not. In theory and ideology, Jewish Studies has followed Jacob Neusner in arguing for the value of a detached knower and propositional knowledge, while Jewish education has tried to inculcate knowers engaged in a different project that has privileged procedural knowledge about how to live Jewishly. In the process, they have established rules and norms of knowing that, in turn, shape Jewish life, how it is understood, lived, and known.

Certainly, the power that Foucault wrote about can be manipulated. It can open people to charges of coercion or "indoctrination," "brainwashing," or, less nefariously but still problematically, taking advantage of the vulnerabilities of learners.[51] Birthright Israel has received its share of criticism on this score, as have other educational approaches that rely on immersive methods to generate short-duration and high-emotion experiences.[52] Scholars of Jewish

Studies have also been accused of using their academic positions to advance political agendas of one sort or another. Anxieties about indoctrination (which, by the way, is harder than it seems if we understand learners as something other than empty vessels) are telling. They reveal that people take the production and transmission of knowledge seriously because it is, at the end of the day, a locus of power. Accounting for power makes the opposition between Jewish education and Jewish Studies murkier in terms of their respective and presumed influence over young minds, and at the same time both epistemes become more significant because of the power they generate (imaginary and real) in shaping the foundations of how people know about Jewish life in the first place.

This chapter is arguing for learning. As an engagement with knowledge, learning is also subject to power. Even sociocultural frameworks have to account for power because every context, every culture makes distinctions between different ways of knowing and different kinds of knowledge. Where does power lie in Jewish life? Does the power to *know* lie in the academy, with its programs of Jewish Studies and their Neusnerian commitments to intellectual and scholarly pursuits? Does that power lie with Jewish education, with its urgency and its claims about how best to ensure the future of the Jewish people? Of course the answer is neither. Or both. To ask these questions in this way reinscribes the binary that lodges Jewish knowledge within one of two frameworks and forecloses the possibility that others might arise or exist already. More to the point of this chapter, asking those questions in those ways locates the action of education with the teachers, scholars, and institutions, not with learners or learning, which is where the action always is.

Turning to learning reminds us that power not only oppresses but makes knowledge possible in the first place. In this regard, it can be thought of as creative and even pleasurable. As Foucault argued, "What makes power hold good, what makes it accepted, is simply the fact that it not only weighs on us as a force that says no but traverses and produces things, induces pleasure, forms knowledge, produces discourse. It needs to be considered as a productive network that runs through the whole social body, much more than as a negative instance whose function is repression."[53] Understanding power only as that which is exerted downward and oppresses is, for Foucault, to misunderstand it. Power is also productive, generative, and even creative. Tethered as it is to knowledge and the creation of epistemes, power makes knowledge possible, and thus makes learning possible, as well.

If the tensions between Jewish Studies and Jewish education can be understood in terms of power, and power produces epistemes and discourse that are central to understanding who Jews are, then both can be understood as projects committed to producing and reproducing Jewish life, culture, memory, history, ritual, religion, practice, and people in ways that extend far beyond their respective domains. As structures for the production and transmission of knowledge, Jewish Studies and Jewish education make the epistemes that make Jewish life knowable and, in the process, make it possible for people to know what it means to be Jewish. Both produced propositional and procedural knowledge. Both have laid foundations for making new ways of being Jewish possible by making them knowable, and thus both have helped create conditions in which people can become knowers by learning.

On Jewish Learning

Centering learning offers an alternative approach to understanding the relationship between knowledge and power in Jewish education and Jewish Studies. Both fields emerged in modernity to provide structure and vision for organizing the production and transmission of knowledge according to a set of largely unwritten and uninterrogated rules. The same is true of many of the examples in the case studies that constitute chapters 2 and 3. But things are changing and changing fast.

Our twenty-first century is saturated with information and abundant in sources. Without much effort, it is possible to know just about anything about how, why, or when to do anything Jewish. Information is readily and widely available: When the Sabbath begins according to one's precise location, full versions of many of the classics of Jewish thought and literature, biographical sketches of famous people, music, narratives, and documentary films. And if it is not already present in your language of choice, there are ample translation platforms that can render it passably. Interested in a vegan challah recipe? Traditional Rosh Hashana foods for Yemenite Jews? The source of the prohibition on Jews getting tattoos? How to conduct a Passover Seder for small children? What the Rambam had to say about repentance? What Jewish celebrities name their children? Ten great shows with Jewish themes to watch from the comfort of your own couch? Much of the knowledge that Rambam organized in the Mishna Torah and that Josef Karo compiled into the Shulchan Aruch can also be found online, hyperlinked to their Talmudic and biblical sources. With a few keystrokes or swipes, it is possible to find a Hebrew lesson, a Jewish date, a b-mitzvah tutor, a GIF, a meme, a podcast, a Star of David necklace, an ugly Chanukah sweater, or whether a certain public figure identifies as Jewish. The internet has made it easy to access all kinds of things from the immanently practical to the utterly arcane—but nearly all of it is available with a few taps on a screen or by hailing the virtual assistant of your choice.

This insight hardly seems worth making: before learners could access them, all of these sources were compiled, copied, digitized, coded, linked, and made searchable (and findable) by people committed to making the knowledge of these sources available at scale. To watch a viral video, someone had to film it. For someone to learn their b-mitzvah portion with the help of an online recording, someone else had to record it. The same is true for undergraduates looking for source material for papers, anyone looking for the Hebrew date for a *yahrzeit*, looking to hear a sermon, or wanting to learn a new melody to an old song. New websites, compendia of sources, fiction, nonfiction, short films, podcasts, music, publications, reference sites, and countless queries posted to online forums and dutifully answered by volunteers have contributed to a rich ecosystem of Jewish knowledge that is more widely available, more representative of the diversity of Jewish experience, and broader than any library previously imaginable. In a radical continuity with ages past, all of this content has been *produced* in order to be *transmitted*.

And, of course, all of this is made possible by the marvels and manipulations of technologies big and small from fragments of code to satellites, in addition to all of the infrastructure in the middle that often works to obscure the materiality of our technologically and informationally mediated world.[54] The production and transmission of Jewish knowledge have been highly mediated for centuries—through the sensorial dimensions of food and song, through the textuality of scrolls, folios, journals, newspapers, and magazines, or the physical properties of buildings or neighborhoods. Jewish education in a new key draws on these earlier modes of mediation and has come to rely on GPS and streaming technologies for source material, to say nothing about email, text messages, digital calendars, or any of the other modalities of communication that people use to do the daily work of Jewish education.

The conditions for Jewish learning are reciprocal and reinforcing. They are less a sharp pivot away from long-developing trends in the production and transmission of knowledge than a transposition of them. To hear Jewish education in a new key means tuning in to new and emergent harmonies that might make the older tonal center sound dissonant. There is room for dissonance, and sometimes dissonance is useful and even beautiful. Shifting the focus of Jewish education toward learning and away from institutions and instruction does not mean ignoring or destroying those structures. Fortunately, it is not an either-or proposition. Schools and synagogues, museums and film festivals, criticism and scholarship, literature, poetry, food, family, folklore should continue to serve as the material from which people construct Jewish knowledge. But in a new key, such elements will no longer anchor the melody or ground the harmony. The notes won't disappear, but their role will change from a place of resolution to a source of tension. Organizing Jewish education around learners and learning requires adapting to new contexts and new surroundings in which older approaches do not harmonize so readily with contemporary practices. It will require muting some of the inclinations, theories, and approaches that served a prior movement but might have fallen out of tune.

Learning is happening anyway and everywhere. Can we hear it? Can we tune the available educational structures to it? Whose voices does it make audi-

ble, and whose does it silence? What once harmonious sounds are now dissonant, and what dissonances can now be heard as harmonies? Does it provide
greater range? What new approaches, structures, instruments might be needed?
How expansive can the chorus be to allow for the creativity of learners across
a range of identities and experiences? Whose Jewish cultural resources can
shape what and how people know? Can both Jewish education and Jewish Studies allow for more fluid and dynamic ways of knowing such that they can
encourage, honor, inspire, challenge, and otherwise allow for all the ways in
which people learn to be Jewish?

In their best versions, Jewish education and Jewish Studies have represented two distinct but overlapping sets of responses to these questions. Jewish
education, in its varied modern forms, from the formal and institutional
(schools of all kinds and orientations) to the more informal but no less informa-
tive (websites, podcasts, curricula written to support recordings of Ladino folk
music or documentary films), can be characterized by efforts to institutional-
ize responses to these questions such that students might develop a deeper
appreciation of Jewish knowledge and thus strengthen their own commitments
to Jewish life. Jewish Studies, too, has evolved to meet these questions, chiefly
by promoting a detached, scholarly approach to the study of Jewish life.

Despite the best intentions of scholars like Neusner, they have a very limited
ability to control what their participants learn in each context. By focusing on
their own intentions and efforts, they substantively avoided any accounting of
what and how students might be learning in their classes. Both Jewish education and Jewish Studies have dedicated so much effort to define their own distinct responses to the questions above that they have largely ignored the
question of how people learn. Hearing Jewish education in a new key shifts the
locus of action regarding the production and transmission of Jewish knowledge away from the intentions, no matter how altruistic, divinely inspired,
kind, or otherwise well-intentioned they might be. It will, hopefully, encourage theorists of Jewish education and Jewish Studies to reconsider and reframe
their efforts around *how* their audiences learn and less around *what* scholars
and teachers think they have to teach their students. Focusing on learning
means attending to the ways in which people come to know about Jewish life
in ways that cannot be determined by the ways in which their teachers present
knowledge to them. Teachers can try to instruct their students as precisely as
possible, but there is simply no guarantee that the encounter they construct is
going to go the way that they intend. At the very least, the terms of a given
learning encounter must be understood as negotiable. And if the encounter is
unstable, so is the knowledge that it has been created to construct.

In the context of a society where learners have access to knowledge through
their nearly ubiquitous digital devices, the authority and ideology of either
scholars of Jewish Studies or professional Jewish educators are much diminished.

Educators already played a relatively small role in the lives of most of their students, but even that portion of the knowledge marketplace has been made even smaller because of the number of sources to which people have access. How people construct, produce, transmit, embed, embody, or explain their understandings of how or why they do what they do or believe what they believe or feel what they feel is only ever partially accounted for by what their teachers intended. This is not a lament about teaching or teachers. But it is an attempt to reckon directly and honestly with Jewish education in a new key that draws on a fuller accounting of all of the ways, settings, and modalities in which people learn.

Neither Jewish Studies nor Jewish education can control the outcomes of their efforts. Perhaps this is why efforts to define them and disagreements between them have been so impassioned. The strength of their assertions exists in inverse proportion to the solidity of their imagined premises. The distinction between them is almost too alluring to resist, even among those who wish to critique or disrupt it. Andrew Bush opens his volume on Jewish Studies with a reference to "learning Jews" (as in Jews who learn), a phrase he attributed to Jacob Neusner.[55] Bush uses Neusner's term as a foil against which to launch his own examination of "studying Jews" as the principal activity of Jewish Studies. "Studying Jews . . . has meant taking Jews and what they do as an object of study, for the purpose of producing, testing, and disseminating knowledge about Jews, regardless of who happens to be doing the studying."[56] Bush's study of Jewish Studies complicates the field, its histories and practices, and ultimately arrives at a conclusion neighboring the one advanced here: that Jewish Studies recognizes "the object of study as a subject in its own right, giving voice to Jews in the understanding and articulation of their own historical experience."[57] Still, he could not resist appealing to the straw man of "learning" to launch his study of "studying." Cautious and supple as he is with his terminology, his treatment of "learning" reinforces the constructed division between Jewish education and Jewish Studies by imagining Jewish Studies to be the terrain of the studying, while Jewish education is the realm of learning. Maybe it was a simple rhetorical move, but his framing reinforces the idea that Jewish Studies cares too little for learning and Jewish education cares too little for studying. This is a reduction, at best. Jewish educators, of course, generally try to teach *something*, while Jewish Studies professors and scholars teach and write so that people might learn something from their efforts. Bush understood this, writing that "the strengthening of solidarities through Jewish Studies between those studying Jews, whoever they are, and the Jews whom they study contributes to the more general humanistic enterprise of the university."[58] Even though he spends the remainder of his book complicating this very notion, his opening gambit nevertheless played on long-standing and well-rehearsed caricatures of the two fields and, in the process, reinforced associated assumptions about learning, the parochial cousin of studying.

I labor on Bush's introduction here because this book is in direct conversation with his, trying as it does to understand Jewish education within and alongside Jewish Studies. As a result, I am interested in how Jewish Studies "thinks" about education and, specifically: learning. I argue that the relationship between learning and studying is not oppositional but compatible, and often in ways that make advocates of Jewish Studies slightly uncomfortable. Studying Jewish Studies by centering learning disrupts and brings Jewish Studies and Jewish education into closer proximity to each other and more direct connection to their historical antecedents. This effort invites people who take pride in their knowledge to adopt a different posture toward their interlocutors that diminishes the emphasis on outcomes and objectivity and instead creates space for people to carve out their own pathways through the mountains of available sources, insights, and knowledge. It also asserts that people have both the cultural resources and the cultural contexts from which to begin building meaningful, informed, active Jewish lives. Allowing them the dignity of doing so and creating conditions under which people might engage in the production and transmission of knowledge might be the first step to hearing Jewish education in a new key.

Focusing on learning is an effort to claw back a bit of the agency and creativity that have been lost during the instrumentalization of Jewish education and its emphasis on outcomes and making up for deficits. It is part of an attempt to balance the scales of power and draw a more comprehensive account of how people produce and transmit knowledge across the range of settings, contexts, and experiences that compose their Jewish lives. It shifts the balance away from schools and institutions and onto the ways in which knowledge work has been central to Jewish life. The preoccupation with identitarian and scholarly outcomes of Jewish education and Jewish Studies has, in some respects, drawn attention away from the role that knowledge work has played in Jewish life across historical and cultural contexts. While it would be anachronistic to claim that "Jewish education" has been a historical constant, it would not be inaccurate to conclude that concerns about what Jewish people know have been central to the constitution and reinvention of Jewish communal life.

The production and transmission of knowledge have long been at the heart of Jewish culture and Jewish life. Schools and programs, curricula and pedagogies, scholarship and study can assume some of the responsibility for the production and transmission of knowledge, but until Jewish education and Jewish Studies can account for learners and learning, they will remain locked in a struggle over whose ideas are better and generally ignorant of how those ideas become meaningful to anyone else. Attending to learning may invert the typical narratives of Jewish Studies, Jewish culture, and Jewish teaching over time. It will center learning in and as Jewish culture. It cannot be a driver of impacts, despite efforts to charge it with the duty of ensuring the survival of the Jewish People. Casting education as the mechanism for sustaining the Jewish People—capital J, capital P—has ironically revealed a profound lack of faith or confidence in Jewish people—capital J, *lowercase* p—to learn on their own. But they have been producing and transmitting knowledge all along, throughout history.

Usually, learning does not take the form of public performances, widely hailed works of scholarship, or achievement tests. More often, it takes the form of bedtime rituals, shared meals, and familial or communal lore. It is the process of producing and transmitting knowledge about what it is to be Jewish and how to be Jewish, if only for oneself. Most learning is never published, shared widely, or turned into a program. Rather, it is retained and shared with intimates when appropriate, and, as such, it refers to the process by which people figure out how to live their lives. Learning cannot be confined to a school or program, and it cannot be isolated like a statistical variable. It is coincident with Jewish life. It is what people do when they are engaging in Jewish life. When they are eating or laughing or arguing. It is what they are doing when they are schmoozing in the back of *shul* or ditching Hebrew school. Learning is what Jewish people do because it is what people do. It is not a source of Jewish life because it *is* Jewish life, and Jewish education can begin to recalibrate itself once people learn how to hear it in a new key.

Conclusion

Neusner knew it. "Judaism does not happen in a classroom," he wrote. "And to begin with it is not learned principally in books."[1] He's right about that. It is learned in people, by people, for people. He knew that even the most meticulous studies would not move people unless they were prepared to be moved. And he knew that no amount of research could surface the learnings acquired in the world outside the archive, the library, the classroom. He knew that the production and transmission of knowledge was, for better and for worse, not an affair for either Jewish education or Jewish Studies and that most people learned what they needed to without consulting their teachers or textbooks. Education is everywhere.

Undoubtedly, the argument of this book will be met by some who find it not academically rigorous enough, not steeped enough in the "traditional sources" of their choosing (empirical, historical, rabbinic), or otherwise inadequate. It may not convince anyone that Jewish Studies is Jewish education, and it might not succeed in laying out a new way of thinking about their shared concerns in terms of the production and transmission of knowledge. For some it will be too theoretical and for others not theoretical enough. It will not answer the question facing countless Jewish educators about what to teach in school tomorrow, and it will not calm the nerves of Jewish Studies scholars about the proximity of their work to the ways their students might choose to engage in the world.

Considering questions of power and context, of the social, sensual, and mediated aspects of knowledge, hopefully opens up new ways for exploring and understanding how people make meaning of Jewish knowledge and how people make Jewish knowledge itself. If we get stuck on the Neusnerian Fallacy and try to parse the difference between learning about Judaism and learning to be Jewish, we will merely reproduce old epistemes of science and modernity. So too will doubling down on particular educational outcomes that are nearly impossible to measure, assess, or ensure. This book has been an exploration of Jewish knowledge making in order to try to envision something different for the future and to offer new frames for understanding long-running debates.

I realize that this might make some of my colleagues in both Jewish Studies and Jewish education nervous, as if I'm proposing that we abandon all of what has come before us and simply allow all learners to decide on their own, willy-nilly, what matters as Jewish knowledge. To be absolutely clear, that is not what I am proposing here. The forms of Jewish knowledge that Jewish communities have inherited—culinary, sonic, literary, embodied, intellectual, practice-based, and so on—are and always have been rich and vital. Attending to what people learn from them opens those same sources up to new directions of creativity and invention through renewed, though not always expected, engagements. It means emphasizing the connections between the ways in which people learn about being Jewish and the ways that people learn to be Jewish. Centering learning does not mean dismissing all of the knowledge that has come before, but it does mean recalibrating people's relationships to it around a new appreciation for how it is transmitted and produced.

Though I hope we've clarified a number of concerns pertaining to the production and transmission of Jewish knowledge, we've not arrived at a definitive answer about what Jewish education is. Raymond Williams told us it was going to be this way (see the introduction). Williams told us that the differences and divergences in meanings were going to be more productive, more illustrative, and more generative than pat, firm answers. As Raymond Williams observed about dictionaries, we can learn more by exploiting the gaps in our knowledge than we can on the firm terrain of facts because there is something to discover in them that seems missing from the places where we feel certain. Differences reveal what we do not know, and they point us in the directions of what is possible to know and to learn. If everything made sense all the time, we would not need to learn anything at all.

Thankfully, the world does not make sense. It is rife with absurdity and tragedy and hilarity and evil and glory and awe and equanimity. We are fortunate to experience moments of sublimity and times of profound revulsion, and to be faced with something new and unexpected is truly one of life's pleasures. To encounter something wholly new is to be shown that we do not know all that we think we do and that we can still learn more. The world is filled with knowledge, and for those of us involved in that enterprise, our job as scholars and teachers is to encourage people to encounter it, metabolize it, poke and prod and discover that the world as they knew it has to make room for something that did not previously belong. The work of Jewish education and Jewish Studies, when done well, changes how people understand the world and their place in it. That is no easy feat. It requires putting oneself (or one's students) in a position where one knows that one does not know, and to begin there. Let us use this new key to turn our attention to learning, away from structures that organize knowledge work around teaching and outcomes, and toward greater care for and understanding of how learners also produce and transmit knowledge.

So, let's follow the Passover Haggadah, one of the most popular Jewish educational texts. The centerpiece of the Haggadah is the partial retelling of the story of the biblical exodus from Egypt. That section begins not with "once upon a time" or "a long time ago in a galaxy far, far away," but with four questions and one gentle exhortation, "go and learn."

Let's go.

Acknowledgments

This book, like every other book, was not a solo effort. I sat myself in the chairs at home, cafés, libraries, and for a single long weekend in the Santa Cruz mountains, but the ideas, references, and everything else that is worthwhile about this book derived from conversations and suggestions with so many people over years—well before I sat down to write the proposal for this project. I chose the words and their order, but the ideas emerged over time and gestated in whatever kinds of magic make new knowledge emerge between people.

My colleagues in the Stanford Graduate School of Education have taught me more than I could have imagined, and my conversations with them have led to so many productive avenues of thought and so many new directions for exploration. Similarly, my colleagues in Jewish Studies at Stanford and elsewhere have helped to crystalize many of the insights in this book. Simply, I would not think the way I do about the things I do were it not for my affinity for and engagement with these two groups of people.

Along the way, lots of people gave me space to talk and gave specific help, when asked. Daniella Farah, Aaron Hahn Tapper, Hillary Falb Kalisman, Eitan Kensky, Rafa Kern, Hannah Kober, Jonathan Krasner, Matthias Lehmann, Akiba Lerner, Jon Levisohn, Jessica Marglin, Marva Shalev Marom, Ray McDermott, Rachel Smith, Sara Smith, Ehud Tsemach, and Laura Yares. Maya Benton came to the rescue with the cover image. My students Jon Ball, Xavi Bugos, Rafa Kern, and Tom Nachtigal served as experimental subjects for so many of the half-baked ideas that ended up here. Nathaniel Deutsch gave the manuscript a brilliantly close read and has been so extraordinarily generous with his insight on Jews and Jewishness more generally (and quick to respond to the occasional random inquiry via text message). Darren Kleinberg has heard more versions of this book than anyone should, but he still patiently read drafts, offered comments, and helped me think through so much of what's here.

I'm grateful for the inspiration and direction of Godspeed You! Black Emperor and Sunn O))), Lee "Scratch" Perry, and random YouTube compilations of dub reggae, which, together, supplied the soundtrack.

I am extraordinarily indebted to Deborah Dash Moore and Jonathan Boyarin, editors of the Key Words series, who read a few proposals and a long, substantially less well-developed draft. They offered just the right measure of criticism and encouragement, which, I hope, has led to the book you have in front of you. Along with two anonymous peer reviewers, they pushed in just the right places to help open up space for the book to grow in new and productive directions. Rutgers University Press acquisitions editors Elisabeth Maselli, Christopher Rios-Sueverkruebbe, and Carah Naseem all helped move this book along its way.

Certainly, this book owes a massive debt to my parents: Vicky and Stuart Kelman are both lifelong Jewish educators in their own rights. My mother helped invent the field of Jewish "family education," for which our immediate family was something of a living laboratory, and in the process she taught my siblings and me (and countless other families) to think about learning outside of schools and synagogues. My father had the audacity to edit a book entitled *What We Know about Jewish Education*. It took me this long to figure out that the title was an invitation, not a conclusion.

Finally, my partner Eva has taken on more than her share of the household duties so that I could run down to the library or sit in the archives or disappear for hours on end and finish this book. I am grateful for her patience, encouragement, curiosity, partnership, and masterful parenting. And Bella and Malachi: When you ask me to explain just what it is that I do all day while I talk about "education: blah, blah, blah." Maybe this book is an answer.

Notes

INTRODUCTION

1. Tehilla Becker, Brian Blumenband, Frayda Gonshor Cohen, Annie Jollymore, and Natasha Nefedyeva, "An Invitation to Action: Findings and Implications across the Career Trajectories of Jewish Educators Study" (Washington, DC: CASJE, 2021), https://www.casje.org/sites/default/files/docs/casje_synthesis_report_designed _final._11.15.21.pdf; Tehilla Becker, Brian Blumenband, Annie Jollymore, Jeffrey Kress, Natasha Nefedyeva, Alex Pomson, and Wendy Rosov, "Preparing for Entry: Fresh Perspectives on How and Why People Become Jewish Educators" (Washington, DC: CASJE, 2021), https://www.casje.org/sites/default/files/docs/casje_p4e_final_report _july_2021.pdf; Rosov Consulting, "On the Journey: Concepts That Support a Study of the Professional Trajectories of Jewish Educators" (Washington, DC: CASJE, 2019), https://www.casje.org/sites/default/files/docs/otj_casje_working_paper_final_3_6 _19.pdf.

2. David Bryfman, *Experience and Jewish Education* (Los Angeles: Torah Aura Productions, 2013); Barry Chazan, "What Is 'Informal Jewish Education'?," in *Principles and Pedagogies in Jewish Education*, ed. Barry Chazan (Cham: Springer, 2022), 51–63, https://doi.org/10.1007/978-3-030-83925-3_7.

3. Even the Jewish Federations, the long-established centralized philanthropic and social service organizations of the Jewish community, include Jewish education in their mission and vision statements. For example, the UJA-Federation of New York includes it on their website: "Jewish Education" (UJA-Federation of New York, n.d.), https://www.ujafedny.org/our-work/strengthening-jewish-life/https.

4. Raymond Williams, *Keywords* (New York: Oxford University Press, 1983), 87. Incidentally, he made a similar observation about the words "alienation" (33) and "empirical" (115).

5. Williams, *Keywords*, 17, emphasis added.

6. Williams, *Keywords*, 24.

7. This is a major component of Heilman's study of adult study circles. Samuel Heilman, *The People of the Book: Drama, Fellowship, and Religion* (Chicago: University of Chicago Press, 1983).

8. For example, see Daniela R. P. Weiner, "Tendentious Texts: Holocaust Representations and Nation-Rebuilding in East German, Italian, and West German Schoolbooks, 1949–1989," *Journal of Modern Jewish Studies* 17, no. 3 (2018): 342–360. For

comparative studies of textbooks across a range of settings, see Patricia Bromley, John W. Meyer, and Francisco O. Ramirez, "Student-Centeredness in Social Science Textbooks, 1970–2008: A Cross-National Study," *Social Forces* 90, no. 2 (2011): 547–570, https://doi.org/10.1093/sf/sor004; Julia Lerch, Patricia Bromley, Francisco O. Ramirez, and John W. Meyer, "The Rise of Individual Agency in Conceptions of Society: Textbooks Worldwide, 1950–2011," *International Sociology* 32, no. 1 (2017): 38–60, https://doi.org/10.1177/0268580916675525; John W. Meyer, Patricia Bromley, and Francisco O. Ramirez, "Human Rights in Social Science Textbooks: Cross-National Analyses, 1970–2008," *Sociology of Education* 83, no. 2 (2010): 111–134, https://doi.org/10.1177/0038040710367936.

9. Ephraim Kanarfogel, *Jewish Education and Society in the High Middle Ages* (Detroit, MI: Wayne State University Press, 1992); Moshe Aberbach, *Jewish Education and History: Continuity, Crisis and Change* (New York: Routledge, 2009). There are many, many other works of scholarship that apply the term "education" to ancient or medieval settings.

10. Aḥad Ha'am, "Hachinuch Haleumi," in *'Al Parashat Derakhim*, Hotsa'ah ḥadashah vol. 4 (Berlin: Yudisher Ferlag, 1930); Rachel Elboim-Dror, *Ha-Ḥinukh Ha-'Ivri Be-Erets-Yiśra'el*, 2 vols., Sifriyah Le-Toldot Ha-Yishuv Ha-Yehudi Be-Erets-Yiśra'el (Yerushalayim: Yad Yitsḥak Ben-Tsevi, 1986).

11. Seymour Fox, Israel Scheffler, and Daniel Marom, eds., *Visions of Jewish Education* (New York: Cambridge University Press, 2003), 14.

12. Still, the keenest insights into the relationship between power and knowledge are from Michel Foucault: Foucault, *The Order of Things: An Archaeology of the Human Sciences* (New York: Vintage, 1970); Foucault, *Power/Knowledge: Selected Interviews and Other Writings, 1972–1977* (New York: Vintage, 1988); Foucault, *The Archaeology of Knowledge: And the Discourse on Language* (New York: Vintage, 2010).

13. Max K. Strassfeld, *Trans Talmud: Androgynes and Eunuchs in Rabbinic Literature* (Oakland: University of California Press, 2022).

14. Max Weber, "Science as a Vocation," *Daedalus* 87, no. 1 (1958): 111–134.

15. For one account of the distinction between scientific and religious ways of knowing, see Peter Harrison, *The Territories of Science and Religion*, repr. ed. (Chicago: University of Chicago Press, 2017). For accounts regarding American higher education, see George Marsden, *The Soul of the American University* (New York: Oxford University Press, 1996). See also Conrad Cherry, *Hurrying toward Zion: Universities, Divinity Schools, and American Protestantism* (Bloomington: Indiana University Press, 1995); Douglas Sloan, *Faith and Knowledge* (Louisville, KY: Westminster John Knox, 1994).

16. The degree to which this was by design or by accident remains the subject of much debate, discussion, and political foment. See, for example, George L. Mosse, *Confronting the Nation: Jewish and Western Nationalism*, Tauber Institute for the Study of European Jewry Series 16 (Hanover, NH: University Press of New England, 1993).

17. David Bezmozgis, *Natasha and Other Stories* (New York: Farrar, Straus and Giroux, 2004), 71.

18. For a classic statement to this effect, see Robert Alter, "What Jewish Studies Can Do," *Commentary*, October 1974. For a more recent indictment of Jewish Studies' communal connections, see Lila Corwin Berman, Kate Rosenblatt, and Ronit Y. Stahl, "Continuity Crisis: The History and Sexual Politics of an American Jewish Communal Project," *American Jewish History* 104, no. 2 (2020): 167–194, https://doi.org/10.1353/ajh .2020.0017.

19. Gilbert Ryle, "Knowing How and Knowing That: The Presidential Address," *Proceedings of the Aristotelian Society* 46 (1945): 1–16.

20. Philip H. Winne and Roger Azevedo, "Metacognition," in *The Cambridge Handbook of the Learning Sciences*, 2nd ed., ed. R. Keith Sawyer (New York: Cambridge University Press, 2014), 63–87.

21. Ryle, "Knowing How and Knowing That," 5.

22. Ryle, "Knowing How and Knowing That," 9.

23. Ann Swidler and Jorge Arditi, "The New Sociology of Knowledge," *Annual Review of Sociology* 20, no. 1 (1994): 305–329, https://doi.org/10.1146/annurev.so.20 .080194.001513. See also E. Doyle McCarthy, *Knowledge as Culture: The New Sociology of Knowledge* (London: Routledge, 2006).

CHAPTER 1 — ESTRANGED SIBLINGS

1. Consider its portrayal in the opening sequence of the Coen Brothers' 2009 film *A Serious Man*, in which an out-of-touch but clearly well-meaning older teacher (a classic caricature of the melamed) totters around a cinderblock Hebrew school classroom quizzing students on Hebrew conjugations while the film's protagonist listens to Jefferson Airplane's "White Rabbit" on a stealthily hidden transistor radio.

2. On Ultra-Orthodox Jewish schools, see Eliza Shapiro, Brian M. Rosenthal, and Jonah Markowitz, "In Hasidic Enclaves, Failing Private Schools Flush with Public Money," *New York Times*, September 11, 2022, sec. New York, https://www.nytimes.com /2022/09/11/nyregion/hasidic-yeshivas-schools-new-york.html. On gender, power, and Jewish summer camps, see Sandra Fox, *The Jews of Summer: Summer Camp and Jewish Culture in Postwar America* (Stanford, CA: Stanford University Press, 2023).

3. Throughout what follows I use the term "b-mitzvah" as a gender-neutral version of the gendered bar (for males) and bat (for females) mitzvah. Hebrew is a language that has gendered terms for objects, and there is not yet a convention for referring to the ritual in nongendered or gender-fluid terms. Perhaps in a few years this term will seem strange and will have been replaced by something more elegant, but until then "b-mitzvah" it is. I am borrowing the term from *Keshet*. See Essie Shachar-Hill, "A Guide for the Gender Neutral B-Mitzvah," *Keshet*, June 19, 2019, https://www .keshetonline.org/resources/a-guide-for-the-gender-neutral-b-mitzvah/.

4. Jonathan Krasner, "On the Origins and Persistence of the Jewish Identity Industry in Jewish Education," *Journal of Jewish Education* 82, no. 2 (2016): 132–158; Michal Kravel-Tovi, "'Continuity Crisis' and Its Instrumentalizing Effects," *American Jewish History* 104, no. 2 (2020): 215–220; Kravel-Tovi, "The Specter of Dwindling Numbers: Population Quantity and Jewish Biopolitics in the United States," *Comparative Studies in Society and History* 62, no. 1 (2020): 35–67.

5. Andrew Bush, *Jewish Studies: A Theoretical Introduction* (New Brunswick, NJ: Rutgers University Press, 2011), 67.

6. The original joke is about the food at a particular resort in which one person says to another, "The food is terrible." To which the other replies, "Yes, and such small portions!"

7. Harvey Shapiro, *Educational Theory and Jewish Studies in Conversation: From Volozhin to Buczacz* (Lanham, MD: Lexington Books, 2012).

8. Shapiro, *Educational Theory and Jewish Studies in Conversation*, 8.

9. There is a grand total of three books that explore the teaching of Jewish Studies in higher education. Google Scholar records three citations for Garber's book from 1986, two of which come from other publications of his. Davis's book fares better, with nine citations. I've never heard any of these books referenced in any paper, panel, or presentation about the teaching of Jewish Studies. Zev Garber, ed., *Methodology in the Academic Teaching of Judaism*, Studies in Judaism (Lanham, MD: University Press of America, 1986); Zev Garber, ed., *Academic Approaches to Teaching Jewish Studies* (Lanham, MD: University Press of America, 2000); Moshe Davis, ed., *Teaching Jewish Civilization: A Global Approach to Higher Education* (New York: New York University Press, 1995).

10. Helena Miller, Lisa D. Grant, and Alex Pomson, eds., *International Handbook of Jewish Education* (New York: Springer, 2011).

11. Stuart L. Kelman, ed., *What We Know about Jewish Education: A Handbook of Today's Research for Tomorrow's Jewish Education* (Los Angeles: Torah Aura Productions, 1992).

12. Jonathan Krasner, "Jewish Education and American Jewish Education, Part I," *Journal of Jewish Education* 71, no. 2 (2005): 121–177; Krasner, "Jewish Education and American Jewish Education, Part II," *Journal of Jewish Education* 71, no. 3 (2005): 279–317; Krasner, "Jewish Education and American Jewish Education, Part III," *Journal of Jewish Education* 72, no. 1 (2005): 29–76.

13. Brandeis University's Cohen Center for Modern Jewish Studies has published numerous program evaluations and studies of Birthright Israel applicants and alumni.

14. Oxford University Press, ed. 2000. *Oxford English Dictionary*. Electronic resource. Oxford, UK: Oxford University Press. https://www.oed.com.

15. David Sorkin, *Jewish Emancipation: A History across Five Centuries* (Princeton, NJ: Princeton University Press, 2021), 1.

16. John Willinsky, *Learning to Divide the World: Education at Empire's End* (Minneapolis: University of Minnesota Press, 1998).

17. John Locke, "Some Thoughts Concerning Education" (1692), in *Fordham University Modern History Sourcebook*, https://sourcebooks.fordham.edu/mod/1692locke-education.asp.

18. Jean-Jacques Rousseau, *Emile*, trans. Allan Bloom (New York: Basic Books, 1979).

19 Immanuel Kant, "Kant. What Is Enlightenment?" (n.d.), http://www.columbia.edu/acis/ets/CCREAD/etscc/kant.html.

20. Kant, "Kant. What Is Enlightenment?"

21. Immanuel Kant, "Kant on Education (Über Pädagogik)" (n.d.), https://oll.libertyfund.org/title/davids-kant-on-education-uber-padagogik.

22. Johann Gottfried von Herder, *Reflections on the Philosophy of the History of Mankind*, trans. T. O. Churchill (Chicago: University of Chicago Press, 1968).

23. Allan Bloom, "Introduction," in Rousseau, *Emile*, 6.

24. Quoted in Willinsky, *Learning to Divide the World*, 89.

25. Sorkin, *Jewish Emancipation*, 149–150, emphasis original.

26. Michael Meyer, "Reflections on the Educated Jew from the Perspective of Reform Judaism," in *Visions of Jewish Education*, ed. Seymour Fox, Israel Scheffler, and Daniel Marom (New York: Cambridge University Press, 2003), 149–161, 151.

27. Steven Gerald Rappaport, "Jewish Education and Jewish Culture in the Russian Empire, 1880–1914" (PhD diss., Stanford University, 2000). For an account of girls schools during this period, see Eliyana R. Adler, *In Her Hands: The Education of Jewish Girls in Tsarist Russia* (Detroit, MI: Wayne State University Press, 2011).

28. David W. Edwards, "Nicholas I and Jewish Education," *History of Education Quarterly* 22, no. 1 (1982): 51.

29. Carl F. Kaestle, *Pillars of the Republic: Common Schools and American Society, 1780–1860*, American Century Series (New York: Hill & Wang, 1983), 5–6.

30. Raymond B. Culver, *Horace Mann and Religion in the Massachusetts Public Schools*, Yale Studies in Religious Education 3 (New Haven, CT: Yale University Press, 1929).

31. Horace Mann, *The Republic and the School: Horace Mann on the Education of Free Men*, ed. Lawrence A. Cremin (New York: Teachers College Press, 1957); Lawrence Cremin, *The Transformation of the School: Progressivism in American Education, 1876–1957* (New York: Vintage, 1964), 5–6. See also James W. Fraser, *Between Church and State: Religion and Public Education in a Multicultural America*, 2nd ed. (Baltimore: Johns Hopkins University Press, 2016).

32. Peter Gay, *The Enlightenment: The Rise of Modern Paganism*, rev. ed. (New York: Norton, 1995), 92.

33. Michael W. Apple, *Education and Power*, 2nd ed. (New York: Routledge, 1995); Stanley Aronowitz and Henry A. Giroux, *Education Under Siege: The Conservative, Liberal and Radical Debate over Schooling* (New York: Routledge, 1987); Samuel Bowles and Herbert Gintis, *Schooling in Capitalist America: Educational Reform and the Contradictions of Economic Life* (New York: Basic Books, 1977); Martin Carnoy, *Education as Cultural Imperialism* (New York: D. McKay, 1974). For a history of critical studies of education, see Isaac Gottesman, *The Critical Turn in Education: From Marxist Critique to Poststructuralist Feminism to Critical Theories of Race* (New York: Routledge, 2016).

34. Overviews of the Alliance Israelite can be found in Michael M. Laskier, *The Alliance Israelite Universelle and the Jewish Communities of Morocco 1862–1962* (Albany: State University of New York Press, 1983); Aron Rodrigue, *French Jews, Turkish Jews: The Alliance Israelite Universelle and the Politics of Jewish Schooling in Turkey 1860–1925* (Bloomington: Indiana University Press, 1990). For historical and biographical information about Rebecca Gratz, see Dianne Ashton, "The Feminization of Jewish Education," *Transformations* 3, no. 2 (1992): 15–23; Dianne Ashton, *Rebecca Gratz: Women and Judaism in Antebellum America* (Detroit, MI: Wayne State University Press, 1998). For Gratz's own writings, see Rebecca Gratz and David Philipson, *Letters of Rebecca Gratz* (Philadelphia: Jewish Publication Society of America, 1929).

35. Eduard Israel Kley, "The Spirit of the Israelite Elementary Schools," ed. David Fränkel, *Sulamith* 6 (1821): 383–398; excerpt from 383–386 in *Key Documents of German-Jewish History*, https://dx.doi.org/10.23691/jgo:source-27.en.vi.

36. Rachel Elboim-Dror, *Ha-Ḥinukh Ha-'Ivri Be-Erets-Yiśra'el*, vol. 1, Sifriyah Le-Toldot Ha-Yishuv Ha-Yehudi Be-Erets-Yiśra'el (Yerushalayim: Yad Yitsḥak Ben-Tsevi, 1986), 3.

37. Stephan F. Brumberg, *Going to America, Going to School: The Jewish Immigrant Public School Encounter in Turn-of-the-Century New York City* (New York: Praeger, 1986); Melissa R. Klapper, *Jewish Girls Coming of Age in America, 1860–1920* (New York: New York University Press, 2005); Ruth Jacknow Markowitz, *My Daughter, the Teacher: Jewish Teachers in the New York City Schools* (New Brunswick, NJ: Rutgers University Press, 1993); Deborah Dash Moore, "Jewish Ethnicity and Acculturation in the 1920s: Public Education in New York City," *Jewish Journal of Sociology* 18 (December 1976): 96–104.

38. Jonathan Krasner, "Jewish Chautauqua, Jewish History, and a Jewish Correspondence School: A Failed Experiment in Jewish Education," *American Jewish Archives Journal* 56, no. 1–2 (2004): 47–93. See also Peggy K. Pearlstein, "Assemblies by the Sea: The Jewish Chautauqua Society in Atlantic City, 1897–1907," *Jewish Political Studies Review* 10, no. 1/2 (1998): 5–17.

39. Jonathan B. Krasner, *The Benderly Boys and American Jewish Education* (Waltham, MA: Brandeis University Press, 2011), 57.

40. Jenna Weissman Joselit, *The Wonders of America: Reinventing Jewish Culture, 1880–1950* (New York: Hill & Wang, 1994). See especially the chapter on "Red Letter Days."

41. David B. Tyack, *The One Best System: A History of American Urban Education* (Cambridge, MA: Harvard University Press, 1974). Jews did not live in geographically bound areas, so Benderly instituted the Bureau of Jewish Education as a means for centralizing and coordinating efforts, meant to mimic public school districts.

42. Klapper, *Jewish Girls Coming of Age in America*, 167.

43. Israel Friedlander, "The Problem of Jewish Education in America and the Bureau of Education of the Jewish Community of New York City," in *Report of the Commissioner of Education for the Year Ending June 30, 1913* (Washington, DC: Government Printing Office, 1914), 365–393, 365.

44. Alexander M. Dushkin, *Jewish Education in New York City* (New York: Bureau of Jewish Education, 1918), 1.

45. Joseph Solomon Bentwich, *Education in Israel* (Philadelphia: Jewish Publication Society of America, 1965), 6.

46. Michael Zeldin, "Preface," in *International Handbook of Jewish Education*, ed. Helena Miller, Lisa D. Grant, and Alex Pomson (The Netherlands: Springer, 2011), v.

47. Zevi Scharfstein, *Toldot Ha-Ḥinukh Be-Yisra'el Be-Dorot Ha-Aḥaronim*, Mahadurah 2, Metukenet ve-Meshukhlelet (Jerusalem: R. Mas, 1960), 1:vi.

48. Barry I. Chazan, Robert Chazan, and Benjamin M. Jacobs, *Cultures and Contexts of Jewish Education* (Cham, Switzerland: Palgrave Macmillan, 2017), xvii.

49. Kevin J. Burke and Avner Segall, *Christian Privilege in U.S. Education: Legacies and Current Issues*, Studies in Curriculum Theory (New York: Routledge, 2017), 11.

50. Moshe Aberbach, *Jewish Education and History: Continuity, Crisis and Change* (New York: Routledge, 2009), 4. See also Aberbach, Moshe. 1988. "The Development of the Jewish Elementary and Secondary School System During the Talmudic Age." In *Studies in Jewish Education*, 290–301, 3. Jerusalem: Magnes Press.

51. Emanuel Gamoran, *Changing Conceptions in Jewish Education* (New York: Macmillan, 1924), viii, vii.

52. Regarding math education, see Jo Boaler, *What's Math Got to Do with It? Helping Children Learn to Love Their Most Hated Subject—and Why It's Important for America* (New York: Viking, 2008); Jo Boaler, *Mathematical Mindsets: Unleashing Students' Potential through Creative Math, Inspiring Messages, and Innovative Teaching* (San Francisco: Jossey-Bass, 2016). Regarding history education, see Samuel S. Wineburg, *Historical Thinking and Other Unnatural Acts: Charting the Future of Teaching the Past*, Critical Perspectives on the Past (Philadelphia: Temple University Press, 2001). Regarding civics education, see Nicole Mirra and Antero Garcia, "Civic Participation Reimagined: Youth Interrogation and Innovation in the Multimodal Public Sphere," *Review of Research in Education* 41, no. 1 (2017): 136–158.

53. Quoted in Samuel M. Blumenfield, "Rashi, the Teacher in Israel (1040–1105)," *Jewish Social Studies* 2, no. 4 (1940): 392.

54. Miriam Eisenstein, *Jewish Schools in Poland, 1919–1939* (New York: King's Crown Press, 1950).

55. Glenn Dynner, "Replenishing the 'Fountain of Judaism': Traditionalist Jewish Education in Interwar Poland," *Jewish History* 31, no. 3–4 (2018): 229–261.

56. Quoted in Naomi Seidman, *Sarah Schenirer and the Bais Yaakov Movement: A Revolution in the Name of Tradition* (London: Littman Library of Jewish Civilization, 2019), 63.

57. Quoted in Hannah Kliger and Rakhmiel Peltz, "The Secular Yiddish School in the United States in Sociohistorical Perspective: Language School or Culture School?," *Linguistics and Education* 2, no. 1 (1990): 5.

58. Krasner, *Benderly Boys and American Jewish Education.* For an account of the women excluded from the "boys" framework, see Carol K. Ingall, ed., *The Women Who Reconstructed American Jewish Education, 1910–1965*, HBI Series on Jewish Women (Waltham, MA: Brandeis University Press, 2010).

59. Samuel Dinin, "An Analysis and Critique of Jewish Education in America," *Jewish Education* 26 (1955): 11.

60. Walter Ackerman, "Some Uses of Justification in Jewish Education," *AJS Review* 2 (1977): 26.

61. Steven Martin Cohen, "The Impact of Jewish Education on Religious Identification and Practice," *Jewish Social Studies* 36, no. 3/4 (1974): 316.

62. Krasner, "On the Origins and Persistence of the Jewish Identity Industry," 97.

63. Lila Corwin Berman, Kate Rosenblatt, and Ronit Y. Stahl, "Continuity Crisis: The History and Sexual Politics of an American Jewish Communal Project," *American Jewish History* 104, no. 2 (2020): 167–194; Jonathan Krasner, "American Jewry at Risk: 'A Time to Act' and the Prioritization of Jewish Education," *Contemporary Jewry* 36, no. 1 (2016): 85–123.

64. Jack Wertheimer, "Jewish Education in the United States: Recent Trends and Issues," *American Jewish Year Book* 99 (1999): 4.

65. Naphtali Herz Wessely, *Sefer Divre Shalom Ve-Emet: Divre Shulem Veemes: Torat Ha-Adam ve-Torat Ha-Ḥinukh* (microform; Varshe: Y.H. Zabelinski, 1886). Full text and translation available as Naphtali Herz Wessely, "Words of Peace and Truth 1:1:8," *Sefaria*, n.d., https://www.sefaria.org/Words_of_Peace_and_Truth.1.1.8?lang=bi.

66. Rodrigue, *French Jews, Turkish Jews*, 80.

67. Aḥad Haʿam, "Hachinuch Haleumi," in *Al Parashat Derakhim*, Hotsaʾah hadashah, 4 vols. (Berlin: Yudisher Ferlag, 1930), 4:133.

68. Paul Mendes-Flohr, "Cultural Zionism's Image of the Educated Jew: Reflections on Creating a Secular Jewish Culture," *Modern Judaism* 18, no. 3 (1998): 236. Louis Brandeis has an essay titled "A Call to the Educated Jew" that argues that Zionism

offers a reconciliation of precisely these tensions. See Brandeis, "A Call to the Educated Jew," *Menorah Journal*, January 1915.

69. John Dewey, *Democracy and Education* (New York: Simon & Brown, 2012).

70. There is quite a bit of scholarship on the relationship and influence of Dewey on Benderly and his circle. See Ronald Kronish, "John Dewey's Influence on Jewish Educators: The Case of Alexander M. Dushkin," *Teachers College Record* 83, no. 3 (1982): 419–433, https://doi.org/10.1177/016146818208300305; Ronald Kronish, "The Influence of John Dewey upon Jewish Education in America," in *Studies in Jewish Education*, vol. 2 (Jerusalem: Magnes Press, 1984), 104–121; Kerry Olitzky, "The Impact of John Dewey on Jewish Education," *Religious Education* 81, no. 1 (1986): 5–18. See also Ben Jacobs, "Socialization into a Civilization: The Dewey-Kaplan Synthesis in American Jewish Schooling in the Early 20th Century," *Religious Education* 104, no. 2 (2009): 149–165.

71. Quoted in "How the Kehillah Worked an Educational Miracle; Faced a Big Problem in Teaching 200,000 Jewish Children, Only One-Quarter of Whom Had Religious Training and Solved It in a Way That Is Pronounced Unique in American Educational History," *New York Times*, January 25, 1914, Magazine sec.

72. For a reassessment of how well Benderly and his circles managed to make good on Dewey's vision, see Miriam Heller Stern, "'A Dream Not Quite Come True': Reassessing the Benderly Era in Jewish Education," *Journal of Jewish Education* 70, no. 3 (2004): 16–26, https://doi.org/10.1080/0021624040700304.

73. Isa Aron, "Instruction and Enculturation in Jewish Education" (paper, Conference of the Network for Research in Jewish Education, 1989).

74. Michael Rosenak, *Commandments and Concerns: Jewish Religious Education in Secular Society* (Philadelphia: Jewish Publication Society, 1987), 256–257.

75. He did write some curriculum for younger children, including a bar or bat mitzvah workbook.

76. Jacob Neusner, *The Academic Study of Judaism: Essays and Reflections* (New York: KTAV, 1975), 41. A note on Neusner and sources: Neusner published so much and would frequently compile essays or articles into volumes that would be published under their own title. He would also publish and republish whole essays or sections under different titles at different times. The sources provided here are sometimes not the only sources in which these quotations appeared but are the ones in which I found them.

77. Conrad Cherry, *Hurrying toward Zion: Universities, Divinity Schools, and American Protestantism* (Bloomington: Indiana University Press, 1995).

78. Susannah Heschel, *Abraham Geiger and the Jewish Jesus* (Chicago: University of Chicago Press, 1998); Susannah Heschel, "Revolt of the Colonized: Abraham Geiger's Wissenschaft Des Judentums as a Challenge to Christian Hegemony in the Academy," *New German Critique*, no. 77 (1999): 61–85, https://doi.org/10.2307/488522.

79. The literature on the Wissenschaft is vast. Amos Bitzan, "Leopold Zunz and the Meanings of Wissenschaft," *Journal of the History of Ideas* 78, no. 2 (2017): 233–254; Harvey Hill, "The Science of Reform: Abraham Geiger and the Wissenschaft Des Judentum," *Modern Judaism* 27, no. 3 (2007): 329–349; Ken Koltun-Fromm, *Abraham Geiger's Liberal Judaism: Personal Meaning and Religious Authority* (Bloomington: Indiana University Press, 2006); Irene E. Zwiep, "Scholarship of Literature and Life: Leopold Zunz and the Invention of Jewish Culture," in *How the West Was Won: Essays on Literary Imagination, the Canon and the Christian Middle Ages for Burcht Pranger*, ed. Willemien Otten, Arjo J. Vanderjagt, and Hent De Vries (Leiden: Brill, 2010), 165–173.

80. Sarah Imhoff, "The Creation Story, or How We Learned to Stop Worrying and Love 'Schempp,'" *Journal of the American Academy of Religion* 84, no. 2 (2016): 466–497.

81. There are a handful of books that tell the histories of these organizations, often from the inside. They include Philip Bernstein, *To Dwell in Unity: The Jewish Federation Movement in America since 1960* (Philadelphia: Jewish Publication Society of America, 1983); Deborah Dash Moore, *B'nai B'rith and the Challenge of Ethnic Leadership*, SUNY Series in Modern Jewish History (Albany: State University of New York Press, 1981); Marianne R. Sanua, *Let Us Prove Strong: The American Jewish Committee, 1945–2006* (Waltham, MA: Brandeis University Press, 2007); Stuart Svonkin, *Jews Against Prejudice* (New York: Columbia University Press, 1999).

82. Ari Y. Kelman, "Identity and Crisis: The Origins of Identity as an Educational Outcome," in *Beyond Jewish Identity: Rethinking Concepts and Imagining Alternatives*, ed. Jon A. Levisohn and Ari Y. Kelman (Boston: Academic Studies Press, 2019), 65–83.

83. Irving Greenberg, "Jewish Survival and the College Campus," *Congress Bi-Weekly*, October 28, 1968, 5, 7.

84. Leon Jick, ed., *The Teaching of Judaica in American Universities: The Proceedings of a Colloquium* (Waltham, MA: Association for Jewish Studies, 1970).

85. Andrew Bush's book on Jewish Studies barely mentions efforts to establish the discipline as a scholarly field.

86. Leon Jick, "Tasks for a Community of Concern," in Jick, *Teaching of Judaica in American Universities*, 83–88, 85.

87. Marshall Sklare, "The Problem of Contemporary Jewish Studies," in Jick, *Teaching of Judaica in American Universities*, 57–72, 69.

88. Gerson Cohen, "An Embarrassment of Riches: Reflections on the Condition of American Jewish Scholarship in 1969," in Jick, *Teaching of Judaica in American Universities*, 120.

89. Robert Chazan, "Teaching Jewish History on the American Campus," in Davis, *Teaching Jewish Civilization*, 110.

90. Quoted in Aaron W. Hughes, *Jacob Neusner: An American Jewish Iconoclast* (New York: New York University Press, 2016), 118.

91 Quoted in Hughes, *Jacob Neusner*, 122.

92. Hughes, *Jacob Neusner*, 137.

93. Jacob Neusner, *"Being Jewish" and Studying about Judaism* (Atlanta: Emory University, 1977), 5, http://archive.org/details/beingjewishstudyoooneus.

94. Jacob Neusner, *How Not to Study Judaism: Examples and Counter-Examples* (Lanham, MD: University Press of America, 2004), iii, http://archive.org/details/hownottostudy judoooneus.

95. For a critique of this perspective, see Berman, Rosenblatt, and Stahl, "Continuity Crisis." For a critical accounting of demographic and reproductive politics, see Michal Kravel-Tovi, "Wet Numbers: The Language of Continuity Crisis and the Work of Care among the Organized American Jewish Community," in *Taking Stock: Cultures of Enumeration in Contemporary Jewish Life*, ed. Michal Kravel-Tovi and Deborah Dash Moore, Modern Jewish Experience (Bloomington: Indiana University Press, 2016); Kravel-Tovi, "Specter of Dwindling Numbers."

96. Neusner, *Academic Study of Judaism*, 43.

97. Neusner, *Academic Study of Judaism*, 67.

98. Neusner, *Academic Study of Judaism*, 44, emphasis original.

99. Neusner, *Academic Study of Judaism*, 177.

100. Neusner, *Academic Study of Judaism*, 205.

101. Jacob Neusner, *Rabbinic Judaism's Generative Logic: The Formation of the Jewish Intellect*, vol. 2, Academic Studies in the History of Judaism (Binghamton, NY: Global Publications, 2002); Jacob Neusner, *Rabbinic Judaism's Generative Logic: The Making of the Mind of Judaism*, vol. 1, Academic Studies in the History of Judaism (Binghamton, NY: Global Publications, 2002).

102. Neusner, *Rabbinic Judaism's Generative Logic: The Formation of the Jewish Intellect*, xix.

103. Russell T. McCutcheon, ed., *The Insider/Outsider Problem in the Study of Religion: A Reader*, Controversies in the Study of Religion (London: Cassell, 1999).

104. Donna J. Haraway, "Situated Knowledges: The Science Question in Feminism and the Privilege of Partial Perspective," *Feminist Studies* 14, no. 3 (1988): 575–599.

105. Haraway, "Situated Knowledges," 585.

106. Haraway, "Situated Knowledges," 586.

107. McCutcheon, *Insider/Outsider Problem*. For an expression of the argument that scholars can never know what religious practitioners do, see Wilfred Cantwell Smith, *The Meaning and End of Religion: A New Approach to the Religious Traditions of Mankind* (New York: New American Library, 1963).

108. Hughes, *Jacob Neusner*, 136.

CHAPTER 2 — LOGICS OF PRODUCTION

1. Of course, scholars of Jewish Studies could apprehend procedural knowledge, but the idea was to engage it almost as if it were propositional knowledge. Within the domain of Jewish Studies, procedural knowledge was not intended to be applied or lived. One could know that marriage rites looked a particular way within a certain community of Jews, so that they married in this or that way. This is technically procedural knowledge, but within the epistemological framework of Jewish Studies, it functioned like propositional knowledge because nobody was getting married in that context.

2. Throughout what follows, I am going to use the modern Israeli pronunciation for terms like *aleph-bet*, instead of the Ashkenazi *aleph-beys* or the English "alphabet." I have no political reason for doing so. I speak both Hebrew and Yiddish, and in each linguistic context I am most comfortable speaking both languages with the pronounced accent of a California-born Jew. To me—and this is my personal preference— saying *aleph-bet* is more natural and more comfortable than saying *aleph-beys*, just as *beit midrash* is more comfortable than *beys midrash* The reason is likely that I learned to speak Hebrew before I learned to speak Yiddish, so the terms come to me more naturally in the former. I am aware of the larger political context of this choice, but understand that my choice to transliterate in this manner is not born of a political ideology that posits the superiority or even propriety of one language over the other. For more on the politics of Yiddish and Hebrew, see Naomi Seidman, *A Marriage Made in Heaven: The Sexual Politics of Hebrew and Yiddish* (Berkeley: University of California Press, 1997).

3. Lawrence Kushner, *Sefer Otiyot: The Book of Letters—A Mystical Alef-Bait* (New York: Harper & Row, 1975).

4. Deuteronomy 6:7.

5. Yaron Ben-Naeh, *Jews in the Realm of the Sultans: Ottoman Jewish Society in the Seventeenth Century*, Texts and Studies in Medieval and Early Modern Judaism 22 (Tübingen: Mohr Siebeck, 2008), 252; Shlomo A. Deshen, *The Mellah Society: Jewish Community Life in Sherifian Morocco* (Chicago: University of Chicago Press, 1989), 86. For more on Jewish families, see Jonathan Boyarin, *Jewish Families*, Key Words in Jewish Studies 4 (New Brunswick, NJ: Rutgers University Press, 2013); Alex Pomson and Randal F. Schnoor, *Jewish Family: Identity and Self-Formation at Home* (Bloomington: Indiana University Press, 2018). The advent of "Jewish family education" is a more recent effort to bring Jewish education to whole families. See Vicky Kelman, *Family Room: Linking Families into a Jewish Learning Community* (Los Angeles: Shirley and Arthur Whizin Institute for Jewish Family Life, University of Judaism, 1995).

6. Robert Alter, *The Hebrew Bible: A Translation with Commentary* (New York: Norton, 2018).

7. Bava Batra 21a, Sefaria translation.

8. Pirke Avot 5:21.

9. Jeffrey L. Rubenstein, "Social and Institutional Settings of Rabbinic Literature," in *The Cambridge Companion to the Talmud and Rabbinic Literature,* ed. Charlotte Elisheva Fonrobert and Martin S. Jaffee, Cambridge Companions to Religion (Cambridge: Cambridge University Press, 2007), 58–74, 58.

10. Robert Brody, *The Geonim of Babylonia and the Shaping of Medieval Jewish Culture* (New Haven, CT: Yale University Press, 1998); Jeffrey L. Rubenstein, "The Rise of the Babylonian Rabbinic Academy: A Reexamination of the Talmudic Evidence," *Jewish Studies an Internet Journal* 1 (2002): 55–68.

11. S. D. Goitein, *A Mediterranean Society: The Jewish Communities of the Arab World as Portrayed in the Documents of the Cairo Geniza,* vol. 2 (Berkeley: University of California Press, 1967), 197. See also S. D. Goitein, "A Jewish Business Woman of the Eleventh Century," *Jewish Quarterly Review* 57 (1967): 225–242; Shlomo Dov Goitein, *Jewish Education in Muslim Countries: Based on Records from the Cairo Geniza* (Jerusalem: Ben-Zvi Institution, Hebrew University, 1962).

12. Moulie Vidas, *Tradition and the Formation of the Talmud* (Princeton, NJ: Princeton University Press, 2014).

13. Proverbs 22:6.

14. A search of the Princeton Geniza Project for various forms of the term in Hebrew returned no results.

15. Yehuda he Chassid and Avraham Yaakov Finkel, *Sefer Hasidim* (Northvale, NJ: Jason Aronson, 1996), 176–197. Sefaria.org contains the entire text of the *Sefer Hasidim* in Hebrew, and a search of the Hebrew text returned no results for the term.

16. *Sefer Hachinuch,* "Author's Introduction," Sefaria translation, https://www.sefaria.org/Sefer_HaChinukh%2C_Author's_Introduction.1?lang=bi&with=all&lang2=en.

17. Frontispiece reproduced in Rachel Elboim-Dror, *Ha-Ḥinukh Ha-'Ivri Be-Erets-Yiśra'el,* 2 vols., Sifriyah Le-Toldot Ha-Yishuv Ha-Yehudi Be-Erets-Yiśra'el (Yerushalayim: Yad Yitsḥak Ben-Tsevi, 1986), 20. From an edition of the book published in Warsaw in 1886.

18. Ahad Ha'am's concerns are often rendered in English as "education," but in the original Hebrew he uses a number of different terms. For the difference, compare the Hebrew in his essay "T'chiyat Haruach" (Cultural Revival) and its English translation. Aḥad Ha'am, *'Al Parashat Derakhim,* ed. Yirmeyahu Frenḳel, Hotsa'ah 'Ivrit (Tel Aviv: Dvir, 1948). Compare with Aḥad Ha'am, *Selected Essays,* trans. Leon Simon (Philadelphia: Jewish Publication Society of America, 1912). Simon uses the term "education" freely, in places where Ahad Ha'am used terms better translated as "school" or "teaching."

19. Steven J. Zipperstein, *Elusive Prophet: Ahad Ha'am and the Origins of Zionism* (London: Halban, 1993).

20. American Hebraist and Hebrew publisher Zvi Scharfstein authored a number of books about the history of Jewish education and educational figures, all of which used the term *chinuch* rather unreflexively or uncritically to refer to schooling, teaching, and instructional efforts across a wide range of settings, communities, countries, languages, and ideologies. Zevi Scharfstein, *Ḥinukh Ve-Ḳiyum* (New York: Shiloh, 1956); Zevi Scharfstein, *Ha-Ḥinukh Veha-Tarbut Ha-ʿIvrit Be-Eropah Ben Shete Milḥamot Ha-Olam* (New York: ʿOgen ʿal yad ha-Histadrut ha-ʿIvrit ba-ʾAmeriḳah, 1957); Zevi Scharfstein, *Toldot Ha-Ḥinukh Be-Yisraʾel Be-Dorot Ha-Aḥaronim*, Mahadurah 2, Metukenet ve-Meshukhlelet (Jerusalem: R. Mas, 1960).

21. Suzanne Schneider, *Mandatory Separation: Religion, Education, and Mass Politics in Palestine* (Stanford, CA: Stanford University Press, 2018), 89.

22. Nirit Raichel and Tali Tadmor-Shimony, "Jewish Philanthropy, Zionist Culture, and the Civilizing Mission of Hebrew Education," *Modern Judaism* 34, no. 1 (2014): 60–85, 69.

23. For more on the role of teachers in establishing Zionist culture, see Tali Tadmor-Shimony and Nirit Raichel, "The Hebrew Teachers as Creators of the Zionist Community in (the Land of) Israel," *Israel Studies Review* 28, no. 1 (2013): 120–141.

24. Quoted in Raichel and Tadmor-Shimony, "Jewish Philanthropy," 74.

25. "State Education Law" (1953), https://www.adalah.org/uploads/oldfiles/Public /files/Discriminatory-Laws-Database/English/24-State-Education-Law-1953.pdf.

26. Zalman Aranne, "Tochnit 'Hatoda'ah Hayehudit' Bema'arechet Hachinuch Hayisraelit," 31–35, and David Ben-Gurion, "Arachim Bechinuch Hayehudi: Hazika Hameshulshelet Letarbut Ivrit, Lamedina Velagolah Hameshikhit," 11–24, both in *Meḳorot Li-Veʿayot Ha-Ḥinukh Ha-Yehudi Be-Dorenu*, ed. David Weinstein and Michael Yizhar, Sifriyah Le-Hagut Yehudit, kerekh 1 (Chicago: ha-Mikhlalah le-madaʿe ha-Yahadut, 1964).

27. Walter Ackerman, "Making Jews: An Enduring Challenge in Israeli Education," *Israel Studies* 2, no. 2 (1997): 7.

28. Uri Ferago, "The Jewish Identity of Israeli Youth," *Yahadut Z'Maneinu* 5 (1989): 259–85 [Hebrew], cited in Ackerman, "Making Jews," 12.

29. Zosa Szajkowski and Tobey B. Gitelle, *Jewish Education in France, 1789–1939*, Jewish Social Studies Monograph Series no. 2 (New York: Conference on Jewish Social Studies, 1980), 4. See also Jeffrey Haus, "Liberte, Egalite, Utilite: Jewish Education and State in Nineteenth-Century France," *Modern Judaism* 22, no. 1 (2002): 1–27. For a more contemporary account of the tensions between Jewish education and French nationalism, see Kimberly A. Arkin, *Rhinestones, Religion, and the Republic: Fashioning Jewishness in France* (Stanford, CA: Stanford University Press, 2014), 99–133. For a similar account of Dutch schools, see N. L. Dodde and M. M. P. Stultjens, "Jewish Education in Schools in the Netherlands from 1815 to 1940," *Studia Rosenthaliana* 30, no. 1 (1996), 67–87.

30. Steven J. Zipperstein, "Jewish Enlightenment in Odessa: Cultural Characteristics, 1794–1871," *Jewish Social Studies* 44, no. 1 (1982): 19–36.

31. Quoted in David W. Edwards, "Nicholas I and Jewish Education," *History of Education Quarterly* 22, no. 1 (1982): 16.

32. Jonathan Krasner, "On the Origins and Persistence of the Jewish Identity Industry in Jewish Education," *Journal of Jewish Education* 82, no. 2 (2016): 132–158.

33. Among the chief proponents of "identity" as a desirable outcome of Jewish communal labor was sociologist Marshall Sklare, for whom the concept recurs throughout his body of work as a bulwark against what he understood to be the benefits and withering effects of life in an "open society." See Marshall Sklare, "Where Are We—Where Are We Going?," in *When Yesterday Becomes Tomorrow: 125th Anniversary Celebration, Congregation Emanu-El of the City of New York, 1845–1970,* ed. Temple Emanu-El (New York: Congregation Emanu-El, 1971), 47–63; Marshall Sklare and Joseph Greenblum, *Jewish Identity on the Suburban Frontier: A Study of Group Survival in the Open Society* (New York: Basic Books, 1967).

34. Ackerman, "Making Jews," 1–2.

35. S. Ilan Troen, "The Construction of a Secular Jewish Identity: European and American Influences in Israeli Education," in *Divergent Jewish Cultures: Israel and America,* ed. Deborah Dash Moore and S. Ilan Troen (New Haven, CT: Yale University Press, 2001), 28.

36. Ministry of Education and Culture, *A People and the World: Jewish Culture in a Changing World* (Jerusalem: Ministry of Education and Culture, 1994), 1 [Hebrew].

37. Geoffrey Bock, *Does Jewish Schooling Matter?* (New York: American Jewish Committee, 1977); Arnold Dashefsky and Cory Lebson, "Does Jewish Schooling Matter? A Review of the Empirical Literature on the Relationship between Jewish Education and Dimensions of Jewish Identity," *Contemporary Jewry* 23, no. 1 (2002): 96–131; Harold S. Himmelfarb, "The Non-Linear Impact of Schooling: Comparing Different Types and Amounts of Jewish Education," *Sociology of Education* 50, no. 2 (1977): 114–132.

38. Rambam echoes this in his chapter in the *Mishne Torah.*

39. See Reb Chaim of Volozhin's *Nefesh Hachaim* for a classic modern exposition of this view. Ḥayyim ben Isaac Volozhiner, *Nefesh Ha-Ḥayim: Rav Chaim of Volozhin's Classic Exploration of the Fundamentals of Jewish Belief* (Brooklyn, NY: Judaica Press, 2009). Also see Norman Lamm, *Torah Lishmah: Torah for Torah's Sake in the Works of Rabbi Hayyim of Volozhin and His Contemporaries* (Hoboken, NJ: KTAV, 1989).

40. Jonathan Boyarin, *Yeshiva Days* (Princeton, NJ: Princeton University Press, 2020), 152. The whole meditation spans thirteen pages, 142–155.

41. Quoted in Goitein, *Mediterranean Society,* 177; Judith Olszowy-Schlanger, "Learning to Read and Write in Medieval Egypt: Children's Exercise Books from the Cairo Geniza," *Journal of Semitic Studies* 48, no. 1 (2003): 47–69.

42. Quoted in Emanuel Gamoran, *Changing Conceptions in Jewish Education* (New York: Macmillan, 1924), 11.

43. Israel Abrahams, *Jewish Life in the Middle Ages* (Philadelphia: Jewish Publication Society, 1993), 365–367.

44. Jacob Marcus, ed., *The Jew in the Medieval World: A Sourcebook, 315–1791* (New York: Jewish Publication Society, 1938), 315; I. Abrahams, "Jewish Ethical Wills," *Jewish Quarterly Review* 3, no. 3 (1891): 436–484.

45. Naomi Seidman, "Legitimizing the Revolution: Sarah Schenirer and the Rhetoric of Torah Study for Girls," in *New Directions in the History of the Jews in the Polish Lands*, ed. Antony Polonsky, Hanna Węgrzynek, and Andrzej Żbikowski (Boston: Academic Studies Press, 2018), 356–365; Naomi Seidman, *Sarah Schenirer and the Bais Yaakov Movement: A Revolution in the Name of Tradition* (London: Littman Library of Jewish Civilization, 2019).

46. Ari Y. Kelman, "Identity and Crisis: The Origins of Identity as an Educational Outcome," in *Beyond Jewish Identity: Rethinking Concepts and Imagining Alternatives*, ed. Jon A. Levisohn and Ari Y. Kelman (Boston: Academic Studies Press, 2019), 65–83.

47. Robert Alter, "What Jewish Studies Can Do," *Commentary*, October 1974.

48. Alter, "What Jewish Studies Can Do," 71.

49. Judith R. Baskin, "Jewish Studies in North American Colleges and Universities: Yesterday, Today, and Tomorrow," *Shofar* 32, no. 4 (2014): 9–26.

50. Samuel C. Heilman, *The People of the Book* (Chicago: University of Chicago Press, 1983), 1.

51. Heilman, *People of the Book*, 261.

52. Phillip Jackson, *Life in Classrooms* (New York: Holt, Rinehart and Winston, 1968).

53. For the question as it pertains to Jewish education, see Oded Schremer, "The Hidden Curriculum of Jewish Education," in *Studies in Jewish Education*, vol. 1 (Jerusalem: Magnes Press, 1982).

54. Zvi Bekerman and Adina Segal, "What Is Taught in Talmud Class: Is It Class or Is It Talmud," *Journal of Jewish Education* 75, no. 1 (2009): 19–46.

55. Dan Ben-Amos, *Folklore Concepts: Histories and Critiques* (Bloomington: Indiana University Press, 2020); David Hajdu, *Love for Sale: Pop Music in America* (New York: Farrar, Straus and Giroux, 2016); David Hajdu, *The Ten-Cent Plague: The Great Comic-Book Scare and How It Changed America* (New York: Macmillan, 2009); Jenna Weissman Joselit, *The Wonders of America: Reinventing Jewish Culture, 1880–1950* (New York: Henry Holt, 1994). For retellings of salacious material from the Yiddish press, see Eddy Portnoy, *Bad Rabbi: And Other Strange but True Stories from the Yiddish Press*, Stanford Studies in Jewish History and Culture (Stanford, CA: Stanford University Press, 2018).

56. Shabbat 112a.

57. Shabbat 112b.

58. Richard A. Lanham, *The Economics of Attention: Style and Substance in the Age of Information* (Chicago: University of Chicago Press, 2006).

59. Elisheva Baumgarten, *Mothers and Children: Jewish Family Life in Medieval Europe* (Princeton, NJ: Princeton University Press, 2007), 184. See also Judith R. Baskin, "Some Parallels in the Education of Medieval Jewish and Christian Women," *Jewish History* 5, no. 1 (1991): 41–51; Judith R. Baskin, "חינוך נשים יהודיותוהשכלתן בימי הביניים באמצעות האסלאם והנצרות", *Pe'amim: Studies in Oriental Jewry* / רבעון לחקר קהילות ישראל במזרח, no. 82 (2000): 31–49.

60. *Sefer Hasidim* 313, quoted from Judith R. Baskin, "Women and Ritual Immersion in Medieval Ashkenaz," in *Judaism in Practice: From the Early Middle Ages through the Early Modern Period*, ed. Lawrence Fine (Princeton, NJ: Princeton University Press, 2001), 142.

61. Quoted in Matthias B. Lehmann, *Ladino Rabbinic Literature and Ottoman Sephardic Culture*, (Bloomington: Indiana University Press, 2005), 76.

62. Rashi on Exodus 16:9, Sefaria translation, https://www.sefaria.org/Mishneh _Torah%2C_Transmission_of_the_Oral_Law.8?ven=Maimonides%27_Mishneh _Torah,_edited_by_Philip_Birnbaum,_New_York,_1967&vhe=Wikisource _Mishneh_Torah&lang=bi.

63. Rashi on Berakhot 28b, author's translation.

64. Rambam, *Mishne Torah*, Transmission of the Oral Law, 8, https://www.sefaria .org/Mishneh_Torah%2C_Transmission_of_the_Oral_Law.8?ven=Maimonides%27 _Mishneh_Torah,_edited_by_Philip_Birnbaum,_New_York,_1967&vhe =Wikisource_Mishneh_Torah&lang=bi.

65. Brachot 11b.

66. Leonard A. Matanky, "The Status of Primary and Elementary School Teachers as Reflected in Rabbinic Responsa and Communal 'Taqqanot' of the Germanic States during the Seventeenth and Eighteenth Centuries" (PhD diss., New York University, 1989); Gamoran, *Changing Conceptions in Jewish Education*; Ephraim Kanarfogel, *Jewish Education and Society in the High Middle Ages* (Detroit, MI: Wayne State University Press, 1992).

67. Mihaly Csikszentmihalyi, *Flow* (New York: HarperCollins, 1991), 4.

68. Hasia R. Diner, *Lower East Side Memories: A Jewish Place in America* (Princeton, NJ: Princeton University Press, 2000); Hasia R. Diner, Jeffrey Shandler, and Beth S. Wenger, *Remembering the Lower East Side* (Bloomington: Indiana University Press, 2000); Rachel B. Gross, *Beyond the Synagogue: Jewish Nostalgia as Religious Practice* (New York: New York University Press, 2021).

69. Jakob Petuchowski, "Manuals and Catechisms of the Jewish Religion in the Early Period of Emancipation," in *Studies in Nineteenth-Century Jewish Intellectual*

History, ed. Alexander Altmann (Cambridge, MA: Harvard University Press, 1964), 47–64. See also Kerstin von der Krone, "The Duty to Know: Nineteenth-Century Jewish Catechisms and Manuals and the Making of Jewish Religious Knowledge," *History of Knowledge*, June 3, 2018, https://historyofknowledge.net/2018/06/03/the -duty-to-know/.

70. Petuchowski, "Manuals and Catechisms," 56.

71. Jonathan B. Krasner, *The Benderly Boys and American Jewish Education* (Waltham, MA: Brandeis University Press, 2011), 269.

72. David Bryfman, *Experience and Jewish Education* (Los Angeles: Torah Aura Productions, 2013); Barry Chazan, "A Philosophy of Informal Jewish Education," Infed .org, 2003, http://www.infed.org/informaljewisheducation/informal_jewish_education .htm; Joe Reimer, "Experiential Jewish Education," in *What We Now Know about Jewish Education: Perspectives on Research for Practice*, ed. Roberta Goodman, Paul Flexner, and L. Bloomberg (Los Angeles: Torah Aura Productions, 2009), 343–352; Joseph Reimer, "Beyond More Jews Doing Jewish: Clarifying the Goals of Informal Jewish Education," *Journal of Jewish Education* 73, no. 1 (2007): 5–23.

73. Quoted in William B. Helmreich, *The World of the Yeshiva: An Intimate Portrait of Orthodox Jewry* (Hoboken, NJ: KTAV, 2000), 43.

74. The Yeshiva in Lakewood can be understood as a continuation of the tradition of Kletzk. Yoel Finkelman, "Haredi Isolation in Changing Environments: A Case Study in Yeshiva Immigration," *Modern Judaism* 22, no. 1 (2002): 61–82. See also Adam Mintz, "From Kletzk to Lakewood: The Yeshiva Moves to America | Rabbi Mintz" (n.d.), http://www.rabbimintz.com/audio/from-kletzk-to-lakewood-the-yeshiva-moves-to -america/.

75. Adam S. Ferziger, "From Lubavitch to Lakewood: The Chabadization of American Orthodoxy," *Modern Judaism* 33, no. 2 (2013): 101–124; Adam S. Ferziger, "The Emergence of the Community Kollel: A New Model for Addressing Assimilation" (Ramat Gan: Rappaport Center for Assimilation Research and Strengthening Jewish Vitality, Bar-Ilan University, 2006); Helmreich, *World of the Yeshiva*; Sidney Rubin Lewitter, "A School for Scholars, the Beth Medrash Govoha, the Rabbi Aaron Kotler Jewish Institute of Higher Learning in Lakewood, New Jersey: A Study of the Development and Theory of One Aspect of Jewish Higher Education in America" (EdD diss., Rutgers University, 1981).

76. Hillel Levine, "To Share a Vision," in *Jewish Radicalism: A Selected Anthology*, ed. Jack Nusan Porter and Peter Dreier (New York: Grove, 1973), 187–188.

77. James A. Sleeper, "Authenticity and Responsiveness in Jewish Education," in *The New Jews*, ed. James A. Sleeper and Alan L. Mintz (New York: Vintage, 1971), 138.

78. For a great discussion of what this looks like in science and religion, see Donovan O. Schaefer, *Wild Experiment: Feeling Science and Secularism after Darwin* (Durham, NC: Duke University Press, 2022).

79. See Psalm 119:103 for the biblical source. But also see Ivan G. Marcus, *Rituals of Childhood: Jewish Acculturation in Medieval Europe* (New Haven, CT: Yale University Press, 1996), 47–73; Diane Roskies, "Alphabet Instruction in the East European Heder," *YIVO Annual of Jewish Social Science* 17 (1978): 21–53.

80. Nathaniel Deutsch, *The Jewish Dark Continent: Life and Death in the Russian Pale of Settlement* (Cambridge, MA: Harvard University Press, 2011), 146. Deutsch presents An-Ski's entire extant survey instrument in translation.

81. In fact, memories of life and learning in the heder of early modern Europe were remembered as anything but sweet, but more on that later. Steven Zipperstein, "Reinventing Heders," in *Imagining Russian Jewry* (Seattle: University of Washington Press, 1999), 41–62.

82. Daniel Boyarin, "Placing Reading: Ancient Israel and Medieval Europe," in *The Ethnography of Reading*, ed. Jonathan Boyarin (Berkeley: University of California Press, 1993), 14.

83. Yosef Fagin, "The Function of Talmudic Chant and Cantillation," *Journal of Jewish Music and Liturgy* 30 (2008): 15–32.

84. Nehemiah 8:2–3.

85. Nehemiah 8:8.

86. David Stern, "The First Jewish Books and the Early History of Jewish Reading," *Jewish Quarterly Review* 98, no. 2 (2007): 163–202, 187.

87. Stern, "First Jewish Books," 174; Aaron ben Moses Ben-Asher and Aron Dotan, *Sefer Dikduke Ha-Teʿamim. Akademyah La-Lashon Ha-ʿIvrit*, Mekorot u-Mehkarim 7 (Yerushalayim: ha-Akademyah la-lashon ha-ʿivrit, 1967).

88. Zecharia Goren, *Taʾamei Hamikra Keparshanut* (Jerusalem: Hakibbutz Hameyuhad, 1995).

89. Jeffrey A. Summit, "Introduction," in *Singing God's Words: The Performance of Biblical Chant in Contemporary Judaism* (Oxford: Oxford University Press, 2016), 10.

90. Mark Kligman, "Liturgical Music in the Jewish Tradition," in *The Oxford Handbook of the Jewish Diaspora*, ed. Hasia R. Diner (New York: Oxford University Press, 2021), 663–675, 665.

91. Edwin Seroussi, "A Common Basis—The Discovery of the Orient and the Uniformity of Jewish Musical Traditions in the Teaching of Abraham Zvi Idelsohn," *Peʾamim: Studies in Oriental Jewry*, no. 100 (2004): 125–146; James Loeffler, "Do Zionists Read Music from Right to Left? Abraham Tsvi Idelsohn and the Invention of Israeli Music," *Jewish Quarterly Review* 100, no. 3 (2010): 385–416; Ido Ramati, "The Orientalized Phonograph: The Mechanical Recording of Oral Jewish Tradition," *Cultural Critique* 102, no. 1 (2019): 61–89.

92. The Karaites remain a small and scattered community, largely excluded from organized Jewish communal efforts in the United States. See Aaron J. Hahn Tapper,

Judaisms: A Twenty-First-Century Introduction to Jews and Jewish Identities (Berkeley: University of California Press, 2016). Also see Talya Fishman, *Becoming the People of the Talmud: Oral Torah as Written Tradition in Medieval Jewish Cultures* (Philadelphia: University of Pennsylvania Press, 2013), chap. 1.

93. Quoted in Fishman, *Becoming the People of the Talmud*, 67.

94. Talya Fishman, "Claims about the Mishna in the Epistle of Sherira Gaon: Islamic Theology and Jewish History," in *Beyond Religious Borders: Interaction and Intellectual Exchange in the Medieval Islamic World*, ed. David M. Freidenreich (Philadelphia: University of Pennsylvania Press, 2011), 65.

95. David M. Carr, *The Formation of the Hebrew Bible: A New Reconstruction* (Oxford: Oxford University Press, 2011).

96. Immanuel Etkes, *Rabbi Israel Salanter and the Mussar Movement: Seeking the Torah of Truth* (Philadelphia: Jewish Publication Society, 1993), 338n2. Etkes uses the transliteration "mussar," which I retained when quoting him.

97. Joseph Dan, *Sifrut Ha-Musar Veha-Derush*, Sifriyat Keter 5 (Yerushalayim: Keter, 1975).

98. Shaul Stampfer, *Lithuanian Yeshivas of the Nineteenth Century: Creating a Tradition of Learning* (Oxford: Littman Library of Jewish Civilization, 2012), 272–273.

99. Etkes, *Rabbi Israel Salanter*, 102.

100. Lehmann, *Ladino Rabbinic Literature*, 5.

101. Lehmann, *Ladino Rabbinic Literature*, 78, 80.

102. Lehmann, *Ladino Rabbinic Literature*, 81. As Lehmann noted, rabbis feared the power and allure of "idle talk" (84).

103. Cantors are clergy, too.

104. Genesis 1:28 and Exodus 12:38.

105. Shaye J. D. Cohen, "Epigraphical Rabbis," *Jewish Quarterly Review* 72, no. 1 (1981): 9.

106. Cohen, "Epigraphical Rabbis," 12.

107. David Ellenson, *Rabbi Esriel Hildesheimer* (Tuscaloosa: University of Alabama Press, 1990); Ismar Schorsch, "Zacharias Frankel and the European Origins of Conservative Judaism," *Judaism* 30, no. 3 (Summer 1981): 344–355; Esther Seidel, "The Jewish Theological Seminary of Breslau (1854–1938)," *European Judaism* 38, no. 1 (2005): 133–144.

108. Tamás Turán and Carsten Wilke, *Modern Jewish Scholarship in Hungary: The "Science of Judaism" between East and West* (Berlin: Walter de Gruyter, 2016), 23.

109. Samuel E. Karff, *Hebrew Union College-Jewish Institute of Religion at One Hundred Years* (Cincinnati: Hebrew Union College Press, 1976); Gilbert Klaperman, "Yeshiva University—Seventy-Five Years in Retrospect," *American Jewish Historical Quarterly*

54, no. 1 (1964): 5–53; Jack Wertheimer, ed., *Tradition Renewed: A History of the Jewish Theological Seminary* (New York: Jewish Theological Seminary of America, 1997). See also Jacob Rader Marcus and Abraham J. Peck, eds., *The American Rabbinate: A Century of Continuity and Change, 1883–1983* (Hoboken, NJ: KTAV, 1985). For an account of women's ordination, see Pamela S. Nadell, *Women Who Would Be Rabbis: A History of Women's Ordination, 1889–1985* (Boston: Beacon, 1998).

110. This was not always the case. Jeffrey S. Gurock, "From Fluidity to Rigidity: The Religious Worlds of Conservative and Orthodox Jews in Twentieth-Century America," in *American Jewish Identity Politics*, ed. Deborah Dash Moore (Ann Arbor: University of Michigan Press, 2009).

111. Pamela S. Nadell, "'Top Down' or 'Bottom Up': Two Movements for Women's Rabbinic Ordination," in *An Inventory of Promises: Essays in Honor of Moses Rischin*, ed. Jeffrey Gurock and Marc Lee Raphael (New York: Carlson, 1995), 179–208; Nadell, *Women Who Would Be Rabbis*.

112. Beth Wenger, "The Politics of Women's Ordination: Jewish Law, Institutional Power and the Debate over Women in the Rabbinate," in Wertheimer, *Tradition Renewed*, 485–523.

113. Reva Clar and William M. Kramer, "The Girl Rabbi of the Golden West: The Adventurous Life of Ray Frank in Nevada, California and the Northwest," *Western States Jewish History* 18 (1986): 99–111, 223–236, 336–351.

114. Michel Foucault, *Power/Knowledge: Selected Interviews and Other Writings, 1972–1977* (New York: Vintage, 1988).

115. Genesis 2:18.

116. Genesis 15:6, 8.

117. Genesis 28:16.

118. Exodus 14:4, Exodus 14:18.

119. The word was invented by science fiction writer Robert Heinlein in his 1961 book, *Stranger in a Strange Land*. It appears without comment or definition, but it has gained purchase in popular culture to refer to a kind of "deep learning." Robert A. Heinlein, *Stranger in a Strange Land*, tenth edition (New York: Penguin, 1987), 18.

120. Mary Helen Immordino-Yang, *Emotions, Learning, and the Brain: Exploring the Educational Implications of Affective Neuroscience*, Norton Series on the Social Neuroscience of Education (New York: Norton, 2016), 21.

121. Mishna Torah 3:3, Sefaria translation.

122. Jodi Eichler-Levine, *Painted Pomegranates and Needlepoint Rabbis: How Jews Craft Resilience and Create Community* (Chapel Hill: University of North Carolina Press, 2020); Colleen McDannell, *Material Christianity: Religion and Popular Culture in America* (New Haven, CT: Yale University Press, 1995); W. David Kingery, *Learning from Things: Method and Theory of Material Culture Studies* (Washington, DC: Smithsonian Institution

Press, 1996); David Morgan, *The Thing about Religion: An Introduction to the Material Study of Religions* (Chapel Hill: University of North Carolina Press, 2021).

123. Natalia Berger, *The Jewish Museum: History and Memory, Identity and Art from Vienna to the Bezalel National Museum, Jerusalem*, Jewish Identities in a Changing World vol. 29 (Leiden: Brill, 2018); Barbara Kirshenblatt-Gimblett, "Theorizing Heritage," *Ethnomusicology* 39, no. 3 (1995): 367–380; Barbara Kirshenblatt-Gimblett, "Destination Culture: Tourism, Museums and Heritage," in *Exhibiting Jews*, ed. Barbara Kirshenblatt-Gimblett (Berkeley: University of California Press, 1998), 79–130; Barbara Kirshenblatt-Gimblett, "From Ethnology to Heritage" (2004), http://www.nyu.edu/classes/bkg/web/SIEF.pdf; Gross, *Beyond the Synagogue*.

124. David Biale, David Assaf, Benjamin Brown, Uriel Gellman, Samuel C. Heilman, Murray Jay Rosman, Gad Sagiv, Marcin Wodziński, and Arthur Green, *Hasidism: A New History* (New York: Oxford University Press, 2018).

125. Martin Kavka, "Religious Experience in Levinas and R. Hayyim of Volozhin," *Philosophy Today* 50, no. 1 (2006): 69–79; Harvey Shapiro, *Educational Theory and Jewish Studies in Conversation: From Volozhin to Buczacz* (Lanham, MD: Lexington Books, 2012).

126. Franz Rosenzweig, *On Jewish Learning* (Madison: University of Wisconsin Press, 2002), 28, emphasis added.

127. Samson Benderly, "Introduction," in Israel Konovitz, *A Brief Survey of Thirty-One Conferences Held by Talmud Torah Principals in New York City* (New York: Bureau of Jewish Education, 1912), 10, quoted in Krasner, *The Benderly Boys*, 96.

128. Judah Pilch, "Changing Patterns in Jewish Education," *Jewish Social Studies* 21, no. 2 (1959): 106, emphasis added.

129. Bryfman, *Experience and Jewish Education*; Reimer, "Experiential Jewish Education"; Reimer, "Beyond More Jews Doing Jewish."

130. Deborah Dash Moore, "Inventing Jewish Identity in California: Shlomo Bardin, Zionism, and the Brandeis Camp Institute," in *National Variations in Jewish Identity: Implications for Jewish Education*, ed. Steven Martin Cohen and Gabriel Horenczyk (Albany: State University of New York Press, 1999), 201–222.

131. Quoted in Moore, "Inventing Jewish Identity in California," 205.

132. Moore, "Inventing Jewish Identity in California," 205.

133. Moore, "Inventing Jewish Identity in California," 216.

134. Erik Cohen, "Travel as a Jewish Educational Tool," in *International Handbook of Jewish Education*, ed. Helena Miller, Lisa D. Grant, and Alex Pomson (Dordrecht: Springer, 2011), 615–632; Jackie Feldman, *Above the Death Pits, Beneath the Flag: Youth Voyages to Poland and the Performance of Israeli National Identity* (New York: Berghahn Books, 2008); Shaul Kelner, *Tours That Bind: Diaspora, Pilgrimage, and Israeli Birthright Tourism* (New York: New York University Press, 2012).

135. Erik Cohen, "Travel as a Jewish Educational Tool," 626.

136. Yosef Blau, *Lomdus: The Conceptual Approach to Jewish Learning* (Hoboken, NJ: KTAV, 2006).

137. Goitein, *Mediterranean Society*, 186. Melamdim who also housed their students was also a feature of nineteenth-century Morocco. Deshen, *Mellah Society*, 87.

138. Avraham Greenbaum, "The Girls' Heder and Girls in the Boys' Heder in Eastern Europe before World War I," *East/West Education* 18, no. 1 (1997): 55–62; Jack Kugelmass and Jonathan Boyarin, eds., *From a Ruined Garden: The Memorial Books of Polish Jewry* (New York: Schocken Books, 1983), 71.

139. Greenbaum, "Girls' Heder"; Kugelmass and Boyarin, *From a Ruined Garden*, 81.

140. Abrahams, "Jewish Ethical Wills," 462.

141. Goitein, "Jewish Business Woman," 232.

142. Kanarfogel, *Jewish Education and Society*, 24–25.

143. Kanarfogel, *Jewish Education and Society*, 19. Gamoran describes *melamdim* with a winsome sweetness. "What he lacked because of his ignorance in child psychology, child hygiene and general secular studies, he often made up by his love for the child, his friendship to the family, and by his simplicity and devotion." Most memoirs and descriptions are less kind about melamdim and their treatment of their pupils. Gamoran, *Changing Conceptions in Jewish Education*, 108.

144. Shaul Stampfer, *Families, Rabbis and Education: Traditional Jewish Society in Nineteenth-Century Eastern Europe* (Oxford: Littman Library of Jewish Civilization, 2010), 149–150.

145. Elisheva Baumgarten, "Ask the Midwives: A Hebrew Manual on Midwifery from Medieval Germany," *Social History of Medicine* 32, no. 4 (2019): 712–733.

146. Translated in Judith R. Baskin, "Dolce of Worms: The Lives and Deaths of an Exemplary Medieval Jewish Woman and Her Daughters," in Fine, *Judaism in Practice*, 429–437; Elisheva Baumgarten, *Practicing Piety in Medieval Ashkenaz: Men, Women, and Everyday Religious Observance*, Jewish Culture and Contexts (Philadelphia: University of Pennsylvania Press, 2014).

147. Howard Adelman, "The Educational and Literary Activities of Jewish Women in Italy during the Renaissance and the Catholic Restoration," in *Sefer Yovel Li-Shelomoh Simonson: Kovets Mehkarim Le-Toldot Ha-Yehudim Bi-Yeme Ha-Benayim Uvi-Tekufat Ha-Renesans*, ed. Daniel Carpi, Moshe Gil, Yosef Gorni, Yehuda Nini, Aharon Oppenheimer, Minna Rozen, and Anita Shapira (Tel Aviv: Universitat Tel Aviv, ha-Fakultah le-madaʻe ha-ruah, Bet ha-sefer le-madaʻe ha-Yahadut ʻa. sh. Hayim Rozenberg, 1993), 9–24, 12–13.

148. Adelman, "Educational and Literary Activities," 15.

149. Goitein, *Mediterranean Society*, 184.

150. Reneé Levine Melammed, "He Said, She Said: A Woman Teacher in Twelfth-Century Cairo," *AJS Review* 22, no. 1 (1997): 19–35.

151. Melammed, "He Said, She Said," 28.

152. Stampfer, *Lithuanian Yeshivas*, 106.

153. Daniel Boyarin, "'Pilpul': The Logic of Commentary," in *The Talmud—A Personal Take: Selected Essays* ed. Tal Hever-Chybowski (Tübingen, Germany: Mohr Siebeck, 2018), 47–48. See also Zalman Dimitrovsky, "'Al derekh ha-pilpul," in *Sefer ha-yovel li-khevod Shalom Ba'ron* (Jerusalem: Nabu Press, 1975), 111–182.

154. Boyarin, "'Pilpul,'" 49.

155. Meir Raffeld, "Pilpul, Censorship and Enlightenment / פלפול, צנזורה והשכלה: לקורותיה מחקרי ירושלים / *Jerusalem Studies in Hebrew Literature* ," של פרשנות אחת לסוגיית תנורו של עכנאי בספרות עברית יח 7–18 (2001); Elchanan Reiner, "Temurot be-Yeshivot Polin ve-Ashkenaz be-meot ha-16ha-18 ve-ha-Vikuach al ha-Pilpul," in *Ke-minhag Ashkenaz ve-Polin: sefer yovel le-Ḥana Shmeruk: ḳovets meḥḳarim be-tarbut Yehudit*, ed. Yiśra'el Barṭal, Chava Turniansky, and Ezra Mendelsohn (Jerusalem: Merkaz Zalman Shazar le-Toldot Yiśra'el, 1993); Shalem Yahalom, "The Pilpul Method of Talmudic Study: Earliest Evidence / הפלפול: עדויות ראשונות," *Tarbiz* / 543–74: תרביץ פד (ד) (2016). Sometimes Canpanton is spelled Kanpanton. Eliyahu Stern renders it Campanton. Eliyahu Stern, *The Genius: Elijah of Vilna and the Making of Modern Judaism* (New Haven, CT: Yale University Press, 2014).

156. Jacques Derrida, *Of Grammatology* (Baltimore: Johns Hopkins University Press, 1998), 158.

157. Simḥa Assaf, *Meḳorot Le-Toldot Ha-Ḥinukh Be-Yi'sra'el: Mi-Teḥilat Yeme-Ha-Benayim 'ad Teḳufat Ha-Ha'skalah* (Tel-Aviv: Hotsa'at "Devir," 1930), 46. See also Carol K. Ingall, "Reform and Redemption: The Maharal of Prague and John Amos Comenius," *Religious Education* 89, no. 3 (1994): 358–375.

158. Everyone, he believed, received the written Torah. Only Jews had access to the Oral Torah, so therefore it contained the keys to the destiny of the Jewish people.

159. Stern, *Genius*, 118–120, 124–125.

160. Reiner, "Temurot be-Yeshivot," 18, author's translation.

CHAPTER 3 — MODES OF TRANSMISSION

1. Olga Litvak, *Haskalah: The Romantic Movement in Judaism* (New Brunswick, NJ: Rutgers University Press, 2012).

2. Here Litvak is echoing other scholarship on the irrationality and spirituality of the Enlightenment. Peter Gay, *The Enlightenment: The Rise of Modern Paganism*, rev. ed. (New York: Norton, 1995); Jason Ānanda Josephson-Storm, *The Myth of Disenchantment: Magic, Modernity, and the Birth of the Human Sciences* (Chicago: University of Chicago Press, 2017).

3. Jacob Katz, *Tradition and Crisis: Jewish Society at the End of the Middle Ages* (Syracuse, NY: Syracuse University Press, 2000), 156.

4. Dan A. Porat, "The Nation Revised: Teaching the Jewish Past in the Zionist Present (1890–1913)," *Jewish Social Studies* 13, no. 1 (2006): 59–88.

5. Marcin Wodziński, *Haskalah and Hasidism in the Kingdom of Poland: A History of Conflict* (Liverpool: Liverpool University Press, 2005), 49.

6. Moses Mendelssohn, letter to Henning, June 29, 1779, cited in Alexander Altmann, *Moses Mendelssohn: A Biographical Study* (Philadelphia: The Jewish Publication Society of America, 1973), 344.

7. Jonathan Sheehan, *The Enlightenment Bible: Translation, Scholarship, Culture* (Princeton, NJ: Princeton University Press, 2007), 180.

8. Edward Breuer, "Naphtali Herz Wessely and the Cultural Dislocations of an Eighteenth-Century Maskil," in *New Perspectives on the Haskalah*, ed. Shmuel Feiner and David Sorkin (Liverpool: Liverpool University Press, 2004), 27–47; Nancy Sinkoff, *Out of the Shtetl: Making Jews Modern in the Polish Borderlands* (Providence, RI: Brown Judaic Studies, 2004), 113–167.

9. Naphtali Herz Wessely, "Words of Peace and Truth," letter 1:1, Sefaria translation, https://www.sefaria.org/Words_of_Peace_and_Truth.1.1?lang=bi. See also letter 1:7.

10. Quoted in Rachel Elboim-Dror, *Ha-Ḥinukh Ha-'Ivri Be-Erets-Yiśra'el*, 2 vols., Sifriyah Le-Toldot Ha-Yishuv Ha-Yehudi Be-Erets-Yiśra'el (Yerushalayim: Yad Yitsḥak Ben-Tsevi, 1986), 19.

11. Quoted in Shaul Stampfer, *Lithuanian Yeshivas of the Nineteenth Century: Creating a Tradition of Learning* (Oxford: Littman Library of Jewish Civilization, 2012), 26–27.

12. Stampfer, *Lithuanian Yeshivas*, 85.

13. Among historians and scholars of Hasidism, there is some debate about the name, as many people during the early modern period were known as *ba'alei shem*, or mystics who could communicate directly with God and provide magical services for people. Gershom Scholem suggested that the moniker *Ba'al Shem Tov* indicates that Rabbi Israel considered himself to be (and was considered to be) a better version of the more common *ba'al shem* and that a better translation of his title would be "Good Master of Names." Historian Moshe Rosman disagrees, noting that "the Besht was not the only, or even the first, ba'al shem tov." Moshe Rosman, *Founder of Hasidism: A Quest for the Historical Ba'al Shem Tov* (Liverpool: Liverpool University Press, 2013), 13–23, 16.

14. Moshe Rinott, "Religion and Education: The Cultural Question and the Zionist Movement, 1897–1913," *Studies in Zionism* 5, no. 1 (1984): 1–17, 1, https://doi.org/10.1080/13531048408575851; Shoshana Sitton, "Zionist Education in an Encounter between the British Colonial and the Hebrew Cultures," *Journal of Educational Administration and*

History 29, no. 2 (1997): 108–120, 110, https://doi.org/10.1080/0022062970290202. See also the earlier discussion of *chinuch*.

15. Solomon Maimon, *The Autobiography of Solomon Maimon*, trans. J. Clark Murray (London: Alexander Gardner, 1888), 36, https://www.gutenberg.org/files/41042/41042 -h/41042-h.htm#Page_22.

16. Steven Zipperstein, "Reinventing Heders," in *Imagining Russian Jewry* (Seattle: University of Washington Press, 1999), 57.

17. Yaron Ben-Naeh, *Jews in the Realm of the Sultans: Ottoman Jewish Society in the Seventeenth Century*, Texts and Studies in Medieval and Early Modern Judaism 22 (Tübingen: Mohr Siebeck, 2008), 252.

18. Sa'adi ben Betsalel Halevi, Aron Rodrigue, Sarah Abrevaya Stein, and Isaac Jerusalmi, *A Jewish Voice from Ottoman Salonica: The Ladino Memoir of Sa'adi Besalel a-Levi*, Stanford Studies in Jewish History and Culture (Stanford, CA: Stanford University Press, 2012).

19. Halevi et al., *Jewish Voice from Ottoman Salonica*, 18.

20. Katz, *Tradition and Crisis*, 163.

21. Shaul Stampfer, "Heder Study, Knowledge of Torah, and the Maintenance of Social Stratification," in *Families, Rabbis and Education: Traditional Jewish Society in Nineteenth-Century Eastern Europe*, ed. Shaul Stampfer (Oxford: Littman Library of Jewish Civilization, 2010), 145–166.

22. Stampfer, "Heder Study," 163.

23. Stampfer, "Heder Study," 165–166.

24. For one such example, see Edward Fram, *My Dear Daughter: Rabbi Benjamin Slonik and the Education of Jewish Women in Sixteenth-Century Poland* (Cincinnati: Hebrew Union College Press, 2007).

25. Stampfer, "Gender Differentiation and the Education of Jewish Women," in Stampfer, *Families, Rabbis and Education*, 169. See also Zevi Scharfstein, *Ha-Ḥeder Be-Ḥaye 'amenu* (New York, 1943). See also the memoirs of girls' heder in *From a Ruined Garden: The Memorial Books of Polish Jewry*, ed. Jack Kugelmass and Jonathan Boyarin (New York: Schocken Books, 1983).

26. Avraham Greenbaum, "The Girls' Heder and Girls in the Boys' Heder in Eastern Europe before World War I," *East/West Education* 18, no. 1 (1997): 55–62, 60; Avraham Greenbaum, "'Girls' Heders and Girls in Boys' Heder in Eastern Europe before World War I" [Hebrew], in *Ḥinukh ve-historyah: heksherim tarbutiyim u-politiyim*, ed. Rivka Feldhay and Immanuel Etkes (Yerushalayim: Merkaz Zalman Shazar le-toldot Yiśra'el, 1999), 297–304.

27. Greenbaum, "Girls' Heder," 60.

28. Greenbaum, "Girls' Heder," 58.

29. Stampfer, *Families, Rabbis and Education*, 181.

30. Iris Parush, *Reading Jewish Women: Marginality and Modernization in Nineteenth-Century Eastern European Jewish Society*, Brandeis Series on Jewish Women (Hanover, NH: Brandeis University Press, 2004), 25; Judith R. Baskin, "Some Parallels in the Education of Medieval Jewish and Christian Women," *Jewish History* 5, no. 1 (1991): 41–51; Avraham Grossman and Jonathan Chipman, *Pious and Rebellious: Jewish Women in Medieval Europe* (Waltham, MA: Brandeis University Press, 2004).

31. Greenbaum, "Girls' Heder," 80; Kugelmass and Boyarin, *From a Ruined Garden*, 71.

32. Kugelmass and Boyarin, *From a Ruined Garden*, 71. For examples from Italy, see Howard Adelman, "The Educational and Literary Activities of Jewish Women in Italy during the Renaissance and the Catholic Restoration," in *Sefer Yovel Li-Shelomoh Simonson: Kovets Mehkarim Le-Toldot Ha-Yehudim Bi-Yeme Ha-Benayim Uvi-Tekufat Ha-Renesans*, ed. Daniel Carpi, Moshe Gil, Yosef Gorni, Yehuda Nini, Aharon Oppenheimer, Minna Rozen, and Anita Shapira (Tel Aviv: Universitat Tel Aviv, ha-Fakultah le-mada'e ha-ruah, Bet ha-sefer le-mada'e ha-Yahadut 'a. sh. Hayim Rozenberg, 1993), 9–24, 14.

33. Kugelmass and Boyarin, *From a Ruined Garden*, 71. The *megillot*, or scrolls, are included in the Bible as "writings," and each is read ritually on a designated holiday. The *haftarot* are selections from Prophets that were added to the weekly Torah portion recitation as a supplemental thematic reading.

34. Parush, *Reading Jewish Women*, 59–61.

35. Quoted in Joseph P. Schultz, "The 'Ze'enah U-Re'enah': Torah for the Folk," *Judaism* 36, no. 1 (1987): 87. See also Chava Weissler, "Women's Studies and Women's Prayers: Reconstructing the Religious History of Ashkenazic Women," *Jewish Social Studies* 1, no. 2 (1995): 28–47.

36. Eliyana R. Adler, *In Her Hands: The Education of Jewish Girls in Tsarist Russia* (Detroit, MI: Wayne State University Press, 2011), 22.

37. Pirke Avot 3:21.

38. Deuteronomy 8:3, recapitulated in Matthew 4:4.

39. Though not solely focused on education, the overlap between philanthropic attention and educational efforts is substantial. Matthew Berkman, "Transforming Philanthropy: Finance and Institutional Evolution at the Jewish Federation of New York, 1917–86," *Jewish Social Studies* 22, no. 2 (2017): 146–195; Lila Corwin Berman, *The American Jewish Philanthropic Complex: The History of a Multibillion-Dollar Institution* (Princeton, NJ: Princeton University Press, 2020); Arnold Dashefsky and Bernard Melvin Lazerwitz, *Charitable Choices: Philanthropic Decisions of Donors in the American Jewish Community* (Lanham, MD: Lexington Books, 2009); Barry Kosmin and Paul Ritterband, *Jewish Philanthropy in Contemporary America* (Lanham, MD: Rowman & Littlefield, 1991); Jack Wertheimer, "Current Trends in American Jewish Philanthropy," *American Jewish Year Book* 97 (1997): 3–92.

40. One of the oldest jokes in this regard is from Ephraim Kishon's 1964 film *Sallah Shabati*. In one scene an American Jewish family comes to visit the tree that they planted in Israel. They find the tree with their name on a sign, and once they leave the tree's caretaker removes the sign and replaces it with another, bearing the next visiting family's name. In the name of full transparency, I am compelled to mention that my current position bears the name of the person who created the foundation that endowed it.

41. Berman, *American Jewish Philanthropic Complex*, 1–2.

42. Pirke Avot 4:5, Sefaria translation. See also Nedarim 37a, which explains that Deuteronomy 4:5 means that people should teach Torah for free.

43. *Mishne Torah*, Talmud Torah 3:10.

44. Yom Tov Assis, "Chinuch Yaldei Yisrael Besefarad hanotzrit be'amot ha yod-gimel-yod dalet: beyn hakehilah lachavurah," in *Hinukh ve-historyah: heksherim tarbutiyim u-politiyim*, ed. Rivka Feldhay and Immanuel Etkes (Yerushalayim: Merkaz Zalman Shazar le-toldot Yiśra'el, 1999), 147–156; Ben-Naeh, *Jews in the Realm of the Sultans*, 251.

45. Isidore Fishman, *The History of Jewish Education in Central Europe, from the End of the Sixteenth to the End of the Eighteenth Century* (London: E. Goldston, 1944), 25–31.

46. Ephraim Kanarfogel, *Jewish Education and Society in the High Middle Ages* (Detroit, MI: Wayne State University Press, 1992), 62. See also Yom Tov Assis, *The Golden Age of Aragonese Jewry: Community and Society in the Crown of Aragon, 1213–1327* (Portland, OR: Littman Library of Jewish Civilization, 1997), 329. See also Shlomo A. Deshen, *The Mellah Society: Jewish Community Life in Sherifian Morocco* (Chicago: University of Chicago Press, 1989).

47. Rachel Simon, "Education," in *The Jews of the Middle East and North Africa in Modern Times*, ed. Reeva S. Simon, Michael M. Laskier, and Sara Reguer (New York: Columbia University Press, 2003), 144.

48. Stampfer, *Lithuanian Yeshivas*, 31–45.

49. Stampfer, *Lithuanian Yeshivas*, 337.

50. Stampfer, *Lithuanian Yeshivas*, 349.

51. Jonathan B. Krasner, *The Benderly Boys and American Jewish Education* (Waltham, MA: Brandeis University Press, 2011), 120–123, 402–408.

52. The question of endowed chairs warranted a contribution to the conference and the volume that helped initiate the Association of Jewish Studies. Harvie Branscomb, "A Note on Establishing Chairs of Jewish Studies," in *The Teaching of Judaica in American Universities: The Proceedings of a Colloquium*, ed. Leon Jick (Waltham, MA: Association for Jewish Studies, 1970), 95–102.

53. Shaul Kelner, *Tours That Bind: Diaspora, Pilgrimage and Israeli Birthright Tourism* (New York: New York University Press, 2010).

54. Incidentally, the growth of Jewish Studies faculty was typically not driven by campus administrations but was made possible, in large measure, through the philanthropic support of Jewish communities and individuals. I do not know how Neusner's various positions or endeavors were funded.

55. Berman, *American Jewish Philanthropic Complex*, 178.

56. Daniel Kahneman, *Thinking, Fast and Slow* (New York: Farrar, Straus and Giroux, 2011).

57. Elizabeth Popp Berman, *Thinking Like an Economist: How Efficiency Replaced Equality in U.S. Public Policy* (Princeton, NJ: Princeton University Press, 2022), 4.

58. To name only a few examples: Hanan A. Alexander, "Mature Zionism: Education and the Scholarly Study of Israel," *Journal of Jewish Education* 81, no. 2 (2015): 136–161; Yoram Bar-Gal, *Propaganda and Zionist Education: The Jewish National Fund, 1924–1947* (Rochester, NY: University Rochester Press, 2003); Barry Chazan, "Palestine in American Jewish Education in the Pre-State Period," *Jewish Social Studies* 42, no. 3/4 (1980): 229–248; Daniel Kupfert Heller, *Jabotinsky's Children: Polish Jews and the Rise of Right-Wing Zionism* (Princeton, NJ: Princeton University Press, 2017); Kelner, *Tours That Bind*; Jonathan Krasner, "New Jews in an Old-New Land," *Journal of Jewish Education* 69, no. 2 (2003): 7–22; Theodore Sasson, *The New American Zionism* (New York: New York University Press, 2013); Alex Sinclair, *Loving the Real Israel: An Educational Agenda for Liberal Zionism* (Teaneck, NJ: Ben Yehuda Press, 2013); Stephan E. C. Wendehorst, "Between Promised Land and Land of Promise: The Radical Socialist Zionism of Hashomer Hatzair," *Jewish Culture and History* 2, no. 1 (1999): 44–57; Sivan Zakai, "Values in Tension: Israel Education at a U.S. Jewish Day School," *Journal of Jewish Education* 77, no. 3 (2011): 239–265; Sivan Zakai, "'My Heart Is in the East and I Am in the West': Enduring Questions of Israel Education in North America," *Journal of Jewish Education* 80, no. 3 (2014); Sivan Zakai, *My Second-Favorite Country: How American Jewish Children Think about Israel* (New York: New York University Press, 2022).

59. Mircea Eliade, *The Sacred and the Profane: The Nature of Religion*, trans. Willard R. Trask (New York: Harcourt Brace Jovanovich, 1987).

60. Micah 4:2.

61. Ari Kelman and Ilan Baron, "Framing Conflict: Why American Congregations Cannot Not Talk about Israel," *Contemporary Jewry* 39 (2019); Dov Waxman, *Trouble in the Tribe: The American Jewish Conflict over Israel* (Princeton, NJ: Princeton University Press, 2016).

62. Barry I. Chazan, *A Philosophy of Israel Education: A Relational Approach* (Cham, Switzerland: Palgrave Macmillan, 2016); Ezra M. Kopelowitz and Lisa D. Grant, *Israel Education Matters: A 21st Century Paradigm for Jewish Education* (Jerusalem: Center for Jewish Peoplehood Education, 2012); Sinclair, *Loving the Real Israel*; Zakai, "Values in Tension."

63. Makom Israel, "About Us" (n.d.), https://makomisrael.org/about-us-2/.

64. Noam Pianko, *Jewish Peoplehood: An American Innovation* (New Brunswick, NJ: Rutgers University Press, 2015).

65. Sinclair, *Loving the Real Israel.*

66. Makom Israel, "The Four Hatikva Questions (4HQ) Explained" (n.d.), https://makomisrael.org/the-four-hatikva-questions-4hq-explained/. The questions all derive from the line in the Israeli National Anthem that says, "To be a free people in our own land." The questions invite people to interrogate each of the key terms: to be, free, people, and land.

67. The iCenter, "Our Impact" (n.d.), https://theicenter.org/our-impact/.

68. This is known as the "distancing hypothesis."

69. Chazan, *Philosophy of Israel Education*, 11.

70. Birthright Israel Foundation, "Educational Approach" (n.d.), https://birthright israel.foundation/approach/.

71. Emily Alice Katz, "Pen Pals, Pilgrims, and Pioneers: Reform Youth and Israel, 1948–1967," *American Jewish History* 95, no. 2 (2009): 249–276; Emily Alice Katz, *Bringing Zion Home: Israel in American Jewish Culture, 1948–1967* (Albany: State University of New York Press, 2015).

72. Kelner, *Tours That Bind.*

73. Leonard Saxe, Benjamin Phillips, and Theodore Sasson, "Intermarriage: The Impact and Lessons of Taglit-Birthright Israel," *Contemporary Jewry* 31, no. 2 (2011): 151–172; Leonard Saxe and Barry Chazan, *Ten Days of Birthright Israel: A Journey in Young Adult Identity* (Waltham, MA: Brandeis University Press, 2008).

74. Kelner mentions the "Birthrate Israel" reference on page 145 of *Tours That Bind.*

75. See Zakai, *My Second-Favorite Country.*

76. Josh Nathan-Kazis, "Canary Mission Blacklist Funded by Jewish Federation," *Forward*, October 3, 2018, https://forward.com/news/411355/revealed-canary-mission-black list-is-secretly-bankrolled-by-major-jewish/; Michael Poliakoff, "Controversy over Israel Studies at University of Washington Did Not Have to Happen," *Forbes*, April 12, 2022, https://www.forbes.com/sites/michaelpoliakoff/2022/04/12/controversy-over-israel -studies-at-university-of-washington-did-not-have-to-happen/.

77. Katz, *Bringing Zion Home.*

78. Stampfer, *Families, Rabbis and Education*, 235.

79. Jonathan Boyarin, "Voices around the Text: The Ethnography of Reading at Mesivta Tifereth Jerusalem," in *The Ethnography of Reading*, ed. Jonathan Boyarin (Berkeley: University of California Press, 1993), 212–237, 229.

80. This quotation, which is reproduced all over the internet, is attributed to Rabi, who was quoted in "Great Minds Start with Questions" in *Parents* magazine (Septem-

ber 1993). Rabi, however, passed away in 1988, which means that the citation, if it is accurate, was published prior to its appearance in the magazine. Extensive searching could not locate the original source.

81. Exodus 13:8.

82. Quoted in Jacques Bigart, "The Alliance Israelite Universelle," *American Jewish Year Book* 2 (1900): 46.

83. Quoted in Aron Rodrigue, *French Jews, Turkish Jews: The Alliance Israelite Universelle and the Politics of Jewish Schooling in Turkey 1860–1925* (Bloomington: Indiana University Press, 1990), 22.

84. Ronald Florence, *Blood Libel: The Damascus Affair of 1840* (Madison: University of Wisconsin Press, 2004); David I. Kertzer, *The Kidnapping of Edgardo Mortara* (New York: Knopf, 1997); Magda Teter, *Blood Libel: On the Trail of an Antisemitic Myth* (Cambridge, MA: Harvard University Press, 2020). See also Allan Tarshish, "The Board of Delegates of American Israelites (1859–1878)," *Publications of the American Jewish Historical Society* 49, no. 1 (1959): 16–32. On the presence of the AIU in the United States and its interactions with the Board of Delegates, see Zosa Szajkowski, "The Alliance Israelite Universelle in the United States, 1860–1949," *Publications of the American Jewish Historical Society* 39, no. 4 (1950): 389–443.

85. Quoted in Rodrigue, *French Jews, Turkish Jews*, 22. 23.

86. Aron Rodrigue and Tsivyah Zemiri, *Ḥinukh, ḥevrah ve-hisṭoryah: "Kol Yiśra'el haverim" vi-Yehude agan ha-Yam ha-Tikhon 1860–1929* (Jerusalem: Makhon Ben Tsevi le-heḳer ḳehilot Yiśra'el ba-mizraḥ, 1991), 81. For a summary, see Simon, "Education."

87. Rodrigue, *French Jews, Turkish Jews*, 24.

88. Rodrigue, *French Jews, Turkish Jews*, 24.

89. Bigart, "Alliance Israelite Universelle."

90. Michael M. Laskier, "Aspects of the Activities of the Alliance Israélite Universelle in the Jewish Communities of the Middle East and North Africa: 1860–1918," *Modern Judaism* 3, no. 2 (1983): 155.

91. Table 1, "Growth of the Educational System of the AIU," in Rodrigue and Zemiri, *Ḥinukh, ḥevrah ve-hisṭoryah*, 33.

92. Aron Rodrigue, "Jewish Society and Schooling in a Thracian Town: The Alliance Israélite Universelle in Demotica, 1897–1924," *Jewish Social Studies* 45, no. 3/4 (1983): 263–286, 270.

93. Rodrigue, *French Jews, Turkish Jews*, 168. See also Michael M. Laskier, *The Alliance Israelite Universelle and the Jewish Communities of Morocco 1862–1962* (Albany: State University of New York Press, 1983), 81.

94. Quoted in Laskier, "Aspects of the Activities of the Alliance Israélite Universelle," 160.

95. Rodrigue, *French Jews, Turkish Jews*, 84.

96. Jewish Women's Archive, "'Report' Female Hebrew Benevolent Society" (n.d.), https://jwa.org/media/report-female-hebrew-benevolent-society.

97. Alvin Irwin Schiff, *The Jewish Day School in America* (New York: Jewish Education Committee Press, 1966), 154.

98. For an investigation into the ancient roots of these overlapping terms, see Dan Urman, "The House of Assembly and the House of Study: Are They One and the Same?," in *Ancient Synagogues: Historical Analysis and Archaeological Discovery*, ed. Dan Urman and Paul Virgil McCracken Flesher (Leiden: Brill, 1998), 232–255. See also Boyarin, "Voices around the Text." For historical accounts, see Immanuel Etkes, ed., *Yeshivot u-vate midrashot* (Yerushalayim: Merkaz Zalman Shazar le-toldot Yiśra'el, Merkaz Dinur le-ḥeker toldot Yiśra'el, ha-Universiṭah ha-'Ivrit bi-Yerushalayim; Shtern, Yekhiel. Ḥeder Un Bet-Midrash. Nyu-York: Yivo, 1950).

99. Deshen, *Mellah Society*, 87.

100. Boyarin, *Yeshiva Days*, 14.

101. Israel Scheffler, *Teachers of My Youth: An American Jewish Experience*, Philosophy and Education vol. 5 (Dordrecht: Kluwer, 1995), 160.

102. Shlomo Guzmen-Carmeli, *Encounters around the Text: Ethnography of Judaism* (Haifa: Pardes and Haifa University Press, 2020) [Hebrew]; Shlomo Guzmen-Carmeli, "Texts as Places, Texts as Mirrors: Anthropology of Judaisms and Jewish Textuality," *Contemporary Jewry* 40, no. 3 (2020): 471–492. For an ethnography of orthodox yeshivot in Israel, see Yohai Hakak, *Young Men in Israeli Haredi Yeshiva Education: The Scholars' Enclave in Unrest* (Leiden: Brill, 2012). For a sociological analysis of the same, see Ehud Spiegel, *Ve-Talmud-Torah Ke-Neged Kulam: Ḥinukh Ḥaredi Le-Vanim Bi-Yerushalyim* (Yerushalayim: Mekhon Yerushalayim le-ḥeker Yiśra'el, 2011).

103. Elie Holzer and Orit Kent, *A Philosophy of Havruta: Understanding and Teaching the Art of Text Study in Pairs* (Boston: Academic Studies Press, 2014).

104. Joseph S. Lukinsky, "Integration within Jewish Studies," *Jewish Education* 46, no. 4 (1978): 39–41; Ira Stephen Brown and Joseph S. Lukinsky, "Integration of Religious Studies and Mathematics in the Day School," *Journal of Jewish Education* 47, no. 3 (1979): 28–35.

105. The most influential of thinkers along these lines continues to be Michel Foucault. See Michel Foucault, *The Order of Things: An Archaeology of the Human Sciences* (New York: Vintage, 1970); Michel Foucault, *The Archaeology of Knowledge* (New York: Pantheon, 1972). Since Foucault, there have been a number of great studies of the Enlightenment practices of knowledge organization. See Henry M. Cowles, *The Scientific Method: An Evolution of Thinking from Darwin to Dewey* (Cambridge, MA: Harvard University Press, 2020); Mary Poovey, *A History of the Modern Fact: Problems of Knowledge in the Sciences of Wealth and Society* (Chicago: University of Chicago Press, 1998); Chad

Wellmon, *Organizing Enlightenment: Information Overload and the Invention of the Modern Research University*, repr. ed. (Baltimore: Johns Hopkins University Press, 2016).

106. Gershon David Hundert, "The Library of the Study Hall in Volozhin, 1762: Some Notes on the Basis of a Newly Discovered Manuscript," *Jewish History* 14, no. 2 (2000): 225–244.

107. Hundert, "Library of the Study Hall in Volozhin," 226.

108. Simha Assaf, "Sifriyot batei midrash," *Yad lakore* 1, no. 7–9 (1946–1947): 170–172. For a comment about public libraries, see Ze'ev Gries, *Sefer, sofer vesipur bereshit hahasidut* (Israel: Hakibuts hame' uhad, 1992).

109. Stampfer, *Families, Rabbis and Education*, 157–158.

110. Stampfer, *Families, Rabbis and Education*, 159–162.

111. Avraham Shaul Amarillio, "The Great 'Talmud Torah' of Salonica / חברת תלמוד תורה הגדול בשאלוניקי," *Sefunot: Studies and Sources on the History of the Jewish Communities in the East / ספונות: מחקרים ומקורות לתולדות קהילות ישראל במזרח* 13: 273–308 (1971).

112. Devin E. Naar, *Jewish Salonica: Between the Ottoman Empire and Modern Greece* (Stanford, CA: Stanford University Press, 2016), 142–143.

113. Samuel C. Heilman, *The People of the Book: Drama, Fellowship, and Religion* (Chicago: University of Chicago Press, 1983).

114. Svara is explicitly queer in its approach. See www.svara.org.

115. Naomi Azulai and E. Tabori, "From a House of Study to a House of Prayer: Cultural-Religious Developments in the Secular Israeli Spectrum," *Social Issues in Israel* 6 (2008): 121–156; Talia Sagiv and Edna Lomsky-Feder, "An Actualization of a Symbolic Conflict: The Arena of Secular 'Batei Midrash' / מהלכה למעשה: מאבק סמלי על הון תרבותי בבתי מדרש חילוניים," *Israeli Sociology* 8, no. 2 (2007): 171–214; I. Troen, "Secular Judaism in Israel," *Society* 53, no. 2 (2016): 153–162; Shlomo Guzmen-Carmeli, "We Also Learn in a Yeshiva: Ethnography in a Secular Yeshiva in Tel Aviv," in *Jewish Revival Inside Out: Remaking Jewishness in a Transnational Age*, ed. Daniel Monterescu and Rachel Werczberger (Detroit, MI: Wayne State University Press, 2022); Adina Newberg, "'Hitchabrut' or Connecting: Liberal Houses of Study in Israel as Political and Spiritual Expression," *Israel Studies Forum* 20, no. 2 (2005): 97–114.

116. Genesis 25:22.

117. Lee S. Shulman, "Pedagogies of Interpretation, Argumentation, and Formation: From Understanding to Identity in Jewish Education," *Journal of Jewish Education* 74, no. 1 (2008): 5–15.

118. Deshen, *Mellah Society*, 86. I've retained Deshen's transliteration of the term out of fidelity with his original.

119. Shaul Regev, "Oral Preaching and Written Sermons in the Middle Ages," *European Journal of Jewish Studies* 9, no. 1 (2015): 85–99; Marc Saperstein, *Jewish Preaching, 1200–1800:*

An Anthology (New Haven, CT: Yale University Press, 1989); Marc Saperstein, *Your Voice Like a Ram's Horn: Themes and Texts in Traditional Jewish Preaching* (Cincinnati: Hebrew Union College Press, 1996).

120. Quoted in Renate Smithuis, "Preaching for His Daughter: Jacob Anatoli's Goad for Students (Malmad HaTalmidim)," in *Jewish Education from Antiquity to the Middle Ages: Studies in Honour of Philip S. Alexander*, ed. George J. Brooke and Renate Smithuis (Leiden: Brill, 2017), 354–355.

121. This is a reference to an encounter made famous by Clifford Geertz in his essay "Thick Description," in *The Interpretation of Cultures: Selected Essays* (New York: Basic Books, 1973). Geertz was referencing Gilbert Ryle.

122. Moshe Idel, *Absorbing Perfections: Kabbalah and Interpretation* (New Haven, CT: Yale University Press, 2002). Specifically, see Appendix 1: Pardes, the Fourfold Method of Interpretation.

123. Tamar El-Or, *Next Year I Will Know More: Literacy and Identity among Young Orthodox Women in Israel*, Raphael Patai Series in Jewish Folklore and Anthropology (Detroit, MI: Wayne State University Press, 2002).

124. Bar-Ilan University, "About Us | Midrasha | Bar-Ilan University" (n.d.), https://midrasha.biu.ac.il/en/node/406.

125. Richard Bauman and Charles L. Briggs, "Poetics and Performance as Critical Perspectives on Language and Social Life," *Annual Review of Anthropology* 19 (1990): 59–88; Charles L. Briggs and Richard Bauman, "Genre, Intertextuality, and Social Power," *Journal of Linguistic Anthropology* 2, no. 2 (1992): 131–172.

126. Daniel Boyarin, "Placing Reading: Ancient Israel and Medieval Europe," in Boyarin, *Ethnography of Reading*, 10–37.

127. David M. Carr, *Writing on the Tablet of the Heart: Origins of Scripture and Literature* (New York: Oxford University Press, 2009); Raymond F. Person, "The Ancient Israelite Scribe as Performer," *Journal of Biblical Literature* 117 (1998): 601–609; Susan Niditch, *Oral World and Written Word: Ancient Israelite Literature*, Library of Ancient Israel (Philadelphia: Westminster John Knox, 1996).

128. Carr, *Writing on the Tablet of the Heart*. See also Martin S. Jaffee, *Torah in the Mouth: Writing and Oral Tradition in Palestinian Judaism 200 B.C.E.–400 C.E.* (Oxford: Oxford University Press, 2001).

129. Just how widespread literacy was in the Ancient Near East is the source of a great deal of ongoing debate. See William V. Harris, *Ancient Literacy* (Cambridge, MA: Harvard University Press, 1991). On the matter of schools specifically, see Graham Davies, "Were There Schools in Ancient Israel?," in *Wisdom in Ancient Israel: Essays in Honor of J. A. Emerton*, ed. John Day, Robert Gordon, and H. G. M. Williamson (Cambridge: Cambridge University Press, 1995), 199–211; E. W. Heaton, *The School Tradition of the Old Testament: The Bampton Lectures for 1994* (Oxford: Oxford University

Press, 1994); Andrè Lemaire, "Schools and Literacy in Ancient Israel and Early Judaism," in *The Blackwell Companion to the Hebrew Bible*, ed. Leo G. Perdue (New York: John Wiley, 2017), 207–217

130. Kanarfogel, *Jewish Education and Society*, 23.

131. Talya Fishman, *Becoming the People of the Talmud: Oral Torah as Written Tradition in Medieval Jewish Cultures* (Philadelphia: University of Pennsylvania Press, 2013).

132. Nahman Danzig, "Mi-Talmud be'al Peh Le-Talmud Be-Khtav," *Sefer Ha-Shana Bar Ilan* 30–31 (2006): 49–112, cited in Fishman, *Becoming the People of the Talmud*, 7.

133. The wares listed refer to Jewish ritual objects: phylacteries, prayer shawls, and mezuzot that are placed on the doorposts of Jewish homes. Ellen Kellman, "Dos Yidishe Bukh Alarmirt! Towards the History of Yiddish Reading in Inter-war Poland," in *Focusing on Jewish Popular Culture in Poland and Its Afterlife*, ed. Michael C. Steinlauf and Antony Polonsky, 1st digital on-demand ed., Polin Studies in Polish Jewry vol. 16 (Oxford: Littman Library of Jewish Civilization, 2012), 215.

134. Seth Wolitz, "The Kiev-Grupe (1918–1920) Debate: The Function of Literature," *Studies in American Jewish Literature (1975–1979)* 4, no. 2 (1978): 97–106; David G. Roskies, *A Bridge of Longing: The Lost Art of Yiddish Storytelling* (Cambridge, MA: Harvard University Press, 1995), 201.

135. Kathryn Lofton, *Consuming Religion* (Chicago: University of Chicago Press, 2017); Ann Taves, *Revelatory Events: Three Case Studies of the Emergence of New Spiritual Paths* (Princeton, NJ: Princeton University Press, 2016). For Harry Potter, listen to the podcast "Harry Potter and the Sacred Text" (n.d.), https://www.harrypottersacredtext.com.

136. For an accessible introduction to the practice of this kind of calligraphy, see Stuart Kelman, "Calligraphy," in *The Jewish Catalog: A Do-It-Yourself Kit*, ed. Richard Siegel, Michael Strassfeld, and Sharon Strassfeld (Philadelphia: Jewish Publication Society, 1973).

137. Exodus 12:49, 15:16.

138. Exodus 24:12.

139. Deuteronomy 1:5, 33:4.

140. Maimonedes, *Mishne Torah*, Torah Study, 1:12, Sefaria translation.

141. *Mishne Torah* 1:13.

142. Geoffrey Claussen, "Repairing Character Traits and Repairing the Jews: The Talmud Torahs of Kelm and Grobin in the Nineteenth Century," *Polin Studies in Polish Jewry* 30 (2018): 15–41.

143. Fishman, *History of Jewish Education*; Emanuel Gamoran, *Changing Conceptions in Jewish Education* (New York: Macmillan, 1924), 59; Kanarfogel, *Jewish Education and Society*, 17–27.

144. For earlier examples of this approach, dating back to Byzantine era, see Nicholas de Lange, "Jewish Education in the Byzantine Empire in the Twelfth Century," in *Jewish Education and Learning: Published in Honour of Dr. David Patterson on the Occasion of His Seventieth Birthday*, ed. Glenda Abramson and Tudor Parfitt (London: Routledge, 1994), 115–142.

145. Gamoran, *Changing Conceptions in Jewish Education*, 124.

146. Joseph B. Soloveitchik, "Redemption, Prayer, Talmud Torah," *Tradition* 17, no. 2 (1978): 69.

147. Clifford Geertz, "Religion as a Cultural System," in *The Interpretation of Culture* (New York: Basic Books, 1973).

148. In a famous saying from the Mishna, "Every dispute that is for the sake of Heaven, will in the end endure; But one that is not for the sake of Heaven, will not endure" (Pirke Avot 5:17).

CHAPTER 4 — LEARNING IN JEWISH TRADITION

1. Jimmy Webb called the bridge the "nuclear weapon of the modern songwriter." Jimmy Webb, *Tunesmith: Inside the Art of Songwriting* (New York: Hyperion, 1999).

2. Samuel C. Heilman, *The People of the Book: Drama, Fellowship, and Religion* (Chicago: University of Chicago Press, 1983). Neusner offered a pretty sharp reply to Heilman's celebration of lernen. Jacob Neusner, "'Lernen' and Learning: Reflections on Samuel C. Heilman's 'The People of the Book,'" in *Israel in America: A Too-Comfortable Exile?* (Boston: Beacon,1985).

3. Jacob Neusner, *Judaism in the American Humanities: Second Series: Jewish Learning and the New Humanities* (Cambridge: Scholars Press, 1983), 84.

4. The field is large, with many subspecialties, but here are a few good places to start: Megan Bang, Douglas L. Medin, and Scott Atran, "Cultural Mosaics and Mental Models of Nature," *Proceedings of the National Academy of Sciences* 104, no. 35 (2007): 13868, https://doi.org/10.1073/pnas.0706627104; Brigid Barron and Dan Schwarz, "Doing with Understanding: Lessons from Research on Problem-and Project-Based Learning," *Journal of the Learning Sciences* 7, no. 3–4 (1998): 271–311; Jerome Bruner, *The Culture of Education* (Cambridge, MA: Harvard University Press, 1997); Indigo Esmonde, and Angela N. Booker, eds., *Power and Privilege in the Learning Sciences: Critical and Sociocultural Theories of Learning* (New York: Routledge, 2017); Jean Lave and Etienne Wenger, *Situated Learning: Legitimate Peripheral Participation* (Cambridge: Cambridge University Press, 1991); Na'ilah Suad Nasir, Carol D. Lee, Roy Pea, and Maxine McKinney de Royston, eds., *Handbook of the Cultural Foundations of Learning* (New York: Routledge, 2020); Barbara Rogoff and Jean Lave, eds., *Everyday Cognition: Development in Social Context* (Cambridge, MA: Harvard University Press, 1984); R. Keith Sawyer, ed., *Handbook of the Learning Sciences*, 2nd ed. (New York: Cambridge University Press, 2014). See also National Research Council, *How People Learn: Brain,*

Mind, Experience, and School: Expanded Edition, 2nd ed. (Washington, DC: National Academies Press, 2000).

5. Franz Rosenzweig, *On Jewish Learning* (Madison: University of Wisconsin Press, 2002), 98.

6. Rosenzweig, *On Jewish Learning,* 101.

7. Jonathan Woocher, "Reinventing Jewish Education for the 21st Century," *Journal of Jewish Education* 78, no. 3 (2012): 182–226.

8. Woocher, "Reinventing Jewish Education," 189.

9. Woocher, "Reinventing Jewish Education," 218, emphasis added.

10. Harold S. Himmelfarb, "The Impact of Religious Schooling: The Effects of Jewish Education upon Adult Religious Involvement" (PhD diss., University of Chicago, 1974).

11. Geoffrey Bock, "The Jewish Schooling of American Jews: A Study of Non-cognitive Educational Effects" (EdD diss., Harvard Graduate School of Education, 1976).

12. Steven Cohen and Laurence Kotler-Berkowitz, "The Impact of Childhood Jewish Education on Adults' Jewish Identity: Schooling, Israel Travel, Camping and Youth Groups" (New York: United Jewish Communities, 2004).

13. Len Saxe, Fern Chertok, Charles Kadushin, Graham Wright, Aron Klein, and Annette Koren, "What Difference Does Day School Make? The Impact of Day School: A Comparative Analysis of Jewish College Students" (Boston: PEJE and the Cohen Center for Modern Jewish Studies, 2007).

14. Alice Goldstein and Sylvia Barack Fishman, "When They Are Grown They Will Not Depart: Jewish Education and the Jewish Behavior of American Adults," *CMJS Research Report* 8 (Waltham, MA: Cohen Center for Modern Jewish Studies, Brandeis University, 1993).

15. Seymour M. Lipset, "The Power of Jewish Education" (Boston: Wilstein Institute, 1994).

16. Lipset, "Power of Jewish Education," 26.

17. Lipset, "Power of Jewish Education," 34.

18. Commission on Jewish Education in North America, *A Time to Act* (Lanham, MD: University Press of America, 1990), 15.

19. Commission on Jewish Education in North America, *Time to Act,* 15.

20. Israel Scheffler, "Jewish Education: Purposes, Problems and Possibilities," in *Curriculum, Community, Commitment: Views on the American Jewish Day School in Memory of Bennett I. Solomon,* ed. Daniel J. Margolis and Elliot Salo Schoenberg (West Orange, NJ: Behrman House, 1992), 20–28, 20.

21. Leonard Saxe and Barry Chazan, *Ten Days of Birthright Israel: A Journey in Young Adult Identity* (Waltham, MA: Brandeis University Press, 2008), 97.

22. Isa Aron, *Becoming a Congregation of Learners: Learning as a Key to Revitalizing Congregational Life* (Woodstock, VT: Jewish Lights, 2000), 32.

23. Barry I. Chazan, *The Language of Jewish Education: Crisis and Hope in the Jewish School* (New York: Hartmore House, 1978), 14.

24. Harold S. Himmelfarb, "Jewish Education for Naught: Educating the Culturally Deprived Jewish Child," *Analysis* 51 (September 1975): 1–11.

25. Edward L. Thorndike, *Human Learning*, Century Psychology Series, ed. R. M. Elliott (New York: Century Co., 1931), 4.

26. Thorndike, *Human Learning*, 4.

27. Chief among the influences in this effort are Jerome Bruner and Jean Piaget. Bruner, *Culture of Education*; Jean Piaget, *The Psychology of Intelligence*, 2nd ed. (London: Routledge, 2001); Jean Piaget and Barbel Inhelder, *The Psychology of the Child*, 2nd ed. (New York: Basic Books, 1969).

28. Russian (and sometimes Jewish) psychologists were central to the emergence of this area of research. A. A. Leontiev, *Problems and Methods of Psycholinguistics in Face-to-Face Communication* (Berlin: De Gruyter Mouton, 2011), 339–354; L. S. Vygotsky, *Mind in Society: The Development of Higher Psychological Processes* (Cambridge, MA: Harvard University Press, 1980).

29. For examples of some of these studies: K. J. Gilhooly and A. J. K. Green, "The Use of Memory by Experts and Novices," in *Cognition and Action in Skilled Behaviour.* Advances in Psychology 55, ed. Ann M. Colley and John R. Beech (Amsterdam: North-Holland, 1988), 379–395; John A. Hughes, Dave Randall, and Dan Shapiro, "From Ethnographic Record to System Design," *Computer Supported Cooperative Work* 1, no. 3 (1992): 123–141; Edwin Hutchins, *Cognition in the Wild* (Cambridge, MA: MIT Press, 1995); Lave and Wenger, *Situated Learning*; Roy Pea, "Practices of Distributed Intelligence and Designs for Education," in *Distributed Cognitions: Psychological and Educational Considerations*, ed. Gavriel Salomon (Cambridge: Cambridge University Press, 1993), 47–87.

30. The expert-novice paradigm has been employed in an incredible variety of settings. Here are two articles I've found particularly useful: Cindy E. Hmelo-Silver, Surabhi Marathe, and Lei Liu, "Fish Swim, Rocks Sit, and Lungs Breathe: Expert-Novice Understanding of Complex Systems," *Journal of the Learning Sciences* 16, no. 3 (2007): 307–331; Michael J. Jacobson and Uri Wilensky, "Complex Systems in Education: Scientific and Educational Importance and Implications for the Learning Sciences," *Journal of the Learning Sciences* 15, no. 1 (2006): 11–34.

31. Sam Wineburg's pathbreaking work in the area of history education has been particularly important, though it still leaves lots of room for future studies of learning in the humanities. Eli Gottlieb and Sam Wineburg, "Between Veritas and Communitas: Epistemic Switching in the Reading of Academic and Sacred History,"

Journal of the Learning Sciences 21, no. 1 (2012): 84–129; Sam Wineburg, Susan Mosborg, Dan Porat, and Ariel Duncan, "Common Belief and the Cultural Curriculum: An Intergenerational Study of Historical Consciousness," *American Educational Research Journal* 44, no. 1 (2007): 40–76, https://doi.org/10.3102/0002831206298677; Samuel S. Wineburg, *Historical Thinking and Other Unnatural Acts: Charting the Future of Teaching the Past*, Critical Perspectives on the Past (Philadelphia: Temple University Press, 2001).

32. Bruner, *Culture of Education*; Jerome Bruner, "A Narrative Model of Self-Construction," *Annals of the New York Academy of Sciences* 818, no. 1 (1997): 145–161; André Kukla, *Social Constructivism and the Philosophy of Science* (London: Routledge, 2000); Vygotsky, *Mind in Society*; James V. Wertsch, *Vygotsky and the Social Formation of Mind* (Cambridge, MA: Harvard University Press, 1985).

33. Paulo Freire and Donaldo Macedo, *Pedagogy of the Oppressed*, trans. Myra Bergman Ramos, 30th anniv. ed. (New York: Bloomsbury, 2000).

34. John H. Falk, *Identity and the Museum Visitor Experience* (Walnut Creek, CA: Left Coast Press, 2009), 76.

35. John Seely Brown, Allan Collins, and Paul Duguid, "Situated Cognition and the Culture of Learning," *Educational Researcher* 18, no. 1 (1989): 33.

36. Kris D. Gutierrez and Barbara Rogoff, "Cultural Ways of Learning: Individual Traits or Repertoires of Practice," *Educational Researcher* 32, no. 5 (2003): 19–25; Barbara Rogoff, *Apprenticeship in Thinking: Cognitive Development in Social Context* (New York: Oxford University Press, 1990); Rogoff and Lave, *Everyday Cognition*.

37. Barbara Rogoff, Karen Topping, Jaquelyn Baker-Sennett, and Pilar Lacasa, "Mutual Contribution of Individuals, Partners, and Institutions: Planning to Remember in Girl Scout Cookie Sales," *Social Development* 11, no. 2 (2002): 266–289.

38. Jean Lave and Etienne Wenger, *Situated Learning: Legitimate Peripheral Participation*, 1st ed. (Cambridge: Cambridge University Press, 1991).

39. Howard S. Becker, *Art Worlds* (Berkeley: University of California Press, 1982).

40. Tia DiNora, *Beethoven and the Construction of Genius Musical Politics in Vienna, 1792–1803* (Berkeley: University of California Press, 1997).

41. Christopher Small, *Musicking: The Meanings of Performing and Listening* (Middletown, CT: Wesleyan University Press, 1998).

42. Andy Clark and David Chalmers, "The Extended Mind," *Analysis* 58, no. 1 (1998): 7–19.

43. Hutchins, *Cognition in the Wild*; Pea, "Practices of Distributed Intelligence."

44. Stuart Schoenfeld, "Folk Judaism, Elite Judaism and the Role of Bar Mitzvah in the Development of the Synagogue and Jewish School in America," *Contemporary Jewry* 9, no. 1 (1987): 67–86.

45. Barbara Rogoff, Karen Topping, Jaquelyn Baker-Sennett, and Pilar Lacasa, "Mutual Contributions of Individuals, Partners, and Institutions: Planning to Remember in Girl Scout Cookie Sales," *Social Development* 11, no. 2 (2002): 266–289.

46. Michel Foucault, *Power/Knowledge: Selected Interviews and Other Writings, 1972–1977* (New York: Vintage, 1988).

47. Eviatar Zerubavel, *The Seven Day Circle: The History and Meaning of the Week* (Chicago: University of Chicago Press, 1985); Eviatar Zerubavel, *The Fine Line: Making Distinctions in Everyday Life* (Chicago: University of Chicago Press, 1991).

48. Max K. Strassfeld, *Trans Talmud: Androgynes and Eunuchs in Rabbinic Literature* (Oakland: University of California Press, 2022).

49. Foucault, *Power/Knowledge*, 112–119.

50. Foucault, *Power/Knowledge*, 131–133.

51. This is one of the preoccupations of philosopher of Jewish education Michael Rosenak. Michael Rosenak, "Jewish Religious Education and Indoctrination," in *Studies in Jewish Education.* ed. Barry Chazan (Jerusalem: Mandel Institute, 1983), 1:117–138; Michael Rosenak, *Commandments and Concerns: Jewish Religious Education in Secular Society* (Philadelphia: Jewish Publication Society, 1987); Michael Rosenak, *Roads to the Palace: Jewish Texts and Teaching* (New York: Berghahn Books, 1995). See also Barry I. Chazan, "'Indoctrination' and Religious Education," *Religious Education* 67, no. 4 (1972): 243–252.

52. Jackie Feldman, "Marking the Boundaries of the Enclave: Defining the Israeli Collective Through the Poland 'Experience,'" *Israel Studies* 7, no. 2 (2002): 84–114; Jackie Feldman, *Above the Death Pits, Beneath the Flag: Youth Voyages to Poland and the Performance of Israeli National Identity* (New York: Berghahn Books, 2008). Doron Bar and Kobi Cohen-Hattab trace the history of tourism back to the Mandatory period and find that some of the same critiques were levied then too. Doron Bar and Kobi Cohen-Hattab, "A New Kind of Pilgrimage: The Modern Tourist Pilgrim of Nineteenth Century and Early Twentieth Century Palestine," *Middle Eastern Studies* 39, no. 2 (2003): 131–148.

53. Foucault, *Power/Knowledge*, 131.

54. The study of infrastructure is its own field, inaugurated by Susan Leigh Star, "The Ethnography of Infrastructure," *American Behavioral Scientist* 43, no. 3 (1999): 377–391, https://doi.org/10.1177/00027649921955326. More recent studies of infrastructure include Paul Dourish and Genevieve Bell, "The Infrastructure of Experience and the Experience of Infrastructure: Meaning and Structure in Everyday Encounters with Space," *Environment and Planning B: Planning and Design* 34, no. 3 (2007): 414–430. On the relationship between infrastructure and information, or to account for the materiality of information, see Paul Dourish, *The Stuff of Bits: An Essay on the Materialities of Information* (Cambridge, MA: MIT Press, 2017); John Durham Peters, *The Marvelous Clouds: Toward a Philosophy of Elemental Media* (Chicago: University of Chicago Press, 2015).

55. Andrew Bush, *Jewish Studies: A Theoretical Introduction* (New Brunswick, NJ: Rutgers University Press, 2011), 1.

56. Bush, *Jewish Studies*, 1.

57. Bush, 5.

58. Bush, 2.

CONCLUSION

1. Jacob Neusner, *"Being Jewish" and Studying about Judaism* (Atlanta: Emory University Press, 1977), 66.

Index

About the Author

ARI Y. KELMAN is the Jim Joseph Professor of Education and Jewish Studies in the Stanford Graduate School of Education. He is the author of several books and articles that explore the production and transmission of religious knowledge.

Printed in the United States
by Baker & Taylor Publisher Services